Technological and Market Innovation

Technological and Market Innovation

Strategies for Product and Company Development

HARRY NYSTRÖM

Professor of Marketing and Organization
Institute for Economics
Uppsala, Sweden

JOHN WILEY & SONS

Chichester · New York · Brisbane · Toronto · Singapore

Copyright © 1990 by John Wiley & Sons Ltd.
Baffins Lane, Chichester
West Sussex PO19 1UD, England

Other Wiley Editorial Offices

John Wiley & Sons, Inc., 605 Third Avenue,
New York, NY 10158-0012, USA

Jacaranda Wiley Ltd, G.P.O. Box 859, Brisbane,
Queensland 4001, Australia

John Wiley & Sons (Canada) Ltd, 22 Worcester Road,
Rexdale, Ontario M9W 1L1, Canada

John Wiley & Sons (SEA) Pte Ltd, 37 Jalan Pemimpin 05-04,
Block B, Union Industrial Building, Singapore 2057

Library of Congress Cataloging-in-Publication Data:

Nyström, Harry, 1936–
    Technological and market innovation : strategies for product and
company development / by Harry Nyström.
        p. cm.
    Includes bibliographical references.
    ISBN 0 471 92054 1
        1. Strategic planning. 2. Industrial management. 3. Industrial
management—Scandinavia. 4. Product management. 5. Marketing.
    I. Title.
HD30.28.N97   1990
658.4'012—dc20
                                                                89–29727
                                                                    CIP

British Library Cataloguing in Publication Data:

Nyström, Harry
    Technological and market innovation : Strategies for
    product and company development.
    1. Companies. Technological innovation. Management
    I. Title
    658.4'063

ISBN 0 471 92054 1

Typeset by Photo-graphics, Honiton, Devon
Printed in Great Britain by Courier International Ltd, Tiptree, Essex

For Agneta, Emanuel and Anette
and to the memory of Jonas

Contents

Preface

The ideas and empirical results presented in the following chapters are the result of ongoing research on a wide range of strategic management issues for more than two decades. Many of the ideas and results have therefore previously been presented in other books and articles. The main objective of the present book is to bring these contributions together and to indicate the implications for future research.

Obviously any attempt such as this must be suggestive rather than definitive and use a broad stroke in painting the picture. At the same time, empirical support must be given for at least some of the main arguments, if the attempt is to be more than merely speculative.

The book may also be seen as suggesting a unified framework for the purpose of organizing ideas from the evolving Scandinavian Management School, to which these contributions belong. The scope of the present approach is much wider, however, than most other approaches to management in and outside Scandinavia. This is both an advantage and a disadvantage— what is gained in overview may be lost in detail. But a broad approach may be used as a background for integrating and positioning other more focused approaches—which is one of the purposes of the book.

At the same time, the ideas presented here have to a large extent been developed independently of other work in the Scandinavian countries. This not withstanding, there is a similarity in viewpoint which makes it natural to compare and to some extent contrast the ideas in this book with those of other Scandinavian writers on management during the 1970s and 1980s.

To what extent the similarities in outlook are due to similarities in business practices within Scandinavia—and differences between Scandinavia and other countries, particularly the USA where most views on modern management originate—is an open question. It is enough for our purpose to acknowledge that there is a similarity in thinking on management questions within Scandinavia, whatever the reasons for this may be.

Over the years I have accumulated a great debt of gratitude to many people in carrying out the research reported on in this book. A large number of executives generously contributed time for interviews and provided other valuable material. Research assistants helped me to organize and carry out the studies and I worked together with colleagues on a number of the projects.

I should like to thank them all, especially Bo Edvardsson and Urban Åhgren, who did their doctoral work on product development and marketing strategies within the research program, and Göran Ekvall, a professor of psychology at the Swedish Council for management and work life issues, with whom I have done joint research on the relationships between strategy, structure, culture and climate. I have received valuable comments also from many people at conferences where I have presented my ideas, and in private communication.

Financial support has been received from the Social Science Research Council of Sweden, the Swedish National Board for Technical Development, Anders Wall's Foundation and the Swedish Council for Agricultural and Forest Research, which is gratefully acknowledged. Last but not least, I should like to thank my family for their great support and patience while I have spent my time researching and writing this book.

Readers with comments or suggestions with regard to developing further the ideas presented here are invited to write to me at the Institute for Economics, Box 7013, 75007 Uppsala, Sweden.

Uppsala, Sweden   HARRY NYSTRÖM
December 1989

*Images rather than established facts
are our main guidance when venturing
into the unknown*

1
Managing the Future

The most critical issue facing companies today is how to manage the future. Since the future is unrealized and basically unpredictable, evolving images rather than established facts are our main guidance when venturing into the unknown. The more uncertain and unstable the world is, the more companies must rely on image management and innovation management to create their desired futures. There is no crystal ball which companies may use to look into the future, but there are ways in which they can help to bring it about by actively pursuing their visions.

Image and innovation therefore are challenging terms. They challenge our imagination and existing ways of doing things. They point to new possibilities and ways of looking at the world. They are open in the sense that the future is open and unrealized and they suggest, but do not prematurely restrict, how we should proceed in order to achieve our dreams and aspirations.

Image and innovation are closely linked to creativity and entrepreneurship, the elusive but decisive ability to break out of existing patterns of thought and action, to find new ways of looking at and handling reality. They point to the future more than they reflect the past and stress the desirable more than the immediately achievable.

In a rapidly changing world (when the obtainable today often is the undesirable tomorrow) managing image and innovation becomes one of the major challenges to, or headaches of management, depending on whether future changes are invited and encouraged or feared and resisted.

What then do I mean by image and innovation? As did Boulding[1] in his inspiring book *'The Image'*, I use that word to refer to the mental picture, that is the subjective knowledge structure that an individual has of some aspect of reality. Images therefore influence how things are perceived, which is what is emphasized in the marketing and advertising literature. In the static sense[2] image management may be viewed as impression management; how to communicate favorable impressions of existing conditions. Dynamic image management on the other hand, involves creating favorable conditions for constructive change.

In the dynamic sense, images influence creativity and creative problem solving. They help in the flexible focusing of thoughts and ideas, so essential at the early stages of the creative process. But images also make it possible for companies to sell that which is not yet realized, in other words, the future.

By influencing images of what they can do, companies make implicit promises to obtain the resources necessary to develop new ideas. By image marketing companies can to some extent free themselves from the present and make room for the future. At the same time they become obligated to fulfill these promises, but they also may gain the time and resources to make this possible.

In our terminology visions, which are the essence of true entrepreneurship, may be seen as wholistic guiding images of future possibilities. This is well stated by Schon[3] in his book, *Technology and Change*:

> In order to move deliberately towards innovation, the organization must have a vision, vividly and broadly perceived, of what it can come to be.

Ideas, on the other hand, may be viewed as more detailed and concrete images of what may and can be done today. Developing visions then becomes a dialectical process,[4] concerned with the interplay between images and ideas.

Innovation, the other conceptual cornerstone of our approach, means the creation of the future. It is the process of bringing new ideas into use. In Drucker's words innovation is, 'the tool of entrepreneurship'.[5] This is consistent with the way the word is used in this book, to refer to how entrepreneurs, viewed as visionary activists, change the world around them. This, as Schumpeter has noted,[6] leads to both creative destruction and constructive change:

> The typical entrepreneur is more self-centered than other types, because he relies less than they do on tradition and connection and because his characteristic task—theoretically as well as historically—consists precisely in breaking up old and creating new tradition.

Innovation management in our approach is closely linked to image management. Images may be viewed as guiding forces and enabling conditions, while innovations are the process by which change takes place and the result of radical change.

Viewed as a result, innovations may be new products, processes, know-how or patents; but they can be new organizational mechanisms, budgeting systems, management techniques or other devices which represent new ways of looking at and changing the world. Innovation need not (and often does not) require invention—as Schumpeter[7] pointed out long ago—but it does involve radical change.

Traditionally, economic theory and management theory has not concerned itself much with creativity and major change, what in this book is called the management of image and innovation. Instead, the focus has been on how to handle the problems of today by utilizing established procedures and technology. This of course is an important issue. Too much attention paid to managing the status quo makes it more difficult to adapt to future change, regardless of whether we ourselves welcome or resist these changes.

To resist change is part of human nature, but so is survival under changing conditions. Many companies have learned this the hard way when market and technological changes have accelerated and they have been left behind in the competitive race.

Today, the management of innovation, and related areas of strategic management such as entrepreneurship and the management of technology and creativity, are becoming increasingly popular topics for management courses and best selling books. Many leading universities have started courses, and a number of centers for teaching and doing research in these areas have been established.[8]

Books stressing the need for creative corporate transformation, such as Peters and Waterman's *'In Search of Excellence'* and Kanter's *'The Change Masters'* have received much attention, particularly from practicing managers. At the same time the theoretical basis for these approaches is largely undeveloped and most current management books and management courses are even today more concerned with the need for control and stability than with the need for radical change.

There is therefore a great need for empirical studies and theory development in this area. While many books deal with some aspects of managing discontinuous change, such as the relationship between strategy and structure[9] there is a lack of comprehensive frameworks and integrated research efforts which view innovative development from an overall company management perspective. Little empirical and theoretical research attempts to link together the different technoeconomic and behavioral factors which may influence company creativity and innovation (for instance, strategy, structure, culture and climate)[10] and relate them to technological and market change and innovative performance.

In the strategic management area there is therefore a need both for more distinctive and inclusive concepts and ideas and empirical evidence as to how they interact. This book argues, for instance, that marketing and technology should not be viewed as isolated aspects of strategic management. It is instead the interplay between these two factors that is most important for product and company development.

We also need to pay more attention to the concept and content of strategy. In our approach strategies are patterns of decisions[11] which evolve over time in largely unpredictable ways. We therefore need to cast our perceptual and conceptual nets widely to capture these patterns and their implications for product and company development. We cannot determine in advance precisely what the dimensions and characteristics of successful strategies will be, but we can increase the likelihood that such strategies will emerge in the interplay between company action and environmental response.

In Scandinavia wholistic, empirically derived views of management have rapidly gained acceptance in leading universities and companies. The number of researchers working in the business area is very small in this part of the world, but a wide range of problems is studied. This has discouraged specialization both within the management area and in relation to other more behavioral or technical disciplines, such as psychology and engineering.

Scandinavian approaches to management[12] are typically wider and more open and crossdisciplinary when compared, for instance, to the American management tradition, and there is less hesitation to cross academic lines of specialization. The result is an emerging distinctive Scandinavian approach to management, blending and transcending traditional functions such as organization and marketing, and looking for more total, empirically based management concepts, which may be applied to new problem areas.

In my own research I have studied strategies for product and company development in a number of research studies since the early 1970s.[13] In the present work I have interviewed representatives for a large number of Swedish companies in various industries ranging from pharmaceuticals and electronics to basic chemicals, steel, wood and paper and food processing.

Based on this data and drawing on earlier research on the importance of image marketing,[14] I have tried to develop a framework for the strategic management of image and innovation which addresses the issue in a wide perspective. This work is highly tentative and explorative, but at least shows one way of looking at the problem.

Since this book deals with image management, it invites comments on what leading images have guided its own development. The answer is 'Building Blocks' versus 'Chinese Boxes'. Traditional management theory, I would argue, is mainly constructed on the theme of building blocks. Each element is viewed as a separate entity, which may be analyzed in splendid isolation and added to other elements without disturbing their internal structures. The resulting edifice is seen as the sum of its parts, rather than as an interacting whole.

This 'Architectural View of Management' may be contrasted with a 'Chinese Box View', where each box has meaning only in relation to the boxes it contains and to those of which it is a part. When constructing an individual box we then need to consider the design and make-up of the box in which it is contained and of those boxes that we want it to be able to include. This permits greater flexibility and creativity in construction at any time, than adding together given building blocks. If initially only the design and structure of a few basic outside boxes are given, this system allows great flexibility and creativity also in conceiving of and constructing the inside boxes. The outer box then becomes a guiding image for each inner box, but it does not determine precisely its content.

This flexible process for guiding, but not strictly determining, development, is consistent with the function of intuition for guiding thinking and behavior.[15] Analysis, on the other hand, may be seen as the assembling and dissembling of given building blocks.

This book is basically about company creativity. For creativity both intuition and analysis are necessary; which means we require both Chinese boxes and building blocks. We need to invite the future—that is envision possibilities— without unduly restricting the ways in which these possibilities may be realized. This is the dynamic role of image in our framework. But we also need to consider existing conditions and build on what we know. We therefore need to use analysis to make sure that there is room for the present in our designs for the future. For this reason it was necessary when carrying out the research for this book (and writing it) to use building blocks from traditional and non-traditional sources in, for instance, management theory and psychological theory. But it also was necessary to remodel these to fit into our intuitively designed Chinese boxes, that is the ideas evolving out of our empirical research.

These boxes contain concepts which are related to strategic outcomes (new products, processes or technologies) and to new ways of organizing innovative product and company development. The specific strategic outcomes of different development situations are largely unpredictable and difficult to control by direct company action. Indirectly, however, companies may influence the likelihood of success, if they understand the creative mechanisms involved, and the ways in which strategic elements may influence the creative process. Recruiting creative personnel may, for instance, have a decisive influence on success, even if the precise outcomes are impossible to predict, as may research cooperation or combining existing technologies in new ways.

The strategist in our view therefore is more an artist working with new images than an artisan using established categories and ideas. At times he may even appear to be a magician. When opening a strategic box a rabbit may jump out, the carrot we put into it having disappeared. This may be due to the fact that the rabbit has entered the box through a trap door and eaten the carrot. But to the uninitiated observer it will look like magic, as the successful strategies of entrepreneurs often do. As in the artist's conception and the conjuror's trick, creativity and innovation require trapdoors to let in new aspects of reality. Image in our framework is a cognitive trapdoor designed to let the future in rather than a cognitive storehouse of memories from the past.

The book as a whole should be viewed as a Chinese box, containing the different chapters nested within it. It should be viewed as an interdependent entity, rather than as being made up of separate parts. At the same time each chapter is a Chinese box containing other boxes, to organize the ideas and set them in relation to each other. This intricate design probably demands a more open mind and a greater willingness to explore possibilities than do most books on management.

Following this introductory chapter, Chapter 2 gives the main ideas and overall framework for our approach, summarized in a 'strategic management box', within which the rest of the book may be located.

Chapter 3 deals with creativity and entrepreneurship as basic mechanisms for managing the future against the background of two case studies, one of radical entrepreneurship and the other of intrapreneurship.

Chapter 4 is concerned with innovation management, how companies may prepare for and help to create the future by employing different technological strategies. It is summarized in an 'innovation management box'. This includes innovation strategies, company creativity, informational diversity and organizational flexibility as major determinants of technological change, seen as the evolvement of implicit and explicit technologies.

Chapter 5 gives some results from an empirical study of an important aspect of innovation management, technological cooperation to find and develop new products. The companies studied are mechanical engineering companies in Sweden manufacturing farm machinery.

Chapter 6 deals with image management and image marketing. In this chapter an 'image management box' and a 'marketing management box' are introduced, based on the distinction between generalization and discrimination as basic psychological mechanisms for image learning, and between explicit and implicit marketing activities.

Chapter 7 gives some empirical data in support of our model of image learning, based on the psychological interplay between generalization and discrimination.

Chapter 8 is about the dynamic management of marketing relationships. It discusses the strategic marketing mix of a company, which is concerned with how companies may strike a balance in their marketing activities between competitive action and buyer–seller interaction. This is summarized in a 'marketing strategy box', which assumes that there are two basic marketing strategies, holding strategies and competitive strategies.

Chapter 9 gives the results of a study of how Swedish newsprint manufacturers balance competitive action and buyer–seller interaction in their strategic marketing mixes.

Chapter 10 presents the results of an extensive, empirical investigation of product development strategies and consumer outcomes in Swedish food processing companies.

Chapter 11 gives the results of a similar, more intensive

study of product development strategies for Swedish pulp and paper companies.

Chapter 12 is about managing company culture and climate against the background of a case study of a leading Swedish chemical company.

Chapter 13 pulls together elements from the other chapters. It looks at product and company development as an integrated process, using a 'strategy development box' and a 'knowledge development box' to summarize the main themes of the book.

Concepts are needed to organize our
thinking and experience

2
Conceptualizing the Strategic Management Box

Chapter 2 is concerned with setting the stage. It presents the main ideas and definitions and the overall framework in which they are organized. These concepts and their implications for our reasoning will then be further elaborated and developed in the following chapters, both from a theoretical and an empirical point of view.

Most of the ideas have evolved in the context of our empirical research, summarized in this book. A full understanding of their meaning and implications requires an understanding of these studies. Since our main purpose is to present an empirically grounded framework, this joint process of concept elaboration and theory generation[1] may be seen as both a result of and major guiding principle for our investigation.

The ideas put forward should be viewed in the context of an evolving strategic management theory. This theory is evolving in the sense that quite a few recent management books deal with different aspects of it, using labels such as strategic marketing management,[2] strategic management of technology[3] and innovation management.[4] At the same time, few attempts have been made to present a more unified overall framework.

A MODEL OF COMPANY DEVELOPMENT

To begin with we will present a model of company development[5] based on how companies respond to or initiate environmental change. This model has been used in our various studies as a help in understanding differences in product and company development and in relating these differences to strategy, technology, market conditions, culture and climate.

Positional and Innovative Companies

A starting point is that companies differ in the extent to which they emphasize their existing technologies and markets or stress new possibilities in their strategic management. Companies which mainly try to do better what they already know how to do, are called more *positional companies* and companies which emphasize creating and utilizing new technological and market opportunities are called more *innovative companies* (Figure 2.1).

Positional companies avoid change and therefore are best suited for stable environments. Their strategies are reactive and basically reflect past conditions: the focus is on short run efficiency based on continuous development. In Leavitt's words they are mainly problem solvers, rather than pathfinders.[6] Their technological and marketing strategies are evolutionary and defensive and R & D and market research is basically used by them to strengthen their existing markets and technologies. Their organization structures are relatively formalized and functionally specialized. In the framework of our analysis we may say that they have very closed technological, marketing and organization strategies.

Innovative companies are best suited for more dynamic, complex, and changing environments, and help to realize such surroundings by their proactive strategies. They actively create their futures by offensive technological and marketing strategies. Their organization structures are flexible and unformalized. In our approach we refer to these companies

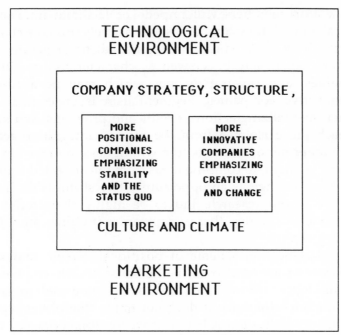

TECHNOLOGICAL
ENVIRONMENT

COMPANY STRATEGY, STRUCTURE,

| MORE POSITIONAL COMPANIES EMPHASIZING STABILITY AND THE STATUS QUO | MORE INNOVATIVE COMPANIES EMPHASIZING CREATIVITY AND CHANGE |

CULTURE AND CLIMATE

MARKETING
ENVIRONMENT

Figure 2.1 Basic company development box

as having very open technological, marketing and organization strategies.

We may compare our typology with other models proposed in the organization literature. Burns and Stalker, for instance, distinguish between mechanistic and organic organizations, based on their empirical studies of electronic and textile companies in England and Scotland.[7] Mechanistic organizations are highly specialized in task performance and employ precise definitions and technical specifications in carrying out operations. Organic organizations build on network interaction with continual adjustment and readjustment of roles and activities. In our framework positional companies may be viewed as employing predominantly mechanistic organization structures and innovative companies organic ones.

Burns and Stalker are, however, not explicitly concerned with strategies for change, which is our main concern. Instead they deal mainly with how relationships between individual organization members will impede or facilitate innovation, rather than with how companies may actively promote change.

Similarly, Kanter[8] speaks of segmentalistic structures and cultures, which may be viewed as characterizing positional companies, and integrative ones which may be attributed to innovative companies. Segmentalism is concerned with 'compartmentalizing actions, events and problems, and keeping each piece isolated from the other'.[9] Integrative action, on the other hand, refers to, 'the willingness to move beyond received wisdom, to combine ideas from unconnected sources, to embrace change as an opportunity to test limits'.[10] This is what we in our research find to be highly characteristic of innovative companies, that is, companies inviting rather than resisting change.

Our classification scheme of positional versus innovative companies is an ideal one, in the sense that it emphasizes and highlights features that are less pronounced in actual development situations. It does not imply that either type of company by definition is better or worse from a development point of view.

As is widely recognized today in the management literature,[11] different environmental conditions lead to different organizational requirements. The strategy, structure, culture and climate of a company determine its capacity for change, but actual success depends on the match between internal capabilities and external needs. Since market and technological requirements are changing rapidly almost everywhere, most companies experience the need to become more innovative, but the need is much more pressing for some companies and industries than for others.

Within companies we find differences also in the possibility and in the need to be more positional or innovative. Operative functions such as production and sales by definition have to be more positional than more strategic functions, such as R & D and market development. Achieving a balance between positional and innovative activities within companies and in relation to the outside environment is the major issue in achieving successful product and company development.

Product and Company Differences in Development Patterns

Our study of Swedish food processing companies presented in Chapter 10 shows, for instance, that most people are quite conservative in their food habits, which make it difficult for companies to successfully pursue innovative product development strategies. By and large, relatively positional technological and marketing strategies are both more common and more profitable in this industry than in most other consumer goods industries. This is one reason why the shift towards higher nutritional values for mass manufactured food items has been so slow.

In the pharmaceutical industry, on the other hand, our interviews indicate that more innovative strategies are both eagerly pursued by the leading companies and closely linked to commercial success. Both doctors and patients are quite likely to view medical innovations as beneficial and accept them, while both food distributors and consumers tend to resist radical food innovations.

These are just two examples of the variation in innovative potential and the need for innovation between product groups and industries. In the area of typical producer goods we find pronounced and successful positional strategies in the pulp and paper industry (see Chapters 9 and 11) and highly pronounced and successful innovative strategies in the industrial electronics industry (Chapter 4).

At the same time, companies tend and need to be more innovative during some time periods and more positional during others. Venture companies—or venture units in established companies trying to undertake more radical technological or marketing diversification—naturally need more innovative strategies than do older companies working along more established lines. As we shall see in our discussion of Inter Innovation in Chapter 3, the greatest strategic need in a highly entrepreneurial firm, after some 5–10 years, often is to change its orientation from highly innovative to more positional. This, then, requires a radical change in strategic leadership and in company organization, and may make necessary a change in top management.

Low-tech Companies

Low-tech companies are relatively positional in their outlook and activities. They are market searchers, rather than market developers. Since they cannot, or do not, want to offer highly creative solutions based on radically new knowledge, they must instead find a market for what they already know how to do. This they may achieve by focusing and differentiating their products the better to relate to their environment and by using sales promotion and advertising to achieve favorable psychological positioning[12] of their offers in the minds of prospective buyers.

In traditional marketing terminology this is called product differentiation and market segmentation.[13] By including overall cost leadership as a third generic strategy, as Porter does,[14] we may extend this framework to apply both to process and to product changes.[15]

All these strategic options are concerned with the marginal adjustment and selective marketing and promotion of existing products to increase their competitiveness, without considering the need to develop radically new technologies and products. Low-tech companies are therefore mainly concerned with how to compete with established products and technologies. Finding existing market opportunities and niches that fit their unique competence then becomes more important than developing new knowledge and markets to solve new customer problems. It is therefore understandable that these highly marketing-dependent companies usually devote a very small proportion of costs to R & D and a large proportion to market research, advertising and sales promotion to locate buyers and to try to make them prefer their offers.

In our terminology, more fully developed in the following chapters, low-tech companies use relatively closed and convergent technological, marketing and organization strategies in product and company development instead of more open and divergent strategies. They thereby tend to defend and exploit the advantages they have achieved rather than try to find and develop new opportunities.

Hi-tech Companies

Hi-tech companies, on the other hand, may be defined as innovative companies which have successfully used open and technological, marketing and organization strategies to gain strong leadership positions for their new products. They are, as Riggs points out, 'companies for which technology is a key—and often the key—competitive tool'.[16] Their strategies are more open and are based on creating and exploiting change rather than consolidating and defending existing conditions.

This means that the interface between technology and marketing[17] becomes of crucial importance to hi-tech companies. While low-tech companies may basically adjust their marketing strategies to reflect relatively unchanging technological conditions, hi-tech companies must recognize that both technological and marketing conditions[18] are rapidly changing.

Hi-tech companies therefore must consider the dynamic impact of technological and marketing strategy on product and company development. But even more importantly they must be aware of the complex interrelationships between these two main strategy components in creating and realizing possibilities. Depending on how this interaction is handled the result may be either friction and frustration or fruition and fulfillment.

The different, but also complementary, implications of technological and marketing strategies are not spelt out and explicitly dealt with in much of the product and company development literature and are often not recognized in company practice[19] either. In our framework, technology mainly widens opportunities and marketing focuses them. The widening and focusing are distinct but mutually dependent mechanisms; balancing the two is the essence both of the creative process and of successful product and company development.

Hi-tech companies must open up and broaden their technological outlook to find new opportunities, but in close conjunction also focus and differentiate their marketing position to satisfy customer needs. They need to 'stretch technological developments to the fullest, but with the restraints of not imposing it on an unready market'.[20] This is the dynamic balancing act in which hi-tech companies must excell to succeed in product and company development. It is quite different from the more static and stable ways in which low-tech companies analyze and explore the market implications of their existing technologies.

Marketing Dependent and Technology Intensive Companies

In summary we may say that positional, low-tech companies by definition utilize very closed and concentrated development strategies, emphasizing their existing products and technologies. Traditional marketing theory, based on product specific competition and given production functions, depicts the situation of such marketing dependent companies quite well.

Hi-tech, innovative companies, on the other hand, have quite different technological and marketing requirements. To understand and evaluate the strategic management situations of research and technology intensive companies, we need to focus on general company based development and more open and flexible concepts of image and innovation management.

For this we need an open model of strategic management based on the development and use of new knowledge and competence. Specific products and technologies then are the outcome of, rather than the basis for, strategic development. Marketing dependent companies, too, need to broaden their strategic thinking and to use more open strategies, if they want to become technologically more innovative (Figure 2.2).

STRATEGY

To understand how and why companies develop and to judge how successful they have been in their search for new products and technologies, we need to be able to define and measure their strategies and strategic outcomes. A number of strategic dimensions have been defined and used in our

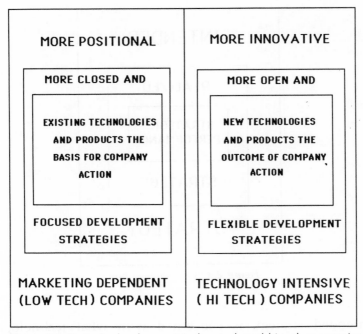

Figure 2.2 *Strategic development in low-tech and hi-tech companies*

studies[21] and the most important are given in this section. Our overall definitions related to strategy are summarized in our basic strategy box (Figure 2.3).

Intended and Realized Strategy

Intended strategy is the overall, often indirect, guidance of company activities, with long run implications for product and company development.[22] It is more concerned with the conditions for change, than with actual outcomes. When intended strategy is dealt with in the management literature it is often called policy.

The word policy, however, is often used to refer to the official goals of a company, even when these goals are detached from actual decision-making.[23] For that reason, since our concern is with what companies want to achieve, although they may not know precisely how to go about it, the phrase intended strategy is used in this book instead of policy.

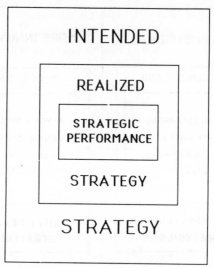

Figure 2.3 Basic strategy box

Intended strategy is concerned with what technologies companies want to develop and what markets they want to focus on, but it need not specify what actual new products they hope to achieve. It may also deal with organizational conditions to stimulate and facilitate change and with company culture and climate to make change possible.

Realized strategy,[24] on the other hand, is the actual evolving pattern of decisions and activities. It is what the company has done, rather than what it has planned to do, and therefore is our main interest when relating strategic action to outcome. Intended strategy may guide and enable, or restrain and delimit, realized strategy by favoring or blocking various learning and development patterns. It will not, however, determine what will actually happen, since this will be influenced also by unpredictable events, such as general technological change, competitive response and changes in buyer attitudes and preferences.

The distinction between intended and realized strategy, and the view of realized strategy as a pattern of evolving decisions, are cornerstones of our approach to strategic management. It was first developed in an empirical study of pricing, employing a number of operational dimensions of strategy.[25] A similar view of strategy has been suggested by

Mintzberg,[26] who also uses the term realized strategy to refer to 'a pattern in a stream of significant decisions' and sees strategic learning as being fostered by emergent strategy.

Company Strategy

Company strategy deals with the configuration and orientation of an enterprise, rather than with its marketable results. This includes dimensions such as the technological and marketing orientation of a company and its organization structure, culture and climate.

A company, for instance, may favor more closed, concentrated strategies or more open, diversified ones.[27] In the case of organization strategy, for instance, both internally and in relation to the external environment, a more closed strategy is fixed and functionally specialized, while a more open strategy is flexible and project based.

Pharmacia, one of the world's leading companies in fine separation and medical diagnosis, has a very open and flexible internal and external organization strategy, based on project specific cooperation and coordination with outside experts and resources. This involves a wide, rather than narrow focus for searching the outside environment, and a strong emphasis on attracting people with unknown ideas and resources, which fit the company's technological and marketing image.

This company has been highly successful in building up and maintaining a challenging and creative culture and climate and a strong company image of technological leadership and of openness and fairness in dealing with external ideas and in research cooperation.

More open marketing strategies may be used by companies to find new markets for exploiting their technological competence. They may, for instance, try to reach new customers by broadening their distribution channels or by licensing product rights to other companies. AGA, for instance, the major Swedish gas and gas equipment company, had to find new distribution channels for gas-based medical applications. They then needed to reach doctors and hospitals, and not only manufacturing firms which are their traditional customers.

In other instances companies may achieve more open marketing strategies by buyer development, making buyers more receptive to change and more competent in taking advantage of new techniques. Eka Nobell, a Swedish chemical company which we shall describe more closely in Chapter 12, stressed this in their marketing strategy, when they developed a new chemical process for paper making, which most paper makers did not have the technical skills or psychological willingness to use. They installed the necessary equipment and helped buyers to run it during extended training periods giving them confidence and competence in using the new system.

An open company development strategy with regard to organization and marketing may lead to even greater innovative potential, if a company also deliberately tries to broaden its internal technological base, its own skills and competences. A very important substrategy then is recruitment. By bringing in people with different technological backgrounds, which may give rise to new technological competences and combinations within the company, a more innovative strategy may be achieved. Food companies may, for instance, employ nutritional experts for their R & D, and not only food chemists; as Wasa, the Swedish Hard Bread company, did to improve the nutritional value of their products, and their product image.

Product Strategy

Strategic management requires, however, that we consider not only different intended and realized strategies on the company level, and the extent to which they support each other, but also strategic outcome, that is the resulting products, processes or marketable know-how. If we use the word product in a wide sense—to include not only hardware, but also software—we may call this the need to look at both company strategy, product strategy and the relationships between company and product strategy.

Typically, strategic management theory[28] has been almost exclusively concerned with the company level and strategic marketing theory[29] with the product level of analysis. In this book the need to consider both levels, and the interaction between them, is emphasized. This is illustrated in our company and product development box (Figure 2.4). In this diagram we distinguish between more open company strategies, which are likely to lead to more innovative technologies and products, and more closed strategies, which are more likely to lead to less innovative ones.

In our empirical work we have studied company strategy mainly by interviewing top management. Product strategies have been dealt with by directly interviewing company representatives about specific instances of product development, which together are used to give a representative picture of realized strategy over an extended time period. From these detailed cases a number of strategic dimensions have been derived, which in our data are closely associated with technological, marketing and commercial success.

These dimensions—for instance, technology use, technology orientation and marketing orientation—and the ways in which they are related to more open and more closed technological

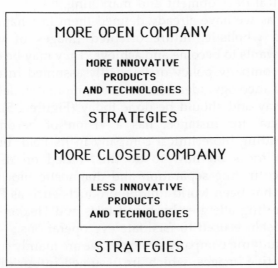

Figure 2.4 *Company and product development box*

and marketing strategies and to success—are discussed more
fully in Chapter 4.

IMAGE AND INNOVATION

Our definition of *image* refers to the mental picture, that is
conceptual representation, that an individual has of some
aspect of reality. This allows for individual creativity in
collecting and processing information. We are thus not only
concerned with cognitive input or perception in our definition
of image, which is the usual way image is defined in the
marketing and communications literature.[30] Our use of the
word image thus assumes an active psychological orientation
towards the environment and allows for psychological interplay both in and between individuals. Image is not merely
seen as the result of passive perception of environmental
cues.

This makes it possible for us to relate the concept of image
to company creativity and innovation. Image management
then becomes a question of how companies can use corporate
images and product images as a basis for strategic learning
and promotional activities, to become more successful in
technological development and marketing.

Visions, as we have already defined them in Chapter 1, are
vivid and wholistic, future oriented images of what the
company wants to become and achieve. They may be explicitly
stated in company policy or implicitly assumed in company
action and ideology. Ideas are concrete, more detailed images
of what may and should be done today (Figure 2.5).

Pharmacia, for instance, has a vision of becoming the
world's leading biotechnical company in its field, but it also
has many ideas on how to do this, based on its unique
competence in fine separation and diagnostic biochemistry.
The result has been world unique products such as Phadebas
Rast for testing allergies by blood tests and Healon, a semi-
liquid substance used to facilitate eye operations.

When studying company strategies we are mainly concerned
with collective images, which are assumed in our discussion
unless otherwise noted. We must remember, however, that

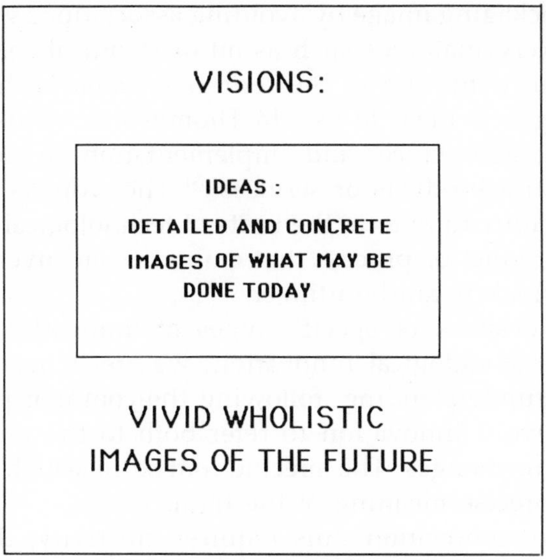

VISIONS:

IDEAS :

DETAILED AND CONCRETE
IMAGES OF WHAT MAY BE
DONE TODAY

VIVID WHOLISTIC
IMAGES OF THE FUTURE

Figure 2.5 Vision and idea

all shared visions and ideas are based on individual thought processes. If we want to study and influence corporate and product image making and image change, which is of crucial importance for company creativity and innovation, we must begin with individual images and creativity.

In our framework, image is related to marketing and to technological innovation. From our data it is clear that companies try to develop specific guiding images on both the strategic and operational levels and that the outcome of these efforts influences success in product and company development.

A good example is Tetra Pak, the world's leading supplier of packaging equipment for edible liquids. This company communicates by its philosophy and corporate advertising clear and consistent images, which have led to highly focused marketing efforts, but also permitted innovative thinking and research. Its liquid packaging concept is based on a geometrical image, the tetraeder. This idea has helped the company to find solutions which decrease material use in production, limit storage space and increase hygiene in distribution and consumption. Tetra Pak's marketing concept is built on restricting the use of its equipment to edible foods: to retain a 'clean' packaging image by avoiding associations with 'dirty' or 'poisonous' materials such as oil or chemical solutions.

Our main definition of the term *innovation* is the process of bringing new ideas to use. In Thompson's words it is 'the generation, acceptance, and implementation of new ideas, processes and products or services'.[31] The word is also used in the literature to refer to the units of technological change,[32] and 'the product or process that embodies an invention in a form by which it can be utilized'.[33]

When we speak of specific types of innovation, such as market or technological innovation, we are, when it cannot lead to misunderstanding, following the common practice of using the word innovation to refer both to the process and the resulting changes. The specific context in which it is used gives the precise meaning of the term.

Successful innovation thus requires creativity, the ability to conceive and develop constructive new ideas. Insightful new images therefore may be seen as manifestations of creativity and as intermediate links between creativity and innovation.

These definitions allow for both individual and company creativity and innovation, which is necessary if we, as in the present book, want to focus on both product and company development and the interaction between these two levels of analysis.

STRATEGIC CREATIVITY MIX

On the company level the term strategic creativity mix is used to refer to the combination of innovation management and image management needed to achieve creative company development. On the product level creativity is seen in terms of the need to combine and recombine knowledge from different areas of technology and use marketing to focus this knowledge and make it commercially valuable.

Creative strategic management thus requires that companies use both image and innovation management to achieve marketing and technological innovation, as a basis for successful product and company development in a changing world.

Image is the psychological basis for strategy guidance and marketing efforts. Successful image management in innovative situations requires both individual creativity and a creative company culture and climate.

Innovation is the technological basis for, and outcome of, marketing and technological strategies. Innovation management requires building up knowledge in the company and combining this knowledge in unique ways to gain competitive advantages and customer satisfaction.

To implement strategy organizational processes[34] are needed and these processes, as well as individual creativity, are influenced by company culture and climate. Culture[35] is defined as values, norms, beliefs and assumptions that a group uses to cope with external adaptation and internal integration. Climate[36] is defined as the feelings, attitudes and behavioral tendencies that characterize organizational life. The interrelationships between culture, climate and strategy are discussed more fully in an empirical context in Chapter 12.

It is by using these and related concepts and definitions that an analytical integration is achieved in our framework between our two main factors, image management and innovation management.

MARKETING

Employing a broad definition, marketing may be viewed as 'the activities that relate an organization successfully to its environment'.[37] These activities lead to exchange relationships between companies and their supportive environment and transactions between buyers and sellers. They also lead to competition with other companies for scarce and valued resources and market share.

Following this definition of marketing as relationship management[38] the short-term handling of relationships should be the concern of day-to-day marketing and the long-term evolving and transforming of relationships the role of strategic marketing.

Strategic marketing models, such as those discussed by Abel and Hammond,[39] do not, however, pay much attention to how companies may handle innovative relationships, for instance, find and develop radically new products and phase out old ones. Instead, as in the Boston Consulting Group model,[40] the need for a balance between old and new products and markets is usually acknowledged, but little attention is paid to the main strategic problem, how companies should proceed to achieve this goal. Essentially, these models do not deal with the role of marketing for product and company development, they merely state the problem.

Our strategic management framework emphasizes the creative process of innovative change, and views marketing strategy as an important part of this process. The creative role of marketing in our approach is handling changing relationships between companies and their environments and contributing to constructive change in these networks; it is the focusing, balancing and integrative mechanism for matching internal organizational possibilities with external opportunities. It is not so much concerned with directly generating these possibilities, the content of change, which is the main role attributed in our framework to technological strategy.

By helping to develop, influence and communicate images within companies and on the market place, marketing strategies guide and coordinate both the process of relating the company to its environment (external marketing) and building company culture and climate (internal marketing). Marketing, as we view the term, therefore plays a major role in strategic management, but we need to carefully consider its relationships to other aspects of strategic change, such as technological strategies.

An example from our data of a company showing a very concentrated and consistent marketing strategy is SCA, a major Swedish wood and paper company. This company has employed a highly consistent marketing strategy, based on strong self sufficiency and large scale mass production, to successfully build and maintain its traditional business. Its external strategy of extending the range of its own activities and controlling its sales, is supported by its internal marketing strategy, and reflected in almost all its activities from the forest to its final customers, which often are its own subsidiaries.

SCA has a very large proportion of sales going to established customers and its R & D and product development are strongly concentrated on existing technologies and products. It has, for instance, been highly successful in reducing the weight per square inch of newsprint paper, while still retaining acceptable strength and printability. Its self image, as a producer of forest products, does not favor the use of any basic raw material for making pulp and paper except 'virgin fibers'. This means nonrecirculated fibers from trees, preferably grown in its own forests in Northern Sweden. It also views itself as almost entirely a mass processor of wood and pulp. Differentiating and upgrading its products by diversifying into related fields, such as prefabricated houses or wooden details, is discouraged by its self image, which is more focused and concentrated than most of its competitors.

An example from our data of a company with a more open and flexible self image guiding its strategy is the chemical company Eka Nobell. Similar to SCA this company works in a large scale, industrial supply industry, but its internal and external marketing strategy—and its technological strategy— put more emphasis on promoting new technologies and products.

Eka has actively used internal marketing to change its company image, climate and culture in an innovative direction and external marketing to find new markets. By combining this with an open technological strategy the company has successfully developed a number of new products, for instance Compozil, a radically new chemical concept for making paper. The idea was successfully marketed internally and externally, although it made necessary substantial technological reorientations, both within the company and in the paper making industry.

Instead of using highly positional internal and external marketing strategies to focus its marketing and technological efforts almost exclusively on its existing products and markets, as in the case of SCA, Eka thus has used its strategies actively to promote innovative development. This has taken place both within the company and in relation to its external environment and has made it possible for Eka to become a more innovative company.

Strategic Marketing Mix

The term strategic marketing mix[41] is used in our approach to refer to the balance between openness and closure in the way companies handle marketing relationships (Figure 2.6). It is seen as basically reflecting the relative use by companies of competitive strategy versus holding strategy.

When using a competitive strategy companies utilize the horizontal complexity in market situations (differences in offers by competing firms) by making frequent moves in the market place to get customers to buy from them rather than from competitors. Buyer mobility and propensity to change

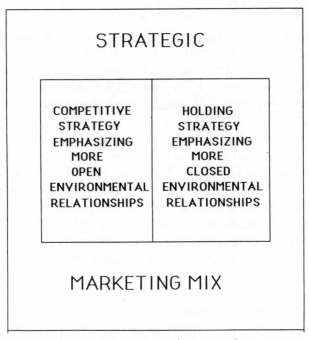

STRATEGIC	
COMPETITIVE STRATEGY EMPHASIZING MORE OPEN ENVIRONMENTAL RELATIONSHIPS	HOLDING STRATEGY EMPHASIZING MORE CLOSED ENVIRONMENTAL RELATIONSHIPS

MARKETING MIX

Figure 2.6 *Strategic marketing mix box*

their patronage to get a better deal is thus the center of interest in this, which is, from a marketing point of view, a relatively open strategy. Holding strategy is based on vertical complexity, tying customers to a company by the active use of various action parameters (such as buyer–seller cooperation and interaction to achieve joint benefits from technological development) which limit customer mobility or willingness to change from one supplier to another. These terms are discussed more in detail in Chapter 8, and applied to an empirical study of marketing strategies in Swedish paper companies in Chapter 9.

Generalization and Discrimination

Image learning in our approach is viewed as a psychological process of generalization and discrimination (Figure 2.7). This model was first developed and presented in the context of pricing strategies,[42] but it is a mechanism which may be used as well to understand image marketing and image competition in general.

Generalization implies jumping between different levels of meaning and points of time, while discrimination means

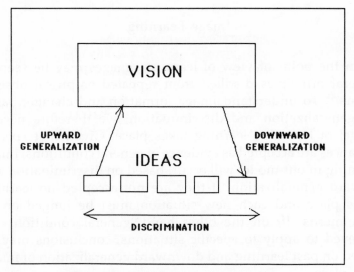

Figure 2.7 Generalization and discrimination

immediately comparing different possibilities and options. Forming visions: images of the future, from ideas: concrete evaluations of present day situations, is an example of upward generalization based on discrimination. These visions should be sufficiently closed in their meanings and implications to provide guidance, but open enough to permit creative thinking. If this is the case, decision makers may take intuitive leaps in their thinking, without losing contact with pre-existing conditions. This is the essence of the creative process and a precondition for innovative strategies. By using flexible images we can stretch our imagination, yet stay within the limits of technological, marketing and organizational restraints.

Upward generalization therefore is concerned with the building up of images to provide guiding visions for creative action in the future, while downward generalization involves breaking down and deconstructing images to make possible direct action today. Discrimination is a selective response to existing conditions. The process of generalization and discrimination may be influenced by company action, as we shall see in the following sections, and image management is our term for this.

Image Learning

From the point of view of learning, images may be seen as general principles distilled from repeated empirical observations.[43] To understand image formation and change, based on generalization and discrimination, we therefore need a model of how this learning takes place. Given that specific instances are accepted as evidence of general conditions, image learning in our model will occur, based on discrimination and upward generalization. If they are not accepted no learning takes place and each new situation must be judged on its own merits. If, on the other hand, general conditions are believed to apply to specific situations, conclusions may be based on past learning and downward generalization of image take place.

In the case of strategy, downward generalization could be from strategic vision to product or project evaluation, and upward generalization from evaluation to strategic vision. Because the Swedish pharmaceutical company Astra has a leading reputation in, and strategic commitment to, heart medicine, its top executives are likely to believe in the strategic vision that the company can develop unique and successful new products in this area and to be willing to commit resources to such R & D projects. This, then, is an example of downward generalization from perceived overall competence to the evaluation of specific projects.

If on the other hand a number of such R & D projects fail, company leaders are likely to reassess their strategic visions on the basis of these specific projects, and be less willing in the future to invest in developing new heart medicines. We then have an example of image learning based on upward generalization from specific instances to general principle. An example of sideward generalization is concluding on the basis of a successful project for developing a new heart medicine that another project for developing a different heart medicine will probably also be successful.

Image Marketing

Image marketing in our framework is closely tied to relationship management. By making explicit or implicit promises, and living up to the resulting expectations, companies can influence buyer images and achieve strong customer ties, based on mutual commitments and psychological trust. This, then, should reduce the company's exposure to competitive attacks in the future and increase buyer willingness to cooperate in product development and other joint ventures.

By marketing agreements, such as contracts and joint ventures, companies can further tighten these relationships. Hopefully both buyers and sellers will benefit from such agreements, which then may be expected to lead to positive feedback and strengthened long-term relationships. Inter Innovation, for instance, succeeded in selling a corporate image of speed and efficiency in developing and delivering technologically advanced banking equipment, while possessing no relevant manufacturing experience or even facilities to produce it. They then bought and converted a factory to successfully fulfill their obligations and on time. This, of course is a spectacular instance of successful image management, but many innovative companies have succeeded less dramatically with this type of strategy.

Tour Agenturer, for instance—a company producing electronic regulation equipment for buildings—stated in our early interviews that they had to be one step ahead of their own accomplishments in making commitments. Owing to rapid technological change, and the demand from contractors to be able to plan ahead for using the most advanced technology in their building projects, they had to contract to deliver their new products up to six months before these were fully developed, and then make sure that they could keep their promises. Maintaining a technological lead over competitors was not enough in this situation. Even future unrealized technological advances had to be sold to stay in business.

External Image Marketing

In the case of external image marketing, if customers or business partners base evaluations of specific products or projects on images of the company's overall ability to satisfy their needs, this is an example of downward generalization. If they build up such images from previous experience this is an example of upward generalization. If they judge one specific instance by another in some way similar one, we may speak of sideward generalization.

If a customer, for instance, thinks a company is a technological leader in biotechnology, because it has developed one or more world unique products or processes (as in the case of Pharmacia) this is an upward generalization, based on discrimination. If the customer thinks that technological leadership *per se* is a guarantee for high and unique technical quality in the case of individual products or processes, this instead is a downward generalization from a higher to a lower level of evaluation. If the customer thinks that a diagnostic kit for cancer developed by Pharmacia is an outstanding new product, because some experience or knowledge of one of Pharmacia's allergy testing kits is favorable, this is an instance of sideward generalization, based on discrimination.

In these examples of external image marketing, the same type of reasoning is applicable, as in the case of internal image marketing. The important thing is not whether images are true representations of reality: often this is an impossible or meaningless question to answer. Instead, it is images that determine behavior, as our empirical data in Chapter 7 clearly show.

It is almost impossible, for instance, to determine objectively and accurately whether a store with a favorable price image really has lower prices than competing stores. This almost always, at least in the case of multiple purchases over time, depends on precisely when, and exactly what, items a customer purchases and in what quantities. Most stores, particularly in the case of convenience goods, usually have higher prices than their competitors for certain types of comparable items and lower prices for others. In addition, there are almost always quality differences between competing items, especially if we use a wide definition of quality to include subjective quality, that is psychological satisfaction.

The main questions from an image marketing point of view are if buyers or business partners have clear images of what they expect, and how these images change as a result of company action and are related to the customers' or partners' behavior and satisfaction. The ethical marketing issue is whether or not companies deliberately try to create misleading expectations by using marketing tricks. These are not easy questions to answer, but if we ask the right questions, we at least do not risk getting the right reply to the wrong enquiry. This is more misleading than not getting any answers at all, but waiting instead with a more open state of mind to see what will happen.

What is important from an image marketing point of view is therefore not whether images truly reflect reality. Instead, the crucial issue is if images are individually and socially acceptable, and if companies believe that they can live up to the expectations they create soon and well enough. If so they should use the most efficient means at their disposal for changing images to make possible their desired futures, and then fulfill the resulting expectations.

Internal Image Marketing

Internal image marketing may be used by company employees who want to promote their own development projects and we may use our model of discrimination and generalization to understand how this may work. Such internal marketing is carried out in many ways. One often used strategy is to try to gain outside support for proposals. This may be done directly by using established external experts to support specific projects (discrimination). Or it may be done indirectly, by company personnel seeking outside acceptance for their overall competence to carry out projects (generalization).

Researchers, for instance, may gain credibility for their ability to carry out specific projects by publishing articles on related topics in scientific journals. Indeed this may be the main reason for company researchers to seek publication, even in obscure journals with limited readership.

Another way to carry out internal image marketing is to use research cooperation with qualified outside experts, to convince superiors that a certain type of research can successfully be carried out within the company. This may be one reason why research cooperation, as our studies show, is fairly common in many companies, despite the 'not invented here' syndrome and other resistance to using outside expertise, not least the fact that this may be taken as a sign of weakness within the company. By using the right argument—that outside cooperation strengthens the company's own ability, rather than shows a lack of internal competence—an apparent inadequacy thus can be turned into an asset, which is what image marketing is really all about.

Image Marketing and Entrepreneurship

Entrepreneurs often view success in one field as evidence of their competence in strikingly different fields (sideward generalization) and surprisingly often they are proved right. This may be part of the entrepreneurial personality, seeing resemblances and strengths where others see only disparities and weaknesses.

Successful entrepreneurs typically employ direct action to achieve changes in image. It is by doing things, rather than talking about them, they try to convince both themselves and others that they are successful. They thus tend to build up both their corporate images and strategic visions by upward generalization based on discrimination of concrete action and ideas. The whole company may be seen as a research project selling the future, but lack of established images and practices from which to generalize, makes it necessary for the company to specify closely what they want to achieve and can achieve and to be sensitive to direct experience rather than to echoes from the past.

The most extreme entrepreneur in our data, Leif Lundblad, with whom we will be concerned more closely in Chapter 3, progressed from repairing television sets to cleaning neon signs and buildings, followed by the hi-tech development and marketing of automatic cash dispensing systems for banks and even invented a back exercising machine. This latter product he put on the market after it had cured his own ailing back, which was the real reason he developed it.

Probably no one but Lundblad could see and explain the links and connections between these, from a conventional point of view, very different projects. Since he was the founder and owner of the companies he was involved in, he had less need for internal image marketing to sell his ideas, than if he had been employed, but he probably would have done well in this respect too, had it been more necessary, at least if we may judge from his success in selling his ideas to other companies.

Leif Lundblad sold his prototype for a cash dispensing machine to a prospective customer, Citibank, by using vivid displays, such as cardboard models of the as yet not fully developed equipment. He thereby sold the rough idea for the product and received advance orders and financial and technical help from his first customer in developing the prototype, without giving up product rights. By successfully completing the project he was able to build a favorable company image and use this to market the banking equipment to other customers. This in our terminology is an example of highly successful external image marketing.

Changing an Established Image

Established companies often try to use corporate advertising, public relations or sponsoring to achieve favorable image changes and favorable downward generalization of image. This requires a consistency between image and perceived reality, within the company as well as in relation to its environment.

If the picture a company tries to paint is viewed as irrelevant (as it may well be in the case of sponsoring) or perceived as invalid (as may be the case in corporate advertising or public relations programs) the result may be confusion, resentment or a lack of interest in the target groups. This may even lead to unfavorable, rather than favorable changes in image, since some people may view it as intentionally misleading.

As an example we may take Alfa Laval, one of Sweden's largest firms, specializing in separation processes with major applications in agriculture and in the food industry. A few years ago this company tried to change its image from relatively low-tech to hi-tech, mainly by using corporate advertising. The company was not very successful in this attempt at external image marketing and by and large gave up its efforts to change its image by mass media communication.

The reason for lack of success in this attempt at external image marketing was most likely that the image communicated did not fit the existing public image of the company and no specific evidence was given to make possible a change in image by upward generalization. Unsubstantiated claims tend not to lead to changes in image since there is no basis for learning based on independent thinking (discrimination).

TECHNOLOGY

If we are mainly interested in existing products and processes, technology may be defined as, 'the set of physical processes, methods, techniques, tools and equipment by which products are made or services rendered'.[44] This is the way the term technology is usually employed in the management literature.

If we want to study innovative product and company development, however, we need a broader and more open definition. In our approach technology means knowledge that is potentially useful for product and company development, even though the immediate implications may not be clear.

We thus stress the open possibilities implied by knowledge, rather than the closed applications we may call techniques. Technological strategies are seen mainly as divergent, knowledge creating devices. They give new content to marketing strategies and successful technological strategies therefore are directly related to, and require, creativity and innovation; that is, novel and constructive thinking and results.

Technology and Innovation

Technological strategy in our framework refers to how companies may directly and indirectly open and extend the knowledge base of the company: the term R & D strategy might be used instead. This term, however, is often used in a narrower sense in the literature, with the emphasis on product development.[45] Since we are interested both in company and product development, and the relationship between the two, we prefer a more open, knowledge based development term, going beyond what is needed to develop specific new products or processes.

As we have noted above there is a direct connection in our framework between technological strategy and innovation, viewed as radical change. Since innovation leads to and demands new knowledge, and technological strategy is concerned with developing new knowledge, this relationship follows directly from the meanings we have given these terms.

There is also a close connection between creativity and technology in our approach.

Creativity is the mechanism for achieving technological breakthroughs and transforming them into innovation, that is constructive change. The earlier stages of the creative process are primarily concerned with developing new technology, that is with broadening the knowledge base of the company. This is the main function of technological strategy in our framework. The later stages are more concerned with focusing this knowledge, and the mechanism for doing this in our approach is marketing strategy.

Technology and Marketing

It must be stressed that this is not at odds with the generally accepted view in the marketing literature,[46] that product development must reflect market needs to gain market acceptance. Market knowledge is one crucial part of the technology base of a company, and we may use the term market technology to reflect this need.

It is at odds, however, with a narrow definition of the marketing concept. It is often said by marketing people that by far the most important requirement for the successful development of new products, is to be sensitive to market needs. This may be the main mechanism for successful product modification. In the case of radically new products, on the other hand, we need a broader knowledge base for finding and developing ideas, than follows from a narrow interpretation of the marketing concept.

We need to know what part of the market it is that can provide us with crucial knowledge on new product needs, and develop this knowledge together with existing and potential users. But we also need new knowledge from many other sources and technological strategy must be concerned with finding and developing all new knowledge which is of value for company and product development.

Customers are important in finding and developing new ideas,[47] especially for industrial products such as scientific instruments,[48] that have highly technically competent users, but so are other companies, universities, consultants and inventors, as our own data shows.

In the food processing companies we have studied (Chapter 10), non-competing companies abroad were most influential in providing new ideas and SIK, the Swedish Food Industries joint research institute, in providing outside research assistance for product development. For the farm machinery companies (Chapter 5), the Agricultural University of Sweden was most important for idea generation and outside research cooperation in developing new products. For Pharmacia, in the area of medical diagnosis, outside inventors, doctors and university researchers played an important role for initiating and helping to develop new products.

What sources of outside cooperation and assistance, and what technological strategies companies need to find and develop this knowledge, therefore depends on product type and industry characteristics and must be determined by research. While customers are important in this respect they may not always know what they want and know even less about how to go about getting it.

Internal and External Technology Orientation

As in the case of marketing strategies, we may distinguish between more internal technological strategies, directed towards and based on using the company's own competence and resources to develop knowledge and more external technological strategies, aiming at utilizing outside help for this purpose.[49]

Around 1975, when our early company interviews took place, Swedish companies seemed to emphasize internal technological strategies to a greater extent than they do today. Sandvik, for instance, the pioneering Swedish company in hard metal tools, had a very internally oriented technological strategy before and during the mid-seventies. They relied almost entirely on their own technological competence and knowledge for finding and developing new products and processes, and had very few contacts with outside consultants, inventors, universities, or even their own customers, for development purposes.

Both the culture and technological strategies of the company reflected a strong belief in 'do-it-yourself', and 'not invented here' had almost the same meaning in the company as 'of no use here'. This strong, internally oriented company culture and development strategy had been built up during periods when the company was commercially very successful. When the company in later years became less successful it changed, with difficulty, to a more externally oriented technological strategy, based more on outside cooperation for development purposes.

We may contrast this very internal technological strategy with an extreme instance of an external technological strategy, again originating in our early interview data. Even before the mid-seventies Pharmacia had shown a strong external orientation, which is usually given as the main reason for the geographical location of the company to Uppsala, to be close to its university. By locating itself at the center of a technological network, it hoped to be able to attract and retain the best ideas and leading technology to generate and develop business possibilities.

By encouraging university researchers, doctors and inventors to view Pharmacia as the best possible partner in developing their ideas, Pharmacia has been able to develop a number of world unique products in the area of medical diagnostics and treatment, based on the synergy between outside ideas and internal company competence. This flexible type of technological networking has also helped to develop the overall technological competence of the company and position it as a leading biotechnological company in the medical area.

Synergistic and Isolated Technology Use

Another related aspect of technological strategy is synergistic or isolated technology use.[50] Synergistic technology use refers to the combining and recombining of existing knowledge to gain new knowledge. This obviously may be viewed as a general definition of creativity, and as a natural requirement for creative management. Since broadening the knowledge base of a company is necessary to achieve synergistic technology use, and an important mechanism for this is cooperation with outside experts, the degree of external orientation is of interest in this context.

Management theory, however, has traditionally focused mainly on the refinement of existing knowledge, what we may call isolated technology use, and not much attention has been paid to the generation and use of radical new knowledge. Since we can find little help in the management literature, the basis for our discussion of this creativity aspect of technological development, as in the case of internal versus external orientation, therefore, is the empirical evidence from our early interviews.

In our very first interview a leading representative for AGA—the Swedish company now specializing in gas and gas equipment, but then interested in a wider range of technologies and products—indicated the need for looking at company technology in a new way. It was company policy, he stated, to require that any new product be based on a combination of at least two of the company's three then leading areas of technology, mechanical engineering, optical measurement, and microelectronics. Knowledge from at least two of these areas jointly had to be viewed as of critical importance in developing a new product or process: otherwise the company was not likely to gain a leading technological advantage—a technological niche—from the development efforts, and was therefore not interested.

Today AGA is more interested in specialization within given areas of technology, that is isolated technology use, than in the combining of previously unrelated knowledge from different areas, that is synergistic technology use. ASEA, another company interviewed in our early research, emphasized isolated technology use in 1975 within areas such as the transmission of electric power, and has a similar technological strategy today.

Pharmacia, on the other hand, has since 1975 continued to pursue its successful technological strategy of creatively combining knowledge from different areas; for example, polymer technology and biotechnical separation. This has led to many radically new products, such as Debrisan, a new medical treatment for sores.

As in the case of our other strategic dimensions it is thus not possible to say that specific aspects of technological development strategies, such as isolated versus synergistic technology use, are always related to success. Our view of strategy assumes instead that different strategies are required to reflect different situations, and a successful strategy in one development context may be unsuccessful in another.

Our empirical results suggest, however, that companies can often succeed in becoming more innovative—in the sense of successfully finding and commercially developing technologically more unique products and processes—by employing a more externally oriented technological strategy to achieve synergistic technology use. There is a clear correlation in our data between using such strategies and finding technologically advanced or unique new products or processes.

On the other hand, if the objective is to be more positional in the sense of finding and developing a large number of new products reflecting the established technology areas and markets of a company, then our results suggest that a more internally oriented strategy and an isolated technology use is more likely to be successful.

Strategic Technology Mix

In our conceptual scheme the term strategic technology mix is used to refer to the combined effect of technology use and technological orientation on how open or closed a technological strategy is. A more external orientation and a more synergistic technology use both tend to lead to a more open and searching technological strategy while a more internal orientation and a more isolated technology use tend to lead to a more closed and consolidated one. These two dimensions of technological strategy are shown in our strategic technology mix box (Figure 2.8).

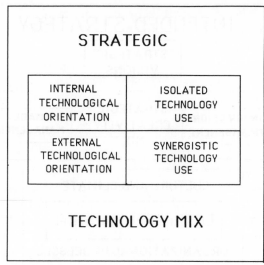

Figure 2.8 *Strategic technology mix box*

STRATEGIC MANAGEMENT BOX

Our basic overall framework is summarized in the 'Strategic Management Box' presented in Figure 2.9. The upper part of this box is concerned with intended strategy and the lower part with realized strategy.

Being an important part of intended strategies, strategic visions are seen as guiding mechanisms for allocating technological marketing resources for product and company development, restrained by technological requirements and marketing requirements. These requirements are partly satisfied by the existing technological and marketing specialization of the company: of dominating importance in highly positional companies. But they also depend on the innovative potential of the company, that is, the possibilities for developing new products, processes and know-how by creative combinations and extensions of the technology base. The greater these possibilities are, the more innovative the company can become if its strategic management utilizes this potential.

The strategic allocations of resources used for innovation management and image management, and the complementary way in which this is done is the strategic creativity mix of

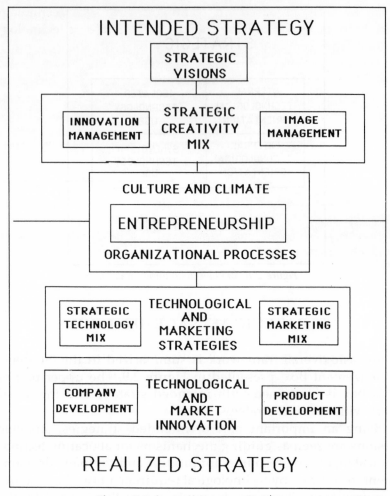

Figure 2.9 *Strategic management box*

the company. More marketing dependent companies need to put more emphasis directly on image management and market development in their strategic creativity mix, while more technologically dependent companies need to put more emphasis directly on innovation management and technology development.

With regard to realized strategy, innovation management is most closely related to technological strategy and image management to marketing strategy. Technological strategy in turn is seen as based on technology use and technology orientation, which together make up the strategic technology mix of the company.

As noted above, technology use may be either synergistic, based on technological combinations, or isolated, based on technological specialization, while technology orientation may be internal, based on company resources or external, based on cooperation with outside resources. Marketing strategy is viewed as the balance between competitive and holding elements, and this as we have noted above is called the strategic marketing mix. Strategic technology mix, finally, is most closely related to company development and strategic marketing mix to product development, and the interaction between these two levels of strategic outcome determines the strategic development of the company over time.

Entrepreneurship

Entrepreneurship is seen as a direct fusion of intended and realized strategy: a shortcutting of the strategic management process. In Figure 2.9 entrepreneurship therefore is located at the center of the strategic management box. More planned approaches to strategic management may be viewed as a process of strategy formulation and implementation, that is of intended strategy and realized strategy. In our framework, however, the entrepreneur does not formulate strategy: instead, he enacts strategy by directly influencing strategic conditions and outcomes.

Entrepreneurship, therefore, does not in general depend upon given visions, but itself creates visions through action. The entrepreneur as seen by us and described in our book is a visionary activist, rather than a visionary planner. This is reflected in Figure 2.9 by the fact that entrepreneurship is located between intended and realized strategy. It is learning by doing, the action based fusion between both these strategic domains. Culture and climate and organizational processes are viewed as intervening variables which help to determine and are themselves determined by the other strategic variables.

All strategic management has some element of planning and some element of entrepreneurship as described above, which is reflected in the strategic possibilities contained in our strategic management box. The purpose of the strategic management box is to relate the different theoretical and empirical contributions in this book to each other, and to give an overall picture of what is meant by our use of the term strategic management.

*Creativity is the intellectual unfolding
and converging of experience*

*Entrepreneurship is the vizualization
and realization of new ideas*

3
Creativity and Entrepreneurship

In this chapter[1] the role of creativity and entrepreneurship for managing the future will be discussed. The creative process is defined as the balanced intellectual unfolding and converging of experience which is necessary to achieve technological and market innovation. We use the term entrepreneurship to refer to the management of radical change. The word is used in the literature by different writers in many ways,[2] to refer either to general management or to innovation management, and we want to stress that we are using the word in the latter sense.

Technology is viewed in its broadest sense as the knowledge required to change social and economic mechanisms and processes, in society as a whole and in individual companies. With this outlook technological innovation becomes the most important factor for the long run transformation of society and the basic condition for market innovation and successful product and company development.

Entrepreneurship, on the other hand, is seen as the visualization and realization of new ideas and processes by insightful individuals, who are able to use information and mobilize resources to implement their visions. It is thus a necessary condition for transforming information into innovation (Figure 3.1).

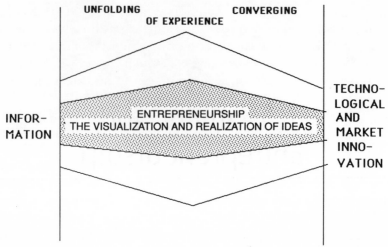

Figure 3.1 *Entrepreneurship as the creative transformation of information into innovation*

This view does not require that entrepreneurs excell in the generation of new ideas. Instead it emphasizes the promotion and implementation of radical change. While such entrepreneurs often are highly creative individuals, they may as well base their entrepreneurship on the ideas of others, as on their own ideas. As our studies of company strategies for innovation summarized in Chapter 4 show, combining knowledge from many sources is more likely to lead to radical change than is concentrated effort.

At the same time, entrepreneurs with many original ideas of their own are usually highly motivated to succeed, but whether or not they do so depends on their ability to assess and market their own ideas, and their sensitivity to and willingness to consider other peoples' viewpoints. Some very successful entrepreneurs, such as Leif Lundblad, who will be introduced further on in this chapter, are also highly creative inventors. Many inventors, however, lack the entrepreneurial skills necessary to evaluate and successfully promote their own ideas.

The entrepreneur in our framework therefore is a visionary activist, a Schumpeterian change agent, who carries out a crucial role in the creative destruction, that is transformation and renewal, of society as a whole and of individual companies. This is quite different from the view of the manager in neoclassical economic theory as an efficient allocator of existing resources, which in effect means a guardian of the status quo. In reaction to orthodox economic theory, a number of economists[3] have pointed out that there is little room for the entrepreneur in this body of thought, and have tried to extend economic theory to include consideration of entrepreneurship.

The most radical attempt was made by Schumpeter who viewed the entrepreneur as carrying out new combinations, thereby introducing spontaneous and discontinuous change and disrupting the circular flow of economic life.[4] He recognized the creative role of the entrepreneur for innovative development and the lack of attention paid to radical change by economists since Ricardo's day. Schumpeter's entrepreneur clearly is innovative in our meaning of the word. His focus is on what we call technological change and his ideas are very interesting in the context of what we call innovation management.

More recently, Klein has argued that there is a need for a more dynamic economic theory, 'based on the assumption of an open system, a system in which entrepreneurs interacting with their technological environments can change both their ideas and their environments by generating new knowledge'.[5] Like Schumpeter he is thus mainly interested in technological change and does not view marketing as an essential part of entrepreneurial decision making.

Other economists, such as Kirzner, view the entrepreneur as responding to opportunities, rather than creating them. According to him the entrepreneur is to be seen as a perceiver, rather than a creator of new opportunities. 'For me the important role of entrepreneurship is not so much the ability to break away from routine as the ability to perceive new opportunities which others have not yet noticed'.[6] Kirzner focuses on some aspects (such as price, advertising and selling efforts) of what we call marketing in our framework, and does not deal with technological change, or the interaction between marketing and technology, which are central to our understanding of entrepreneurship.

Casson's definition of an entrepreneur is someone who specializes in taking judgemental decisions about the coordination of scarce resources.[7] He is an active planner and skillful negotiator who synthesizes information to recognize and exploit opportunities in uncertain conditions. He is not a radical new thinker, but someone who can vizualize the probable consequences of fairly marginal changes in resource allocation. From the point of view of our approach, Casson stresses the organizational aspect of entrepreneurship, and pays much less attention to the technological or market aspects.

While these economists more or less recognize the need for creative action for entrepreneurship, they do not explicitly deal with the main issue from a product and company development point of view, what creative management is and how companies may stimulate and facilitate innovative change. Instead, they focus on the development issues, rather than on strategies for change. They basically assume that the determinants of radical change are outside the range of economic theory.

Their views of entrepreneurship are more partial than our approach and do not consider the need to balance different, often contradictory aspects of change, which is at the heart of the creative process. The entrepreneur in our framework is concerned with the perceiving, opening up and exploiting of technological, marketing and organizational possibilities, excelling in the creative process of balancing these activities.

Our view of entrepreneurship is consistent with the spirit and tone of a number of recent books on innovation in the management literature. These approaches, however, usually do not systematically try to relate entrepreneurship to technological and market change. Instead they typically focus on the organizational potential for entrepreneurship,[8] organizational change,[9] creative leadership[10] or sources for innovation.[11] While strategies for change are dealt with in general terms or are implicit in their reasoning, these writers do not explicitly tell us how such strategies should be measured and related to performance. There are various ways, as we shall see in the following chapters, by which entrepreneurs and companies can increase their likelihood of success by achieving a

constructive balance between openness and closure in technological, marketing and organizational relationships. We need
a wide approach to strategic management to capture the
relevant factors, but also we must focus attention on what
can be done to implement and evaluate change.

CREATIVITY—GENERATING NEW KNOWLEDGE

Our view of creativity[12] focuses on the need for providing
guidance for action in erratically changing and changeable
situations, when a great deal of radically new knowledge is
needed to accommodate change.

Among psychologists, individual creativity used to be a
neglected area of research, owing to prevailing research
doctrines—behaviorism and stimulus response theories—
emphasizing measurement and predictability. This by and
large precluded creativity from consideration, since it is an
elusive and complicated phenomenon difficult to define
precisely and control.[13]

During the recent decades the situation has changed and
research on creativity has become accepted and grown in
importance. This has been accompanied by a change in
emphasis in explaining this type of intellectual activity.
Instead of viewing creativity as essentially a passive random
process of association, it is increasingly seen as the result of
active directed thought.[14] This makes it easier to understand
both the creative process and individual differences in
creativity. It also makes theories of creativity highly relevant
for studying entrepreneurship.

The creative process implies initially widening and then
condensing experience in an ongoing interaction with the
environment. This in order to generate possibilities and to
provide guidance and insight in handling and evaluating
their evolving implications. It is hoped that future events will
validate our tentative views and our actions based on these
views will meet our criteria for success. There is no guarantee
for this, however, in the real world.

We therefore need flexibility in thinking and acting to be
able to rapidly reassess and reevaluate situations and change

our action when things turn out differently, as they often do. All dogmatic closure[15] in our thinking patterns needs to be avoided, but at the same time, our thoughts need a focus and a direction to achieve concentration and determination in our efforts.

This need for constructive vagueness, to be open for future change yet maintain a clear sense of direction, makes the creative process a very difficult balancing act, with seemingly conflicting or even impossible demands (Figure 3.2). To be creative we need to be open minded and determined, flexible and unveering, both withholding judgement and jumping to conclusions.

In a static and analytical approach to decision-making these are clearly contradictory and impossible demands. Once we realize, however, that real creativity by its very nature can only be viewed as a dynamic process, a fluid and changing pattern of activities rather than a fixed mechanism or momentary activity, this apparent paradox resolves itself.

The early stages of the creative process are characterized by fuzzy and implicit ideas allowing for many degrees of intellectual freedom, and should be so, to make room for divergent thinking and wide ranging inspiration from various sources (Figure 3.3). A total 'Gestalt'[16] perspective dominates over a more limited, detailed focus. At this stage it is also important that resistance towards redefining[17] existing concepts is not too strong.

Intuition[18] (drawing implications from many vaguely perceived sources) and visual thinking (which may be an

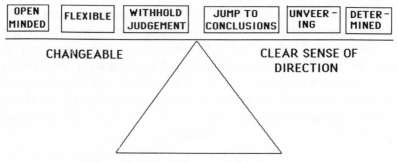

Figure 3.2 *Creativity as a balancing act*

CREATIVE PROCESS	
EARLY STAGES	LATE STAGES
FUZZY IMPLICIT IDEAS MANY DEGREES OF INTELLECTUAL FREEDOM DIVERGENT THINKING WIDE RANGING INSPIRATION VISUAL THINKING INTUITION TOLERANCE OF AMBIGUITY EXPERIMENTS RETHINKING	PRECISE EXPLICIT IDEAS FEW DEGREES OF INTELLECTUAL FREEDOM CONVERGENT THINKING FOCUSED ATTENTION FORMALIZED THINKING ANALYSIS CLEAR CUT RESULTS CONSISTENCY TESTS PERSISTENCE

Figure 3.3 Early and late stages of the creative process

important part of intuitive thinking, by permitting highly open ended interpretations) are extremely flexible and open thought processes, which may be expected to be important at these early stages.

Psychologists interested in the creative process speak, for instance, of the need for tolerating ambiguity, experimenting and rethinking during the early stages of the creative process. In essence this implies what Rogers[19] has called an openness to experience, which characterizes pioneering business men, judging from our own interviews and the literature on innovative entrepreneurship.

The later stages of the creative process, on the other hand, are basically analytical and characterized by convergent thinking and formalized analysis. Highly focused and explicit thought processes are necessary to make more precise and to evaluate the solutions generated during the earlier stages.

This also enables improved communication of results to other people, which is an extremely important aspect of the creative process at its later stages, when verification and implementation are central functions. Being precise and consistent aids the later stages of the creative process, but may be detrimental to the earlier stages by leading to prematurely closed thinking and nonconsideration of other critical, but as yet uncrystallized ideas.

While it is useful to think of the creative process[20] as consisting of different stages, these stages, of course, in practice, are interwoven and there is much moving back and forth between stages as part of the creative process itself. Realizing that different thought patterns and mechanisms may serve different functions in the creative process is more important than dividing it up into clear stages, but at the same time the different stages serve a purpose in communicating this idea. From our data, innovative entrepreneurs appear to be particularly good at balancing; that is, actively timing and coordinating the different stages of the creative process.

As we shall see in the following chapters, our view of technological strategies as basically knowledge creating mechanisms, means that they emphasize the early stages of product and company development processes. Our view of marketing strategies (Chapter 8) as primarily focusing devices means, on the other hand, that they are relatively more important during the later stages of these processes, when adapting to and influencing customer needs tends to be the main consideration.

At the same time it follows from our discussion that more open technological strategies, based for instance on external orientation and synergistic technology use, better reflect what is needed at early stages of development. This is compared to more closed technological strategies, based for instance on internal orientation and isolated technology use, which are better adapted to what is needed during later stages. In Chapter 4, we shall further discuss the implications of more open and closed technological strategies for product and company development against the background of our empirical studies.

ENTREPRENEURSHIP—THE VISUALIZATION AND REALIZATION OF NEW IDEAS

Our view of entrepreneurship is based on the visualization and realization of new ideas. The entrepreneur need not be the inventor or main developer of the ideas, though successful entrepreneurs often are highly creative individuals with many original ideas of their own. The entrepreneurial role, as we see it, is mainly to guide and forcefully carry out innovation. This means that 'innovation, not invention is the specific tool of the entrepreneur'.[21] The result of successful entrepreneurship is the constructive transformation and renewal of different aspects of business and society.

Our approach emphasizes the active handling of risks and uncertainties.[22] It is in sharp contrast, however, with the popular view of the entrepreneur as a risk seeking gambler, who loves risk and finds the business world a more attractive . betting ground than the casino or the race track. Obviously, risk taking plays an important role in entrepreneurship, but the way in which successful entrepreneurs handle such situations is quite different from the commonsense view of the reckless gambler betting the companies resources on wild ideas and projects. It is also different from the calculating way in which businessmen eliminate risk by collecting more information on future possibilities by the use of information theory based economic models.

Our research indicates that entrepreneurship is a balancing act between strong risk creation and strong risk elimination. It is in the timing and balancing of risk that the successful innovative entrepreneur excels. This, then, provides a bridge between our view of the creative process and our view of entrepreneurship. As we have noted, successfully handling counteracting tendencies is a key ability of creative individuals.

The creative person initially increases creative potential in a problem solving situation by actively widening the information base and scope for action. This, however, also leads to subjective uncertainty and anxiety as to the outcome. At the same time, such a personality is cognitively and emotionally able to handle this situation. In the later stages of the creative process the ambiguity and psychological strain are reduced to arrive at clear cut results.

Similarly the entrepreneur, according to our data, initially increases business risk by actively searching for new opportunities, and experimenting to find out if they are worth the effort. Simultaneously, and later on in the creative process, he or she is, however, strongly engaged in reducing risk by actively changing the prevailing conditions.

This dualism and active switch in behavior is difficult to capture in traditional normative models of decision making, which usually assume a continuous process of risk reduction by the gathering of more information on given alternatives. The sequential broadening and narrowing of experience and risk is an important element of the creative process and of creative management and entrepreneurship as we view these terms.

Normal management is mainly concerned with problem solving and knowledge utilization; that is, using existing technology to further given ends. Innovative entrepreneurship, on the other hand is basically concerned with guiding the development and management of new knowledge to find and exploit new opportunities.

Our view of entrepreneurship thus leads to a realization of the need to stimulate and enact an open and flexible intellectual and organizational orientation—both within the enterprise and in relation to the outside environment—and clear but highly changeable mechanisms of strategic direction and control. It also implies an open view of technology, to make possible the constructive conjoining of previously unrelated elements of knowledge, which is the purpose of creative management.

But just as importantly, it involves creative knowledge management: knowing when and how to move from more open knowledge creating action to more closed ways of knowledge utilization. As should be clear by now, exploring these possibilities is the main objective of the empirical research reported in this book and the strategic management framework developed from this data.

In the remainder of this chapter we shall now illustrate and further develop our discussion by presenting two case studies of entrepreneurship from our data. The first we shall call radical entrepreneurship, since it involves starting from scratch a company based on new technology. The second we shall call intrapreneurship,[23] since it involves creating a more favorable internal environment and more innovative strategies for promoting entrepreneurship within an established company.

RADICAL ENTREPRENEURSHIP—THE CASE OF INTER INNOVATION

Inter Innovation is an outstanding example of successful radical entrepreneurship in starting a new company based on new ideas. It was started in 1973 by Leif Lundblad as a one man operation and in 1982–83, when our interviews took place, it had 450 employees and annual sales of 150 million Swedish crowns. Today its stock market value is about 700 million Swedish crowns (about 110 million $US). Its founder had previously built up a successful business in renting construction machines and skylifts and cleaning the fronts of buildings, and now put some of his profits into his new venture.

Although, or perhaps because, he had had almost no formal technical training, Lundblad had a number of original technical ideas which he wanted to develop in his new company. His earliest experience with business was running a television repair shop at the age of 17, and his technical interest was strong. Initially, the objective of Inter Innovation was to develop new technology based on Lundblad's ideas and license this to other companies.

Inter Innovation's first product was a money cassette for use in automatic payment systems at gasoline stations. This made money handling and control easier and their first licensing was successful. At this time, self-service cash dispensing systems were also being developed for banks and Inter Innovation decided to develop their cassette for this market too. The first attempt at commercializing this product was by licensing agreements with large English and German companies for use as a component in their own systems. This was not successful.

As Inter Innovation was to find out the hard way, larger firms are not always interested in actively promoting the use of technology, for which they obtain the right by licensing agreements with smaller companies. Sometimes licensing is used instead as a way of eliminating future competition by buying and then downplaying the use of the acquired technology. The smaller company then usually has a weak bargaining position in relation to larger more established companies, if they question the carrying out of licensing agreements.

Inter Innovation therefore decided in 1977 to give up licensing as a strategy and instead develop, manufacture and sell their own money handling systems. This soon resulted in a multi-denominational cash dispenser for banks, called Cash Adapter, which was developed in close cooperation with their first customer, Citibank in the US. The result was an order from this company for 20 machines, and a letter of intent for 761 machines, which was far beyond Inter Innovation's wildest expectations. Only prototypes had been developed so far, and the company now needed to finance and complete the development and manufacturing of almost 800 banking systems, with no production and service facilities of their own. The capital stock in the company was less than one-tenth the price of a single machine.

To begin with, Inter Innovation cooperated with more established companies in producing and selling the machines, but without giving up any rights to the product. Quite soon the company acquired an electrotechnical manufacturing company and very rapidly converted it to its own manufacturing needs. Inter Innovation quickly established itself as a highly successful, research intensive international company selling almost all its products outside Sweden.

Obviously, Inter Innovation is a highly successful instance of radical entrepreneurship, and it is therefore interesting to listen to what Leif Lundblad has to say about his formula for success. In our interviews he very eloquently described his way of doing business, which we have summarized below. These quotations bring out clearly a number of points about innovative entrepreneurship, developed above. While each statement viewed in isolation appears self evident, it is not easy to see how they may be achieved together; achieving a workable balance between the various demands certainly must be a challenge to any businessman.

To begin with the need to balance risk is shown in the following statements:

Run one business while developing a new one and leaving an old one

Sell the future and provide for the present

The seemingly contradictory nature of entrepreneurship is brought out in several quotes:

Be over optimistic but realistic

Demand the impossible to achieve the necessary

Mistakes create opportunities

Make plans for failure

The need for speed and flexibility shows up in the following:

Time is the main opponent

Tricks provide tempo

The need to consider both technological and marketing considerations is stressed:

Attack the basic problems and provide general solutions

Unique products necessary for success

Simplicity in use more important than technological sophistication

The customer's gain is our profit

Our second case of entrepreneurship within an established company, Eka Kemi, we have called intrapreneurship to distinguish it from our more radical type of entrepreneurship.

INTRAPRENEURSHIP—THE CASE OF EKA NOBELL

Eka Nobell is an established producer of industrial chemicals in Sweden. In 1983, the year before our interviews took place, the company had sales of 546 million Swedish crowns and more than 700 employees. The company mainly produces and sells basic chemicals, for instance to the detergent and paper industries. Until the early 1970s the company was highly positional in its intended and realized strategies, emphasizing the large scale production and sales of standardized established commodities.

Finding it increasingly difficult to expand in its traditional markets and areas of technology, the company in the 1970s intensified its search for new products and applications. Under new top management it started to devote upwards of 10% of sales to product development, which is a very high percentage in this type of basic industry. It also diversified, which made possible more innovative strategies for product areas with high market and technological potential, such as paper chemicals. By supporting both basic and applied research the Managing Director, J. G. Montgomery, with support from the board, had succeeded in creating a favorable climate for innovation in the company.

In 1979 the company made a strategic decision to try to find new applications for silicic acid. It recruited an outside consultant, Per Båtelson, from the paper industry to help to find new applications of this acid in paper making. He was soon appointed as head of a new venture division. The main task of this group was to develop a new system of chemicals, Compozil, for making filled fine paper. This was quite a new technological concept in the industry with great potential for improving paper quality and reducing cost.

Contingent events in and outside the company had led to the discovery of the basic concept. Shortly after starting a pilot plant for producing silicic acid, Eka Nobell acquired the Agency for another chemical, which they found could be used in combination with silicic acid to improve paper making.

After experiments based on trial and error a process was found for making a 'super filled' paper with high dry strength. This production process was patented and an early unsuccessful attempt was made to market the general concept. The potential market was overestimated, however, as was the ability and willingness of prospects to adopt the new process. It was initially not sufficiently adapted to market needs and a number of technical problems remained to be solved.

Eka Nobell then changed its marketing strategy for Compozil to a holding strategy, and began to focus on customer-specific applications and selling know-how, rather than on marketing the general process. This was much more successful and in 1984 a substantial and growing number of paper mills were using Compozil. A number of customers had also used the process to develop their own new products, such as a low-weight bible paper and a better paper for pocket books.

IMPLICATIONS OF THE CASE STUDIES

Our case studies clearly show the need for organizational flexibility to facilitate the early broadening of the creative process as a basis for entrepreneurship and technological change. In Inter Innovation this flexibility was introduced by the founding entrepreneur running the whole company as a development project. By and large there were no boundaries between different functions in the company and all activities were subordinated to the need for radical technological development.

In Eka Nobell the necessary organizational flexibility was made possible by the umbrella which the managing director, figuratively speaking, gave the intrapreneur in his Venture Division. His decentralized leadership helped to produce both the necessary freedom and psychological support to make possible creativity and innovation. The freedom was provided by a hands-off policy for an extended period of time, during which the intrapreneur and his staff were given a chance to prove themselves even when the going was rough. This made possible the type of independence that creative individuals demand and innovative performance requires. Clearly, flexibility is the name of the game if we want to make possible radical change.

These cases also clearly demonstrate how the flexible combining and recombining of different elements of technology may lead to new knowledge and successful new products and processes which we will discuss more fully in Chapter 4. Inter Innovation created a new technology, 'the separation of paper money' by combining elements of, for instance, mechanical engineering, data processing and microelectronics in new ways. Eka Nobell linked chemistry with paper making technology in a novel fashion to develop its Compozil technology. Viewed against the background of the creative process, this gives content to the broadening of knowledge, made possible by organizational flexibility and a wide search inside and outside the company.

This combining and recombining of knowledge, as is shown in our case studies, is facilitated by action based experimentation, learning and relearning. It is also facilitated by an external orientation in the development process, seeking and assimilating from outside the organization what is lacking in its own technological base.

As the case of Eka Nobell shows, this is particularly important when an established company wants to achieve technological diversification, for instance by promoting intrapreneurship. In Inter Innovation this broadening of the technological base of the company was mainly achieved by joint product development with a highly competent prospective customer. Even when customers are not as technologically advanced, as in the case of Eka Nobell, they may be used for testing purposes and thereby aid the experimentation and learning process without actively taking part in it.

The need for action based learning—experimentation, learning by mistakes, rapid evaluation and reevaluation—to promote creative innovative entrepreneurship is basic to our approach. The importance of this for both radical entrepreneurship and intrapreneurship is well illustrated in our two cases.

Apparently both Leif Lundblad and Per Båtelson essentially knew what they wanted to do as soon as they saw the results of what they had done. When licensing did not work, Inter Innovation quickly changed to manufacturing and selling their own products; and when selling a general product did not prove successful, Eka Nobell rapidly changed strategies to provide highly customer specific applications. In neither case was it possible to know all this in advance, but by using entrepreneurship and maintaining organizational flexibility, both companies were quickly able to adapt to what they found out. This also shows the importance of timing and accelerating change in innovative entrepreneurship, well put in Leif Lundblads motto, 'Tricks provide tempo'.

SUMMARY

In this chapter the importance of creativity and entrepreneurship for radical product and company development has been stressed. Creating favorable conditions for entrepreneurship is a highly challenging and difficult task for management, which is not dealt with very much in the traditional management literature. To understand this type of action-based decision making we need to draw on the results of other disciplines, such as creativity research. We also need to talk to successful practitioners and learn from their experience. For this reason our approach is based on what is known about the creative process and on results from our interviews with company representatives.

*Innovation is the creation of the
future*

4
Innovation Management— Handling Technological Change

In our approach[1] innovation refers to the creation of the future. It is a complex process, the totality of which may not be captured in precise and isolated blocks of meaning. Innovation management is the handling of technological change[2] and also the outcome of this process. Strategic management is concerned with innovation strategies and innovative performance: our main interest lies in the relationship between the two.

Successful innovation strategies demand creative efforts to understand and influence future conditions. They result in technological innovation, new knowledge, which by using marketing strategies may be turned into market innovation, the introduction of new products, processes and services to serve new customer needs.

Sometimes in the literature a clear distinction is drawn between invention (conceiving ideas) and innovation (using and implementing ideas).[3] Doing so we may neglect the fact that both the conception and implementation of ideas are integral parts of the innovation process. In our definition of innovation all fundamental changes which may affect product and company development are included.

In our terminology technological innovation therefore is used to refer to the use of new knowledge for both product and company development. This is a broader and more open concept than product or process innovation[4] which often is used to refer to the use of new knowledge to improve given, identified products or production processes.

While we are interested in specific product and process innovation, we need to consider more general technological innovation. Changes in basic knowledge may lead to future marketable results in the form of specific new products or production processes. A wide and open approach to technological change is therefore necessary, if we want to be able to study more long run, indirect implications of technological strategies for company and product development, and not only more direct and immediate prespecified results.

We may therefore speak of an innovation management box (Figure 4.1) including informational diversity and organizational flexibility and openness to provide the innovative potential for company creativity, and innovation strategies to give direction to company efforts. As we have noted before, innovation management and image management in our framework together make up the strategic creativity mix of a company. This mix is realized in technological and marketing strategies for product and company development and if

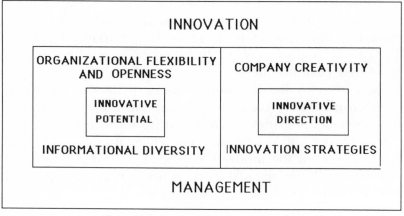

Figure 4.1 Innovation management box

successful leads to innovative development in the form of new products or processes.

Innovation management therefore basically implies preparing for the future. It is the link between company capabilities and environmental possibilities. Company creativity and innovation strategies are the driving forces in innovation management and marketing is the realization of technological potential. While marketing strategies focus on promoting specific offers and relationships, technological strategies are aimed at changing underlying, more general company conditions to stimulate technological change and innovative development.

EXPLICIT AND IMPLICIT TECHNOLOGIES

For our purposes explicit technologies are defined as specialized areas of knowledge—usually separate disciplines at universities—which define and delimit the areas of competence of most researchers. Within such technologies we find specialization in terminology, research instruments, technical facilities and procedures. This creates barriers to interdisciplinary research and to the development of new technologies, based on the merging and intermingling of existing ones.

Since explicit technologies are largely based on established forms of knowledge, reflecting the past more than presaging the future, they are deeply entrenched in organizational and personal knowledge structures, particularly in positional companies.

Implicit technologies, on the other hand, are the evolving knowledge packages of the future. Their contents are not yet firmly fixed in established and conceptually captured form. They are image based, rather than information based, and rely on individual intuition more than analysis and interpersonal communication. In other words, they reflect the early stages of the creative process. Since implicit technologies are problem specific, rather than discipline oriented, they tend to evolve together with the dynamics of creative problem solving, rather than follow the structure and direction of thinking along more established lines.

Today we find many highly implicit technologies, with as yet largely unrealized and unanticipated possibilities, in technology intensive industries, for instance in biotechnology and genetic engineering. An example from genetic engineering is 'spider web technology', using gene technology to copy spiders in making superstrong and highly elastic fibers, five times as strong as steel in relation to their diameter. The potential uses for this implicit technology are multitudinous, from shotproof vests to jet airplanes, difficult to detect by radar.

Another example is 'ice crystallization technology', where the use of 'snow bacteria' to make snow for ski resorts in above freezing temperatures, has already been commercialized by the Californian biotech firm, DNAP. Many other applications, for instance in deep freeze food technology, are likely to unfold, as this technology develops, and a large number are being investigated by the company.

At the same time more implicit technologies, if successful, sooner or later become more explicit technologies. We must keep in mind, however, that the resulting more formalized and established knowledge no longer has the same innovative potential as the more tentative open knowledge inherent in implicit technologies.

We thus need a technological life cycle model emphasizing the development of and relationships between implicit and explicit technologies, to understand technological strategies and technological change (Figure 4.2). While this type of thinking may sometimes be found in the technological forecasting literature,[5] it has hardly been recognized at all in the strategic management literature.

To make possible the empirical study of technological strategy, as a vital component of strategic management, an operational definition of technology has been employed in our research. Companies were asked what critical new knowledge they had been forced to acquire to achieve technological success in specific instances of product and process development, and their responses were used as a basis for our technological classifications.

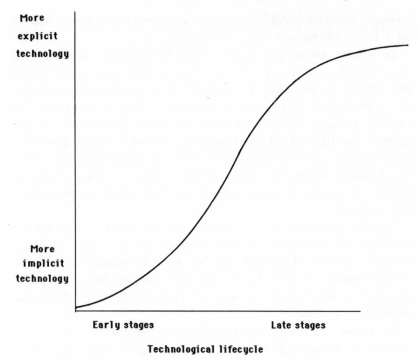

Figure 4.2 *Technological life cycle model*

In the case of more explicit areas of knowledge, such as micro-electronics or organic chemistry, companies were usually able to refer to established terminology in stating their technological needs. In the case of radically new or rapidly evolving, more implicit technologies, on the other hand, such as genetic engineering, ready classifications to fit perceived reality were obviously more difficult or impossible to find.

There are many other examples from our data of new more implicit technologies which are difficult to capture in existing technological classifications. Pharmacia for instance has developed many world unique products for medical diagnosis by combining previously unrelated areas of technology: for example, Phadebas Rast for using blood tests instead of skin tests for allergy testing; Tetra Pak has similarly developed a unique packaging technology for liquid foods and Eka Nobell a new chemical process, Compozil, for paper making. In these and many other instances, companies have been able to break existing technological boundaries and create new technologies as a basis for new products and processes.

In these situations using established classifications to describe the company's technological strategies would have missed the point. Their technological uniqueness would then not have been apparent. Instead, we should have had to attribute their success to a much more positional factor, namely the utilization of common knowledge. While this type of technology use is important, it has little explanatory value in distinguishing the innovative strategic management of highly innovative companies from that of more positional companies.

Highly innovative companies rely to a large extent on implicit technologies, which evolves as a result of their creative efforts. In order to be able to study innovative development we therefore need operational definitions and measurements which are able to capture both implicit and explicit technologies.

In some instances companies had developed their own names for new highly implicit technologies, although these names were usually part of company language, rather than accepted usage outside the firm. Separating paper money is an example of such an implicit technology, which was the basis for Inter Innovation's striking success in developing (from a technological and marketing point of view) highly unique cash handling equipment for banks.

In other instances companies appeared to have had highly intuitive and unformalized knowledge of evolving new technologies, without even having given them names. Technologies for transforming traditional food products into medical products, such as yoghurt for stomach ailments, is an example of this from our data. In some instances when interviewing, by asking unexpected questions, we could even make company representatives aware of what they had not explicitly considered before, and help them to find appropriate labels for their new technologies. Or we could tell them what names other companies had given to similar areas of technology and thereby help them to translate their experiences to broader frames of reference.

STRATEGIC PERFORMANCE

Ultimately the success of a strategy is its effect on company performance. Three measures of success are used in our framework, technological, competitive and commercial.

Our main measure of technological success is the *achieved level of technological innovation*. This is defined as the degree of creativity companies have had to employ to solve the critical technical problems when developing new products or processes. The underlying assumption is that achieving a relatively high level of technological innovation is usually a necessary, but not a sufficient condition for developing highly unique and competitive new products, particularly in research and technology intensive industries. A high level of technological innovation also usually makes it easier to achieve patent protection. Furthermore, as a rule, it requires a longer development time than routine technical development.

In our research the level of technological innovation was directly estimated for each new product or process after intensive discussions with the people who had been involved in developing it. A scale from 1–5 was used with higher values indicating a higher level. The more radical the need for creative thinking and the more successful a company had been in solving the critical problems in a specific development project, the higher the level of technological innovation was taken to be.

Our ratings of the level of technological innovation are highly correlated in our data with our other two measures of technological success, degree of patent protection and development time. Such protection is an imperfect indicator of the level of technological success, since for competitive reasons, companies often do not apply for patents and therefore should not be used as a single indicator. Development time is also an imperfect indicator, since it reflects effort applied rather than success achieved. The high correlations of these more indirect measures with our more valid but less operational measure based on the direct questioning of company researchers, gives us greater confidence, however, in our direct measure of technological success.

In our framework, the measure of market success is *market uniqueness*. The less interchangeable a product is perceived to be by buyers when it is introduced on the market, the higher the degree of market uniqueness. The assumption is that the more unique it is—the more that buyers see it as different in features and performance from competing products—the greater the market potential. An implicit assumption, which usually found support in our interviews, is that companies do not introduce highly unique new products if they have not by pre-testing or market research convinced themselves that customers value the ways in which a unique product differs from existing ones.

Commercial success for new products is ultimately based on the profitability of products over their life cycles. In our research this was measured by estimates of these profitabilities, as judged and justified to the researchers by company executives. Profitability, of course, depends on many factors other than our strategic measures, but it is interesting to look at this relationship if we keep this in mind.

MAIN DETERMINANTS OF TECHNOLOGICAL SUCCESS

Our data points to three main strategic variables directly linked to technological success and indirectly to market and commercial success, one on the organizational or company level and the other two on the product level. The first is organizational flexibility and openness. This determines the ability of the organization to respond to change. The second and third variables, which in our study are directly related to technological success on the product level, are technology orientation and technology use.

ORGANIZATIONAL FLEXIBILITY AND OPENNESS

Companies need organizational flexibility and openness[6] both internally and in relation to the outside environment, to make possible radical change. Judging from our studies, some type of project organization is the usual way in which innovative companies achieve the organizational conditions necessary to make possible radical change.

Internal Organization

The pharmaceutical companies in our data, for instance, were early in recognizing the need for flexible project groups, with variations over time in project membership, to reflect differences in innovative requirements. Usually technical experts dominate at the earlier stages, while marketing experts are more numerous and influential at later stages. This is in line with our discussion of the relative importance of technological and marketing strategies during different stages of the creative process. Integration is usually carried out by a responsible project leader reporting directly to top management.

In more positional companies, such as the food processing companies and the wood and paper companies we have studied, organizational flexibility and openness is not as necessary for development purposes, nor functionally integrated project groups as common. Our interviews indicate that such project groups are used less frequently for development purposes in these companies and that functionally specialized development activities are more common.

Product development, for instance, is often carried out by marketing departments in the food processing companies and by technical departments in the wood and paper companies. Innovative change is difficult to handle in this type of segmented organization, however, since the interface beween technology and marketing is crucial to success. Relatively continuous product or process change, on the other hand, may be carried out efficiently, since specialized attention to market or technological needs then is a more adequate way to handle change than in more innovative companies.

The demand on internal company organization for innovation has been studied in 49 large Swedish companies by Vedin.[7] Using our distinction between positional and

innovative companies he concludes that 'innovative organizations are more complex, also in goals and display multiple
idea paths'. He looks at the location of new product development units in company organization, and concludes that
'innovation appears to be only a secondary concern when
organizing'.[8]

The foremost Swedish companies in his study thus appeared
to need to pay more attention to the relationship between
organization and innovation, which is the impression we
gained in our interviews.

We typically find the most radical type of project organization in entrepreneurial companies or venture divisions within
established firms. In these instances the whole company, such
as Inter Innovation or the whole Division, such as The PK
Division in Eka Nobell, are basically run as development
projects with the owner/entrepreneur or intrapreneur as
project leader. These organizations are described more closely
in Chapters 3 and 12.

Our data show that venture divisions have not been very
common in Sweden during the periods we have looked at.
The first one we found in our study was Aga Innovation,
which was established to bring together and develop new
ideas from more operational divisions in AGA, especially
ideas which went beyond the interest and internal competence
of these more specialized divisions. When we interviewed
representatives for the company in 1972, it was technologically
highly diversified, with products ranging from gas and
welding equipment to electronic instruments and medical
diagnosis units. It subsequently concentrated its activities to
the area of gas and welding, and the role of AGA Innovation
changed from promoting technological diversification to
developing existing technologies.

The most successful example of using a venture division to
promote technological diversification in our data is Pernovo,
started by Perstorp to find and exploit new external ideas and
to integrate ideas emerging in different parts of its parent
company. The orientation of this company, as has been the
case in most venture divisions or venture companies, at least
in Sweden, has changed from hunting for original ideas from
outside inventors to further developing more established, yet

highly innovative companies. Nevertheless, Pernovo has played a key role in transforming Perstorp from a relatively positional and low-tech, basic chemicals company to a more innovative company with its roots in chemistry but branching out into hi-tech applications in, for instance, electronics and pharmaceuticals.

Organizational Mechanisms

With regard to organizational mechanisms for increasing internal flexibility and openness to change in product and company development, the ways in which ideas and projects are evaluated is important. Decentralized and informal evaluation procedures, largely based on intuition, may be expected to lead to greater flexibility and openness in anticipating and reacting to environmental change and opportunity, than centralized, formal and analytical criteria for selecting and following up projects.

In the late 1960s and early 1970s quantitative mathematical and statistical models for product screening and program evaluation and review were common in the management literature.[9] Today, judging from our research, many innovative companies do not even try to use such analytical models and they are seldom mentioned in the strategic management literature.

Innovative companies try most often to achieve organizational flexibility and openness in handling new opportunities by a flexible project organization, combined with informal, intuitive evaluation procedures for selecting and implementing ideas.

External Organization

Not only internal but also external organizational flexibility and openness is crucial, however, for achieving success in technological innovation. While the role of internal organization for change has been paid much and early attention in the literature on organizational innovation, external organization for relating to the outside environment has been relatively neglected. Our interviews almost immediately pointed to the need for stressing this aspect of innovation management and led to an early focus in our research on the relationship between external organization and innovative success.

Once again, Pharmacia initially provided the most persuasive empirical argument for the need to extend our framework. It has positioned itself in the center of a wide information and contact network and developed highly open and flexible organizational mechanisms for communicating and interacting with this outside environment. The company has learned to use many different channels to search widely for ideas and assistance from university researchers, inventors, doctors, other companies and consultants. It also has highly flexible and open internal organizational mechanisms to cope with diversity and change. As we have noted, Pharmacia's flexible and open internal and external organization has led to a highly successful strategy of environmental prospecting to find and utilize unique technological possibilities.

Our early explorative interviews showed, however, that most companies employed much more closed and fixed organizational mechanisms for focusing on and interacting with the outside environment. Typically, they would consistently rely on the same experts or reference groups to evaluate and follow established technologies. This was usually done via existing formal channels, such as specialized journals, publications, research organizations or conferences, focusing on intra- rather than multi-disciplinary issues and problems. This type of environmental search tends to lead to a convergence of knowledge in companies and inflexible focusing of opportunities, which may be highly suited for strengthening positional tendencies, but far more unlikely to stimulate innovative change.

EXTERNAL AND INTERNAL TECHNOLOGY ORIENTATION

Our second strategic variable related to technological success is internal versus external technology orientation. In the search for new ideas and the development of new technology, internally oriented companies emphasize their own competence and their own expertise. Externally oriented companies, on the other hand, rely to a large extent on knowledge carriers and generators in the outside environment.

Operationally we have measured technology orientation by data on new products, developed by companies over an extended time period. The length of this period has been long enough to give a balanced view of long run strategic tendencies in environmental orientation, usually five years or more.

Both idea generation and technical product development are included in our operational definition and measurement of technology orientation. In the first respect the question is whether the idea for a new product has originated inside or outside a company. In the second respect we are interested in whether a company utilizes substantial outside help in developing the idea or basically develops it on its own (joint or internal development).

Our earlier explorative interviews covered 11 companies in a wide range of industries, from industrial electronics and pharmaceutical companies to industrial chemical and steel companies. We then found that differences in technology orientation reflected differences between companies rather than between industries.

Two of the three pharmaceutical companies, however, were quite externally oriented in their product development, while the two steel companies both showed a strong internal orientation. Of the four electronic companies one had a highly internal orientation and one a highly external, while the other two had a somewhat more internal than external orientation. Of the two chemical companies one had a more internal orientation and the other a more external one.

In this study we measured technology orientation by where the ideas for new products came from, to simplify the analysis. This gave basically the same results as combining outside ideas with outside technical cooperation, and gave a more total picture of technology orientation.

Combining all new products we see in Table 4.1 that external ideas led to new products which on the average were technologically much more successful compared to internal

Table 4.1 Technology use and technology orientation in relation to technological success based on 91 products from 11 companies in different industries

	All companies	Pharmaceutical companies	Steel companies	Electronic companies	Chemical companies
Synergistic technology use	4.0 (33)	4.3 (8)	4.0 (3)	3.6 (18)	4.5 (6)
Isolated technology use	3.5 (58)	3.5 (16)	3.4 (20)	3.5 (15)	3.9 (7)
External technology orientation	4.0 (37)	4.0 (15)	3.0 (3)	4.0 (12)	4.3 (7)
Internal technology orientation	3.4 (54)	3.3 (9)	3.6 (20)	3.2 (19)	4.0 (6)

Higher numbers indicate higher levels of technological success.
Technological success is measured by the level of technological innovation.
The number of products in each group is given within parentheses.

ideas, based on our estimates of the level of technological innovation (4.0 compared to 3.4). Looking at our groups of companies from different industries, we found this same pattern: that external ideas were associated with greater technological success than internal ideas—except for the steel companies, where internal ideas were related to greater success (3.6 compared to 3.0).

Internal ideas, however, had led to a larger number of new products, 54 compared to 37, for all companies combined. This was largely due to the steel companies, where 20 of the 23 new products were based on internal ideas. In the pharmaceutical companies, on the other hand, 15 of the 24 new products were based on outside ideas.

In our data there appeared to be some connection between company size and technology orientation. Astra, the largest and also most traditional pharmaceutical company in our sample, showed a stronger internal orientation than the other medical companies, Pharmacia and Kabi. Asea, our largest company in industrial electronics, also had a much more internal orientation than the smaller electronic companies studied. This probably reflects the fact that large companies in relatively stable environments tend to have strongly established explicit technologies of their own and less need than small companies for outside ideas or joint development to strengthen or diversify their positions.

Some large companies, however, may need a more external technology orientation to keep up with rapid technological change or to diversify by developing new, more implicit technologies. Pharmacia, fighting to find new and world unique technological niches in medical diagnosis is an example of the former strategic situation. Perstorp, successfully diversifying from a narrow methanol and formalin based chemistry to a much wider technological competence involving new processes and materials, such as ultra thin copper laminate for integrated circuits, is an example of the latter situation from our data.

Small companies on the other hand, if they have a lot of good ideas of their own and specialize in narrow areas of technology, may be highly innovative in product development, even with a strong internal technology orientation in both idea generation and technical development, as is evident in our farm machinery study dealt with in Chapter 5.

This study looked more closely at the importance of external technology orientation for product development, but used a different approach from our main line of investigation. It was based on an extensive study of 139 companies, using telephone interviews rather than intensive personal interviews. The results further demonstrated the need for considering the role of technology orientation in strategic management and indicated that company size is strongly related to the outcome of different strategies for technological cooperation.

From our extensive sample of farm machinery companies, four companies were chosen for more intensive study (Table 4.2). In this investigation 27 new products were chosen to reflect the strategic outcome of the companies. This sample was chosen together with company people to be as representative as possible for the period 1968 to 1977. Again, as in our explorative study of 11 companies, internal technology orientation was more common than external orientation.

Table 4.2 Technology use and technology orientation in relation to technological, market and commercial success for 27 products from 4 Swedish companies manufacturing and selling farm machinery

	Number of products	Technological success	Market success	Commercial success
Synergistic technology use	16	3.4	3.6	3.2
Isolated technology use	11	2.5	3.4	2.3
External technology orientation	11	3.2	3.6	1.8
Internal technology orientation	16	2.9	3.4	3.4

Higher numbers indicate higher technological, market and commercial success.
Technological success is measured by the level of technological innovation.
Market success is measured by the market situation at product introduction.
Commercial success is measured by estimated profitability.

Sixteen of the new products mainly had their origin in the companies' own ideas and external technology orientation, drawing on outside sources for vital ideas accounted for the other 11 new products.

While there was no difference in market success attributable to internal versus external orientation, we did find a clear difference in commercial and technological success. The new products based on internal technology orientation had been associated with much greater commercial success on the average (3.4 versus 1.8) which may be interpreted as meaning that the companies had a strong internal technological basis, or that there was little possibility in this industry for improving the commercial potential of new products by outside ideas. Technological success, however, was lower for internal than external orientation (2.9 versus 3.2).

In our large study of product development in Swedish food processing companies, described in more detail in Chapter 10, we found that internal technology orientation was much more frequently associated with new products than was external orientation (Table 4.3). Of the 121 new products studied, reflecting the time period 1965–1975, 94 were the

Table 4.3 Technology use and technology orientation in relation to technological, market and commercial success for 121 products from 20 Swedish food processing companies

	Number of products	Technological success	Market success	Commercial success
Synergistic technology use	54	2.9	3.8	3.4
Isolated technology use	67	2.0	3.3	3.3
External technology orientation	27	2.7	3.5	3.1
Internal technology orientation	94	2.4	3.4	3.4

Higher numbers indicate higher technological, market and commercial success.
Technological success is measured by the level of technological innovation.
Market success is measured by the situation at product introduction.
Commercial success is measured by estimated profitability.

result of internal orientation in idea generation and only 27 the result of external orientation. The level of technological success, however, was again higher for new products based on external orientation (2.7) compared to new products based on internal orientation (2.4). Market success, on the other hand, was somewhat higher for external orientation than for internal orientation (3.5 versus 3.4) while commercial success was substantially lower (3.1 versus 3.4).

In this industry, companies were evidently highly self sufficient in their idea generation, which is hardly surprising given the very low research intensity and low rate of technological change in food processing. At the same time, the most innovative companies used external technology orientation more than the most positional ones and the most successful new products—such as *lätt och lagom*, a new low fat bread spread—were often based on external orientation even in this industry.

Similarly, our study of the Swedish pulp and paper industry during the 1970s and early 1980s, described in Chapter 11, also showed that internal technology orientation was more common in developing new products than external orientation

(Table 4.4). The difference, however, was not as pronounced as in the food study. Of the 14 new products chosen to represent product development in the four leading companies, eight were attributed to mainly internal idea generation and six to external. Again, external orientation was associated with far greater technological success than internal orientation (3.5 versus 2.5) and also with greater market success (3.7 versus 3.4). The level of commercial success, however, was the same for external and internal orientation.

Table 4.4 *Technology use and technology orientation in relation to technological, market and commercial success for 28 products from 4 Swedish pulp and paper companies*

	Number of products	Technological success	Market success	Commercial success
External orientation	3	4.0	3.7	3.7
Internal orientation	11	2.6	3.5	3.7
Synergistic technology use	6	3.5	3.7	3.7
Isolated technology use	8	2.5	3.4	3.7

Higher numbers indicate higher technological, market and commercial success. Technological success is measured by the level of technological innovation. Market success is measured by the market situation at product introduction. Commercial success is measured by estimated profitability.

ISOLATED AND SYNERGISTIC TECHNOLOGY USE

Our third strategic variable related to technological success, technology use, refers to the way technologies are applied to the critical technical problems in developing new products and processes. Working within an established technology area, such as micro electronics or optical measurement, is called isolated technology use. Combining knowledge from different areas of technology is called synergistic technology use.

Isolated technology use is intradisciplinary and can be carried out by individuals or firms working in relative isolation from each other. The more explicit technologies are, the greater the pressure to stay within their limits usually will be. Knowledge is power and recognized experts and organizations, with vested interests in established technologies, often stake out and are guardians of technological boundaries. Within companies explicit technologies are engrained in practice and principles, which further enhance their permanency.

In our data we particularly find such highly explicit, isolated technology use in very positional industries, such as steel, pulp and paper and food processing. In these instances the cost of change is high, owing to large scale economics in established production technologies and distribution channels. Companies, therefore, are usually reluctant to expand and diversify their technological base. For instance, in pulp and paper we find strongly established chemical and mechanical processes for converting wood fibers to cellulosa.

In industries such as this it is not easy to consider new technologies, based, for instance, on fibers from the field rather than the forest, such as kenaf. This is a plant which can be used to produce high quality, low cost paper and a paper mill using kenaf is, after 40 years of development work, finally under construction in Texas. There is also great resistance in the forest industry towards developing and testing new, smaller scale production processes, with less negative effects on the environment than traditional, larger scale ones. Such implicit technologies exist, for instance the organosolv method, based on promising, but as yet relatively undocumented knowledge.

Synergistic technology use is interdisciplinary in nature and requires the bridging of gaps between specialized experts from otherwise disjunct areas of knowledge. It demands that good contacts be maintained among people with a quite different technological outlook and competence, to facilitate effective communication and coupling of ideas.

Wide and flexible approaches to problems increase the likelihood of innovative solutions. By employing more variegated company strategies, such as recruiting personnel with differing experience and educational backgrounds and making them work closely together in project groups, companies may achieve more synergistic technology use and increase their innovative potential.

In our explorative study of 11 companies in various industries, synergistic technology use is usually associated with far fewer new products than is isolated technology use. Of the 91 new products studied, 33 were based on combining different areas of technology, while 58 were based on staying within established technological boundaries (Table 4.1). For all groups of companies synergistic technology use is related to a smaller number of new products; except for the electronic companies, where synergistic technology use had led to a slightly larger number (18 compared to 15). In the steel companies, synergistic technology use had accounted for only 3 of 23 new products, while in the pharmaceutical companies the relation was 8 of 24 and in the chemical companies 6 of 13.

We see in Table 4.1 that synergistic technology use was associated with greater technological success in developing new products for all the industry groups. For all groups of companies except for the electronic companies the difference was also pronounced.

Many of the most innovative companies tended to employ synergistic technology use to develop radically new implicit technologies and products which could not otherwise have been attained. Leading examples of this in the pharmaceutical companies were Pharmacia's blood tests for allergies (Phadebas Rast) and Astras asthma medicine (Bricanyl). In the industrial electronics area, LKB's world unique laboratory systems, such as Tachophor, and ASEA's industrial robots were the result of synergistic technology use. In the industrial chemicals area Perstorp's plastic laminates are the result of combining different technologies in new ways.

All of these have been world unique or technologically leading products in their fields, illustrating our thesis that developing implicit new technologies based on synergistic technology use is a major route to technological success in product and process development. As we mentioned in the previous sections, organizational flexibility and external orientation may usually be expected to facilitate synergistic technology use, and these three strategic dimensions therefore should be viewed together. Later on in this chapter we shall combine the various dimensions into an integrated view of technological strategy.

In our intensive study of four farm machinery companies (Table 4.2) we found, on the other hand, that synergistic technology use was more frequently linked to new products than isolated technology use, which is surprising, since this is not usually viewed as a very innovative industry. From our data we classified 16 of the 27 new products studied as based on technological combinations. This may either reflect the fact that the four companies differ from the rest of the industry or some industry related factor, such as a need at the time to combine mechanical construction with new electromechanical principles to gain competitiveness.

In either case this study supports the view that new technological combinations are essential to success even in an industry which is not usually viewed as hi-tech. The products based on synergistic technology use were technologically far more successful than were those based on isolated technology use (3.4 compared to 2.5). They were also associated with greater market success, that is they were unique on the market at the time of their introduction (3.6 versus 3.4), and commercially far more successful than products based on isolated technology use (3.2 versus 2.3).

In our study of 20 major Swedish food processing companies (Table 4.3) we found that synergistic technology use had led less frequently to new products, than had isolated technology use. Of 111 new products, 54 were classified as being the result of synergistic technology use, while 67 were the result of isolated technology use. It is interesting to note that even in this highly positional industry, almost one half of the new products were based on finding new ways to combine old technological knowledge. Again, the new products based on synergistic technology use were technologically much more successful than those based on isolated technology use (2.9 compared to 2.0). They were also notably more successful from a market introduction point of view (3.8 versus 3.3) and slightly more successful commercially (3.4 versus 3.3).

In our pulp and paper study, finally, we found that isolated technology use was associated with far more new products than was synergistic technology use (11 compared to 3). As in all our other studies, however, we found that synergistic technology use was related to far greater technological success than was isolated use (4.0 versus 2.6). Market success was somewhat higher for synergistic compared to isolated technology use (3.7 versus 3.5), while the commercial outcome was the same for both types of technology use (Table 4.4).

STRATEGIC OUTCOME

From an innovation management point of view, the strategic outcome on the product marketing level can be defined in terms of the product and customer focus of the company.

On the dimension of product focus, a company can concentrate on developing products that are essentially variations of existing products (*product modifications*), or it can focus on products that fall outside the established product line (*product diversifications*).

With regard to the second dimension of realized marketing strategy, customer focus, new products may either be primarily aimed at getting new customers or directed towards tying existing customers closer to the company. In the first case the result is a more *offensive, competitive strategy*. In the second case it is a more *defensive, holding strategy*.

Whether the marketing strategy is offensive or defensive it may be implemented through products that are directed toward a wide range of customer needs—a *general product design*; or it may result in products that are aimed at a more narrow spectrum of customer needs—a *specific product design*.

The choice of product modification versus product diversification on the one hand, and a general or specific product design orientation on the other, are important marketing dimensions in strategic management. In our framework they are intervening variables, that relate indirect strategic dimensions on the company level, such as technology use and technology orientation, to direct strategic outcomes on the product level. While product diversification, competitive strategy and general product design are seen primarily as ways of increasing innovative potential (strategic degrees of freedom) product modification, holding strategy and specific product design are mainly viewed as ways of strengthening inherent positional tendencies.

On the technological level, strategic outcome may be defined in terms of the choice of process, especially in industries such as steel, chemicals, pulp and paper and food processing, where product and process innovations are closely connected. A *general process* is used for producing many types of end products. A *specific process* is one designed to produce a narrow range of end products, or even just one. In this sense, the process design can also be considered to be an intervening variable, linking overall intended strategy to specific realized outcomes. General processes then may be viewed as increasing innovative potential by containing more possibilities and specific processes as strengthening positional tendencies by technological focusing.

OPEN AND CLOSED STRATEGIES

From a technological, as well as from a marketing and organizational point of view, innovation strategies may be viewed as lying along the dimension of open or closed (Figure 4.3). Organizational flexibility and openness, synergistic technology use and external technology orientation contribute to an open technological strategy. Conversely, product diversification and an emphasis on new customers are open aspects of realized marketing strategy. Organizational fixedness, isolated technology use, an internal technology orientation, product modification and an emphasis on existing customers are all elements of a more closed strategy.

General product design, to suit a wide range of customer needs, and general process design, for a wide range of production operations, can also be considered to be part of a more open strategic orientation. Specific product and process design indicate a more closed strategic orientation.

The main innovation management assumption that underlies our research is that more open strategies offer a greater

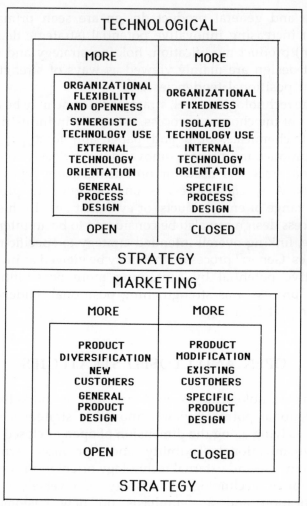

Figure 4.3 *Elements of more open and more closed strategies*

creative potential, and therefore should be more appropriate for innovative companies in highly changing and uncertain environments. More closed strategies on the other hand, should focus the efforts of a company more efficiently and therefore should be better suited for positional companies who want to maintain their more stable and predictable environments. Even in relatively stable environments, however, more open strategies are a way for positional companies to become more innovative to gain competitive advantage.

Initially, we believed that more open strategies would mainly characterize product and company development in industries with rapidly evolving technologies and high research intensity, such as industrial electronics and medical products. Rapid technological change then should make it necessary, but also difficult, for companies to update their technologies, and more open strategies should be an attractive choice. While this is brought out by our research, our results also indicate the strategic opportunity to use more open strategies also in more mature industries.

Our main dimensions of more open company strategies, organizational flexibility and openness, external technology orientation and synergistic technology use appear to be important contributing factors for technological and market success, as in low research and less technology intensive industries, such as farm machinery, food processing and pulp and paper. While we find relatively fewer new products as the result of more innovative strategies in this type of industry, these new products often appear to be competitively successful. Even in quite positional industries we thus find companies who successfully employ elements of more innovative strategies for product and company development.

SUMMARY

In our framework, companies can and should use different technological and marketing strategies to promote different types and degrees of innovation. Thus, highly open and innovative strategies should be used by companies when future products and services are difficult or impossible to define. In more stable situations, on the other hand, companies may need more closed and positional strategies to modify and strengthen their existing product mixes and competitive positions.

In our data we often find strategic, success-related differences between companies, which do not appear to be related to the general differences between industries in their requirements for new knowledge, nor to R & D intensity. Instead, they appear to be related to the availability of suitable innovation partners in the outside environment, for instance university researchers, consultants or other companies working in areas which are complementary to the development of the company's own technology base.

From our point of view, classifying overall industries or technologies as hi-tech or low-tech, as is commonly done, can therefore be highly misleading, if used as a basis for innovation management in individual companies, or for drawing general conclusions with regard to what development strategies should be pursued in different industries or companies.

Our studies indicate that it is the specific technology base of a company in relation to environmental possibilities, which determines what technological strategies should be used to achieve technological and marketing success. Organizational flexibility and openness, external technology orientation and synergistic technology use are important aspects of such company specific strategies for innovation.

We need to distinguish between spontaneous and temporary and systematic and organized technological cooperation strategies for finding and developing new products

5
Technological Cooperation Strategies for Swedish Mechanical Engineering Companies

This chapter[1] deals with an important aspect of innovation management and product development. It looks at how companies cooperate with different parties outside the firm in order to find ideas for new products and their technical development. The companies studied were Swedish mechanical engineering companies and the focus was on their manufacturing and selling of farm machinery.

Technological cooperation between a company and its outside environment is an important aspect of innovation management according to our previous discussion. A company may, for instance, cooperate with customers, universities, outside consultants or other companies in searching for and developing new products. As we have seen in Chapter 4, our research studies indicate that cooperation between a company and its external environmental network is a good strategy for finding and developing successful new products.

This chapter gives some detailed results in support of this thesis, but also points to some exceptions to this general rule.[1] In particular, our data indicate that smaller companies were not as dependent on cooperation as were larger companies. This in spite of the fact that they might be expected to have been more dependent, owing to their smaller, narrower resource base.

Our main findings are consistent with the results of a number of other empirical studies which show the importance of technological cooperation for successful product innovation. Better coupling between a firm and its environment was found to be an important factor correlated with new product success in the SAPPHO[2] study of 58 industrial products. Good inter-firm cooperation was shown to be associated with more successful new products in the Queen's Award[3] study of 84 technological innovations in a wide range of industries.

Cooperation between firms was also shown by Gerstenfeld to be correlated with innovation success in a study of 22 innovations in 11 R & D intensive West German companies.[4] Cooperation between firms and people in their outside research environment was furthermore found to be related to success in a study of 164 R & D projects[5] in five research intensive industries in Europe and Japan. The importance of user–firm cooperation for product innovation has been documented in two studies of 166 high technology products, such as scientific instruments.[6]

None of these studies, however, stresses the aspects of cooperation stressed in this chapter, nor analyze differences between large and small firms with regard to the type of cooperation carried out and their success in doing so. When analyzing the success of technological cooperation it is necessary to consider company size. The innovation literature indicates that differences in company size are often related to differences in R & D success.[7] Our study also shows, as we shall see later on in this chapter, that companies of different size tended to employ different cooperation strategies.

DESIGN OF THE STUDY

Our study of technological cooperation strategies is based on data for 166 new products from 140 companies manufacturing and selling farm machines in Sweden. Farm machines are defined as equipment for crop and animal production, such as sowing and harvesting machines, grain driers, milking machines and manure handling systems.

The investigation was carried out as a total study of this industry. The basis for the selection of companies was a list of firms compiled by the Swedish Board of Agriculture in 1976. Of the 141 companies on this list, only one company did not supply the necessary data. The data was mainly collected by telephone interviews. In the case of ten companies who wanted to give written replies, a mail questionnaire was used instead.

For some of the companies studied, farm machines were the only line of business, but for others this type of product represented only a small part of the total assortment. In the latter case only data on R & D for the farm machine products were collected. Since in most of the diversified companies farm machines was a division or separate profit unit with its own R & D, it did not prove too difficult in these instances to isolate R & D expenditures and efforts for the farm machine products.

BASIC APPROACH AND ASSUMPTIONS

Our own earlier research indicates that it is not only the number and variety of contacts that are related to new product success, but also the way in which the contact network between a company and its environment is organized. Some companies tend to have systematic and organized environmental contacts while others tend to have spontaneous and temporary relationships. Many different types of cooperation between a company and its outside environment may contribute to new product success. Therefore we wanted to include a wide range of contacts related to product development in our study.

In the Swedish farm machine industry an important aspect of systematic and organized cooperation strategies is long term research contracts with universities. Another example of systematic and organized cooperation in this industry is joint research between companies, for instance between suppliers and manufacturers.

An illustration of what we mean by a spontaneous and temporary cooperation strategy is when a company temporarily uses consultants to help solve specific problems in connection with product development. Another example is when a company encourages inventors to offer it ideas for new products.

To analyze the importance of technological cooperation strategies in our study, we first distinguished between companies which stressed cooperation with the outside environment in developing new products and those which did not. Among companies emphasizing cooperation with the outside environment in their product development, we then tried to evaluate the relative success for the two types of cooperation strategies.

We looked at differences in new product success for companies with and without significant technological cooperation. We then checked to see if there were differences in success for companies with a systematic and organized cooperation strategy compared to companies with a spontaneous and temporary one.

Two indicators of technological success in developing new products were used in our study. The first more quantitative criterion was the number of new products introduced on the market during a ten-year period and the second, more qualitative criterion, the number of these products for which patent protection had been achieved.

Our definition of a new product required it to be new both from a technical and from a marketing point of view. This means that it had to be based on a new technical solution, which also satisfied customer needs in a new and better way. It was not necessary, however, that companies should have originated the ideas for the new products themselves, but we required that they had actively participated in their technical and market development.

In measuring the success of technological strategies we assumed that companies usually do not introduce new products on the market unless these are judged to be good prospects for commercial success. We may then expect a company's commercial success to increase with the number of new products successfully launched on the market, and use this number as an indicator of success. Furthermore, since patent protection makes it more difficult for competitors to imitate successful new products, a larger rather than a smaller number of patented new products should usually tend to be associated with greater commercial success for a company.

To estimate technological success for new products it is not enough, however, merely to consider new product outcome. We also need to relate this outcome to R & D effort to achieve a measure of effectiveness. As our estimate of resource input in R & D we have chosen the time spent on R & D by company employees, adding together full and part time work to man–year equivalents.

For each company we thus calculated both the number of new products and the number of patented new products for the ten-year period in relation to R & D effort. These two measures we then used to evaluate new product success for our two types of technological cooperation strategies.

When analyzing the success of technological cooperation strategies it is, however, also necessary to consider company size. To begin with it was, as we shall see, evident from our data that companies of different size employed different types of strategies. Furthermore the innovation literature indicates that differences in company size are often related to differences in R & D success.

In our study, companies were divided into three size groups, based on their total number of employees. In Table 5.1 we see that the distribution of companies with regard to size is relatively even, with 38% for the smallest companies, 34% for the middle-sized and 28% for the largest ones. Small companies were companies with up to nine employees, middle-sized companies had 10–49 employees and large companies more than 50 employees.

RESULTS

Our data show clear differences in the frequency and type of research cooperation between companies of different size

Table 5.1 Company size and technological cooperation

	Company size (total number of employees 1977)		
	Small companies	Middle-sized companies	Large companies
Number of companies	53	48	39
(per cent of all companies)	(38%)	(34%)	(28%)
No technological cooperation	41	26	15
(per cent of same size companies)	(77%)	(54%)	(38%)
Technological cooperation	12	22	24
(per cent of same size companies)	(23%)	(46%)	(62%)
Cooperation strategy:			
Spontaneous and temporary	9	16	12
(per cent of same size companies with technological cooperation)	(75%)	(73%)	(50%)
Systematic and organized cooperation	3	6	12
(per cent of same size companies with technological cooperation)	(25%)	(27%)	(50%)

Small companies: Up to 9 employees.
Middle-sized companies: 10–49 employees.
Large companies: 50 employees and more.

(Table 5.1). At first, we found that technological cooperation had been more frequently used in the larger companies, than in the smaller ones. In the group of large companies 62% had made substantial use of such cooperation strategies for product development, in the group of middle-sized companies 46% and in the group of small companies 23%.

A majority of the large companies thus claimed to have made significant use of technological cooperation strategies, but only a minority of the small and middle-sized ones. For the companies favoring cooperation we found that of the large companies 50% could be classified as having employed a spontaneous and temporary strategy and 50% a systematic and organized one during the time period studied. With regard to the group of middle-sized companies, 73% were classified as having emphasized the former type and 27% the latter type of strategy. For the small companies the corresponding figures were 75% and 25%. We thus found that systematic and organized cooperation was the preferred strategy among the larger companies and spontaneous and temporary cooperation among the smaller ones.

Our next step in the analysis was to find if differences in company size were related to differences in new product success. If this was the case we needed to adjust for company size when estimating the success of different cooperation strategies.

Table 5.2 shows the relationship between company size and new product success. We see that smaller company size

Table 5.2 Company size and new product success

| | Company size (total number of employees 1977) | | |
	Small companies	Middle-sized companies	Large companies
Number of companies in each size group	53	48	30
(per cent of all companies)	(38%)	(34%)	(28%)
Total number of new products per company during the 10-year period	0.8	1.2	1.7
Number of patented new products per company during the 10-year period	0.2	0.4	0.9
Total number of new products per full time R & D employee during the 10-year period	2.6	1.5	0.1
Number of patented new products per full time R & D employee during the 10-year period	0.8	0.5	0.1

Small companies: Up to 9 employees.
Middle-sized companies: 10–49 employees.
Large companies: 50 employees and more.

Table 5.3 New product success for smaller and larger companies with and without technological cooperation

		No technological cooperation	Technological cooperation
Total number of new products developed per full time R & D employee during the 10-year period	small companies	2.7 (41)	2.9 (12)
	middle-sized companies	1.3 (26)	1.8 (22)
	large companies	0.4 (15)	0.4 (24)
Number of patented new products developed per full time R & D employee during the 10-year period	small companies	0.8 (41)	0.4 (12)
	middle-sized companies	0.4 (26)	0.4 (22)
	large companies	0.2 (15)	0.2 (24)

Small companies: Up to 9 employees.
Middle-sized companies: 10–49 employees.
Large companies: 50 employees and more.
Number of companies within parentheses.

in our data is consistently related to a larger number of new products in relation to R & D effort than was larger company size. Small companies had succeeded in developing 2.6 new products per R & D employee during the ten-year period, while middle-sized companies achieved 1.5 and large companies 0.2 new products. Smaller and middle-sized companies did not usually have a full time R & D employee, so the average number of new products per company is much lower.

If we look at the number of patented new products we again see that the smaller companies had a larger number of new products than the larger companies. The small companies achieved 0.7 patented new products per R & D employee during the ten-year period, the middle-sized companies 0.5 and the larger companies one.

We may now summarize the relationship in our data between company size and new product success. Smaller companies consistently achieved a larger number of new products, unpatented and patented, in relation to R & D effort, than did larger companies. When evaluating the success of cooperation strategies we thus need to consider company size, since we have found size-related differences both in the type of cooperation strategy used and in their success. We shall do this by carrying out the analysis for different strategies within and between size-groups.

In Table 5.3 we may compare new product success for companies emphasizing or not emphasizing technological cooperation. Using our quantitative measure of success—the total number of new products—we find that cooperation was more successful or as successful as no cooperation for all size-groups of companies. We find the greatest difference in success between cooperation and no cooperation for the middle-sized companies, a small difference for the small companies and no difference for the large companies.

With regard to our qualitative measure of new product success—the number of patented new products—we find no differences in success between cooperation and no cooperation for the middle-sized and large companies. For the small companies no cooperation is more successful than cooperation.

We thus find with regard to the total number of new products that technological cooperation is associated with as

Table 5.4 Technological cooperation strategy and new product success for smaller and larger companies

	Technological cooperation	
	Spontaneous and temporary cooperation	Systematic and organized cooperation
Total number of new products developed per full time R & D employee during the 10-year period		
small companies	3.2 (9)	1.9 (3)
middle-sized companies	2.0 (16)	1.2 (6)
large companies	0.5 (12)	0.2 (12)
Number of patented new products developed per full time R & D employee during the 10-year period		
small companies	0.3 (9)	0.6 (3)
middle-sized companies	0.3 (16)	0.8 (6)
large companies	0.2 (12)	0.1 (12)

Small companies: Up to 9 employees.
Middle-sized companies: 10–49 employees.
Large companies: 50 employees and more.
Number of companies within parentheses.

great as or greater success than no cooperation. With regard to the number of patented new products, on the other hand, no cooperation is more successful than or as successful as cooperation.

Table 5.4 shows new product success for our two types of technological cooperation strategies. With regard to our quantitative measure of new product success we see that spontaneous and temporary cooperation is associated with a larger total number of new products for all size-groups of companies. With our qualitative measure, however, we find that a systematic and organized technological cooperation strategy is associated with a larger number of patented new products, except for the group of large companies, where spontaneous and temporary cooperation is slightly more successful.

SUMMARY

Our results indicate that it is of great value in product development for companies to utilize the outside environment for finding and developing new products. We therefore conclude that companies need explicitly to consider technological networking and technological cooperation strategies in innovation management.

How companies cooperate is of major importance for new product success. We have shown differences in outcome between two types of strategies. Spontaneous and temporary technological cooperation seems to have been a good strategy for companies which wanted many new products. A systematic and organized strategy, on the other hand, appears to have been a better strategy for achieving a larger number of technologically advanced, patented new products, except for the largest companies.

If we look at differences between smaller and larger companies we see that, with our measures of new product success, smaller companies were much more successful in relation to their R & D efforts than were larger companies. This is the case whether we look at patented or unpatented products, but the difference in success is more pronounced with regard to the latter type of products. It also appears that smaller companies had, in general, used technological cooperation less than larger companies, and in particular had made little use of systematic and organized technological cooperation to find and develop new products.

Images are the fabric of the future and reflections of the creative mind

6
Image Management— Marketing the Future

All approaches to managerial decision making must employ focusing mechanisms. From a creativity point of view, these devices should direct rather than restrict our efforts to understand and influence the future. Furthermore, since we can never look into the future, but can help to bring it about, an action based creative entrepreneurial view of management is better suited for studying radical change than is a more analytical planning approach.

The inevitable question then confronts us: Will tomorrow be like today, but more so, as economic theory has always assumed, or will it be a venture capitalist's dream; quite different and surprising, with new challenges and opportunities? In traditional economic theory and related management approaches the status quo rules the waves, and the dawn tomorrow reflects the sunset today. The starting point then is defined in terms of given products, technologies and other fixed resources, which are assumed to change only slowly and gradually.

In our framework,[1] as in other more creativity and innovation based approaches to management, change is challenge and tomorrow is what we make of it. Creative strategic guidance is provided by visions of the future, wholistic images which may guide and influence behavior. Such visions must be based on open expectations and possibilities—previews of the future—rather than more closed views and projections of present day conditions. They are reflections of the creative mind and the way in which the future is invented and made meaningful, or anticipated and made manageable.

At the same time, managing the future in a changing world requires company procedures and organizational mechanisms for creative image management to give more precise innovative content to intuitive expectations and to make possible successful implementation of innovative strategies. We view images[2] as the fabric of the future, based on the structuring of experience, and image management as concerned with the weaving of this fabric by company decision makers.

Image management in this perspective deals both with product marketing and company management. Marketing strategies must consider how companies should apply their thinking to and market the future by developing new products and know-how. Management theory in turn should be concerned with the marketing of the future, both as a practice and a discipline, and include image marketing and image competition as vital components of strategic management.

TRADITIONAL MARKETING—MANAGING MARKET INFORMATION

In an historical perspective, marketing theory[3] has largely been based on the economic theory of the firm. This theory assumes given, well defined offers, called products, and is mainly concerned with their efficient promotion and distribution to buyers who know what they want and can evaluate what they get.

This is an information based planning approach to marketing management.[4] It assumes that it is possible for firms and customers to obtain, in advance, accurate market information, which makes clear the differences in how competing offers may fulfill given buyer needs. This means that all parties concerned can and do evaluate this information[5] to their own best advantage. In this framework differentiating the offer to gain competitive advantages, and helping buyers to discriminate between competing alternatives to choose what suits them best, is what marketing is all about.

This view emphasizing the management of market information is relatively static and closed, since it does not consider radical changes in technology or in marketing conditions. Neither does it deal with company and environmental conditions related to creativity and innovation. All this means that it is not possible to treat adequately, radical product and company development in this framework without extending it.

The focus in marketing theory differs from the perspective of economic theory[6] by reflecting the viewpoint of the individual enterprise rather than that of industries or of the overall economy. Much of the analytical framework of orthodox economics has been retained, however, and even today most approaches to marketing management show a strong heritage to traditional economic thinking.

The traditional marketing approach also is relatively closed with regard to marketing output, because it starts with individual products, that is, given means for satisfying existing needs. In a wider, more innovative context, we need, instead, to begin with future needs. We must then focus on the possibility of developing products and know-how to satisfy these needs, which may not even yet be recognized by potential customers. For this purpose we need a more open and creative approch to anticipate and evolve what is not yet apparent.

From a psychological[7] point of view, also, the traditional market information approach is relatively closed, since it basically assumes, as in economic theory, that potential customers can discriminate between and evaluate competing offers. The assumption of comparability and rational choice, based on specific market information, makes this type of theory mainly applicable to the marketing of relatively standardized and established goods and commodities in highly competitive and relatively unchanging situations.

In more innovative marketing situations, involving radical change, we need to extend this framework to consider the role of image management and image marketing. This in order to consider how companies build expectations and market potential, and how they realize this potential by using marketing strategy.

IMAGE MANAGEMENT AND IMAGE MARKETING—MANAGING MARKET EXPECTATIONS AND MARKET UNCERTAINTY

By image management and image marketing—making implicit promises rather than explicit commitments—innovative companies may increase their strategic freedom in product and company development. The more they rely on image management for the psychological packaging and promotion of their offers, the more their strategic creativity mix is based on market expectations rather than market information and the more their marketing strategies are directed towards managing market uncertainty and change rather than considering clearly perceived existing differences in market conditions.

Image generalization (the shifting of expectations between different levels of meaning) and image learning (the psychological interplay between discerning the present and implying the future) then take precedence over detailing and comparing, that is, discriminating between offers on the basis of product specific information such as price and quality. This is summarized in our image management box (Figure 6.1).

Innovative companies need to keep running both to stay ahead of their competitors in the technological race and to

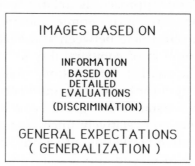

IMAGES BASED ON

INFORMATION
BASED ON
DETAILED
EVALUATIONS
(DISCRIMINATION)

GENERAL EXPECTATIONS
(GENERALIZATION)

Figure 6.1 Image management box

maintain their innovative company and market images. The technological requirement leads to a need for innovation management and the marketing requirement to a need for image management. The joint management and balancing of these requirements is what we refer to as the strategic creativity mix of the company.

Tour Agenturer, a Swedish company making electronic regulators for the building industry, claimed in one of our early interviews that they needed to provide technical specifications and contract their new products to construction firms six months before they had been fully developed, so that these customers could integrate them in their own building plans. They also had to retain a technological lead on competitors to maintain their image of technological leadership.

The company's strategic marketing mix thus included a strong competitive element with regard to technology and a strong holding element with regard to marketing. By combining strong innovation management—to maintain and sustain an innovative lead on competitors—and strong image management—to attract and keep customers—they were very successful in their strategic development with regard to new products and processes, as well as in the satisfaction they were able to provide to their customers. This required high speed and flexibility in their technological strategy for developing products and know-how.

It also required a strong implicit marketing strategy to maintain the image that their as yet not fully developed products would be superior to what competitors could offer, now or in the near future. By succeeding in both these respects, the company could and did achieve a very high profit level. By failing in either their technological or marketing strategy, their new products and services would not have satisfied their customers. This no doubt would rapidly have led to a deterioration of image and a resulting loss of business.

Similarly, the case of Inter Innovation shows that strong image management and image marketing may lead to an extremely successful innovative strategy, when the strategic creativity mix is strong also on handling innovation. By selling the idea for its main product (a cash handling machine for banks) before it was fully developed, this company gained both technological and marketing momentum, and sold machines worth many times its own equity, before it had the technical facilities to manufacture the machines. By buying an existing plant and converting it in six months to its own manufacturing needs, the company was able to fulfill its promises and now is a major Swedish company.

In contrast to these successful examples, the spectacular rise and fall of Fermenta, a Swedish drug fermentation company, illustrates the need for a balanced strategic creativity mix, and what may happen if image management promises too much, and there is a lack of innovative potential and innovation management to back up the claims made. Initially this company was able to establish a hi-tech image and build enormous market expectations, mainly by associating itself with the biotechnical industry and acquiring companies to expand its production and sales. This favorable image deteriorated overnight, however, when the doctoral degree of the supposed financial and technical wizard leading the company was shown to be fictitious, and the company went bankrupt.

Particularly in the case of new ventures and companies newly formed for the development of new technology,[8] strong image management will usually be necessary to launch an enterprise successfully. If there is a well-functioning capital venture market, it will, for instance, be necessary to use image marketing to compete with other investment possibilities. The day of reckoning may then be advanced, as has been the case in the biotechnology business, where few venture companies have yet generated strong sales. If the company is skillful in making and promoting research promises, additional financing may often be obtained, even when results are projected further and further into the future.

When this type of venture financing is more difficult to find, as it is in Sweden, alternative strategies are needed to make possible innovative development. Frequently the strategy is to cooperate with more established companies, which may or may not be potential customers, to develop the technological possibilities. Or universities or other research centers might be approached for this same purpose. This, then, is a holding strategy for promoting innovation, where image management plays an important part in molding and maintaining the joint venture relationships; lack of attention to this aspect can quickly break up the cooperation.

Regardless of how innovative development is organized and financed, creating the right expectations by image marketing, in both potential customers and cooperation partners, will be a main strategic concern of new venture companies. In particular, this will be the case at early stages of their development. Companies which do not succeed in this respect will usually find it extremely difficult to realize their technological potential. At the same time, image management may be of crucial importance even in more positional development situations, with little or no need for innovation management. In this case, the need for image management is due to market complexity. In many purchase situations it is difficult, or even impossible, for customers to use transaction specific information as a basis for discriminating between competing offers.

Convenience goods retailing is one such example, where it is clear that customers often tend to generalize from image, rather than discriminate by basing their purchase decisions on price and quality comparisons for individual items.[9] This either because it is too time consuming or too difficult to compare prices and quality differences between stores or because individual prices are misleading, when 'market baskets', that is, combinations of items, are purchased from one store, rather than single items.

Image management and price and quality expectations then become of utmost importance for marketing success and retailers use a variety of marketing methods to influence (directly or indirectly) price and quality images. They may try to use image advertising to convince customers that their overall price level is lower, or quality level higher, than in the case of competitors, without giving any specific information on prices or qualities. Or they may try to lower prices on certain products with great attention value, such as coffee, and advertise them, hoping that buyers will notice these low prices and conclude that the overall price level of the store is low. The former is an example of downward generalization from image to item level, while the latter is an example of upward generalization to price image based on price discrimination on the item level.

Another example of a relatively positional need for image management is in service marketing.[10] In the present book this term is used to refer to the marketing of open, situation specific possibilities, which are only realized if an offer is accepted. By definition the customer then has to base purchase decisions on expectations of what will take place, rather than on precise knowledge and information of competing possibilities. If one alternative is chosen, the other possibilities will usually remain hypothetical, and will not be available for use as a basis for evaluating the choice.

Management consulting[11] is an example of this type of service management. Image management is often combined with innovation management to develop new knowledge, but even in less innovative consulting situations, expectations are of crucial importance for marketing success. In both instances customers usually base their decisions to do business on image, that is on the perceived capacity of the company to serve their needs, rather than on offer specific information.

Image management, then, is concerned both with building expectations favorable to the company and buyer confidence in it. Creating and fulfilling these obligations is necessary for successful product and company development and the basis for innovative strategic management. Image therefore serves a dual function. It serves both as a marketing magnet, a way to attract buyers, and as a vision or strategic preview of the future, to help companies to direct and focus their innovative efforts.

EXPLICIT AND IMPLICIT MARKETING ACTIVITIES

In this section two alternative views of marketing activities will be presented,[12] which consider the differences between traditional product management and product marketing on the one hand and image management and image marketing on the other. The aim of this approach is to suggest a more wholistic, temporally integrated and balanced view of marketing, looking both to the present and to the future. To achieve this objective, and an understanding of the underlying principles, both economic and psychological mechanisms will be employed.

The starting point is a theoretical distinction between the two extreme types of activities, explicit and implicit marketing, which are shown in our marketing management box (Figure 6.2). Real marketing, of course, is almost always a combination

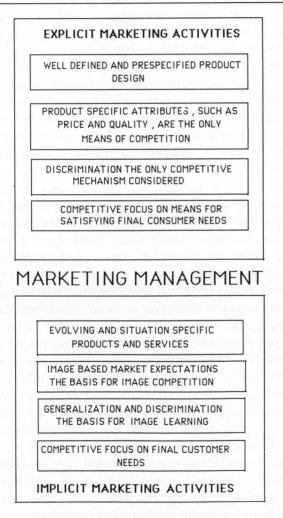

EXPLICIT MARKETING ACTIVITIES

WELL DEFINED AND PRESPECIFIED PRODUCT DESIGN

PRODUCT SPECIFIC ATTRIBUTES , SUCH AS PRICE AND QUALITY , ARE THE ONLY MEANS OF COMPETITION

DISCRIMINATION THE ONLY COMPETITIVE MECHANISM CONSIDERED

COMPETITIVE FOCUS ON MEANS FOR SATISFYING FINAL CONSUMER NEEDS

MARKETING MANAGEMENT

EVOLVING AND SITUATION SPECIFIC PRODUCTS AND SERVICES

IMAGE BASED MARKET EXPECTATIONS THE BASIS FOR IMAGE COMPETITION

GENERALIZATION AND DISCRIMINATION THE BASIS FOR IMAGE LEARNING

COMPETITIVE FOCUS ON FINAL CUSTOMER NEEDS

IMPLICIT MARKETING ACTIVITIES

Figure 6.2 Marketing management box

of these two basic activities. To appreciate the differences it is useful, however, to begin by discussing each in turn.

Explicit Marketing—Prespecified and Well-Defined Marketing

Explicit marketing activities are usually assumed as basic controllable factors in models of marketing management. This is the case in the marketing mix concept[13] stressing combinations of marketing elements, and in the popular '4 Ps' model of marketing,[14] focusing on price, place, promotion and product as the main competitive variables. These approaches, therefore, from our point of view, represent relatively closed and static views of product based marketing. Most general marketing textbooks are mainly concerned with what we call explicit marketing activities, which by and large reflect the relatively short run implications to companies and customers of highly competitive marketing situations, with given product alternatives.

Products in these models may be seen as prespecified and well-defined means for fulfilling given buyer needs. Variations in need fulfillment for specific products, depending on how they are used, are not dealt with. Basic value to consumers of product offerings are tied to given product designs, not to the ways in which products are actually used. While marginal variations in product design are permitted, this is not assumed to lead to radical differences in need fulfillment. A car is a car, regardless of whether it is used to drive to work or as a sleeping place for someone without an apartment.

Standardized commodities, such as oil, paper or wheat, sold on the world market are examples of product situations where pronounced explicit marketing activities usually are emphasized in practice. Variations in use between customers are then not considered, and no attempts are made to adapt products to specific user needs. Even in the case of less standardized products—mass produced consumer goods such as toiletries or TV sets—strong elements of explicit marketing activities can usually be discerned, but they are not as dominant as in the world marketing of industrial commodities.

Only smooth and continuous variations in product variables, such as price and quality, are dealt with in explicit marketing. These variations by definition do not change the competitive situation, that is, the number and types of competing products available on the market place to fulfill the same need, nor do they lead to changes in what competitive variables are used. Merely the intensity of competition, not its direction and basic nature, may thus be influenced by using explicit marketing.

Explicit marketing further requires that buyers and consumers can and do discriminate between partial aspects of products, with regard to their need fulfilling properties. By lowering price, or making more attractive some objective measures of quality, products are assumed to become more attractive to buyers. Competitors are assumed to respond by making corresponding changes, to try to restore the original competitive balance. Competitive price reductions in the retail price of gasoline, for instance, usually lead to much customer switching to lower priced stations if competitors do not respond, and to price wars if they do.

Explicit marketing, therefore, is based on a mechanistic, equilibrium view of competition and buyer response. Attempts by companies to become more competitive lead to offsetting responses by other companies and basically the status quo is maintained and no innovative product or company development takes place. Radical product development and image based marketing aiming at increasing the degrees of freedom and innovative potential in marketing and buyer response, cannot be considered in this framework. In other words, truly creative learning on the part of both buyers and sellers is precluded by definition, and the only learning that can take place is learning to adapt to marginal changes in existing conditions.

Explicit marketing activities reflect what we have called positional company strategy. Everyone loses by competing, since everyone competes in the same way, and no one company can or wants to find a way out of the competitive deadlock. In boxing terminology, the competitors enter into a clinch, with no referee to push them apart, or a coach to teach them new ways to fight. We may, therefore, call explicit marketing unimaginative marketing, since there is little room for imagination, creative learning and the development of new knowledge.

We may also call explicit marketing a building block approach. All companies are assumed to use the same competitive elements to build their marketing. It is possible to make marginal adjustments: for instance, retailers may add some doors or windows to provide better access to customers or a more pleasant indoor climate without redesigning the whole store. Of course sometimes a building will collapse if environmental conditions change dramatically, either owing to internal pressure or to external disturbances. But after a bomb has exploded or a storm erupted it is usually too late to save a building by redesigning its basic structure, even if some belated creative thinking indicates how it might have been done.

Implicit Marketing—Image Based Marketing

In the case of implicit marketing the emphasis is on broadly conceived needs rather than specific means (products or services) to satisfy these needs. Individual needs typically vary more than predefined products or services, as a result of companies trying to achieve benefits of scale and specialization in their production and marketing.

Since needs reflect, rather than determine, individual life styles and consumption patterns, they are an integral part of buyer behavior, difficult to isolate and directly relate to individual products and services, and to explicit marketing dimensions, such as product specific price and quality. In particular it becomes difficult, if not impossible, to specify in advance precisely what needs a given product or service can satisfy, and which individuals will display a certain need at any time.

Implicit marketing recognizes the need for more wholistic concepts and indirect mechanisms to deal with image based marketing, focusing on broadly conceived needs. Essentially, this implies a Chinese box approach to marketing. Perceived needs provide the guidance and outside boundaries for marketing strategies, but do not determine in advance the precise contents of the box, that is, the specific products or services rendered. Within each box many different ways of fulfilling needs are possible, which give companies and consumers considerable freedom with regard to choosing and implementing development patterns and patterns of use.

Instead of directly varying the dimensions of specific offers, such as price and quality, as in the case of explicit marketing,it becomes necessary in the case of implicit marketing strategies to try to achieve favorable, more wholistic buyer expectations, related to future need fulfillment, the precise nature of which cannot be determined in advance.

These expectations are images of company performance held by prospective customers. By generalizing from such images, which provide indirect clues to future need fulfillment, customers may anticipate, rather than evaluate their future satisfaction from entering into a deal.

Implicit marketing, therefore, is based on and assumes image marketing and image competition, which are quite different competitive mechanisms, compared to traditional competitive mechanisms, based on explicit marketing activities. Image marketing, if successful, may for instance usually be expected to lead to more far ranging and lasting effects than traditional product based marketing.

To begin with, images, as defined in our approach, encompass more potential needs than do products, and in creative minds they may therefore accommodate more radical change. Predefined products—whether hardware or software—are, on the other hand, usually quite fixed in their design and subject to strong technical and marketing restraints. This makes them more difficult to change, and they may more easily become obsolete.

Successful image marketing is also more difficult to imitate than successful product marketing, since it is less clear to competitors what dimensions and mechanisms are effective in implicit image competition, than in explicit product competition. Images are also more complex phenomena than product attributes, they may be more centrally integrated in personality and life style, which in general should make them more resistant to change and difficult to imitate.

A management consulting company, for instance, which develops a strong image and competence in general problem solving, will find it easier to accommodate radical change in consulting needs than will one which develops a narrower competence, based on highly specific and predefined product offers.

At the same time it is probably more difficult and time consuming to develop a strong image in general consulting, than a competitive strength in specific applications. The former strategy requires a strong emphasis on implicit marketing, to show and to document general ability. The latter can usually be carried out successfully, at least in the short run, by using a more explicit marketing strategy, emphasizing specific skills. When using a more implicit marketing strategy a company also needs to show concrete results, but this then is mainly to demonstrate the overall competence of a company, not its specialized abilities.

Indeed, being extremely successful in specific applications may even lead to suspicion of overspecialization and doubts as to general competence. A company with a strong agribusiness image, highly skilled in making farm machinery, may, for instance, experience a lack of credibility when trying to establish itself as a hi-tech company in other areas of application, such as biotechnology, as Alfa Laval has found out in recent years.

Disassociating those parts of the company pursuing a different technological strategy from the overall image of the company by divisionalization, joint ventures with companies with a more compatible image or renaming, may then be used to achieve more favorable conditions for successful image marketing.

AGA, for instance, with a strong image in gas and gas related equipment tried to use divisionalization in the early 1970s to achieve technological diversification into quite different areas of technology, such as industrial electronics and medical equipment. It retained the name AGA, however, for its divisions, and called them, for instance, Aga Electronics and Aga Medical. This probably made it more difficult for these divisions to develop their own images. It may have been one reason why most of these divisions did not live up to company expectations, and were later sold off to other companies or absorbed in the gas and welding division.

Successful image marketing also requires that a company devotes much organizational work to gain innovative ability. This involves integrating knowledge and building a culture with high creative potential. It also involves using innovation management and technological strategy to build a broad knowledge base, which may be creatively focused to develop unique products and services with high market potential.

Implicit marketing and successful image marketing thus require creative technological strategies and strong innovation management to be successful. As we have seen in Chapter 4, this may be achieved by more open strategies, combining technological possibilities and directing company efforts to utilize as fully as possible the research and development potential both inside and outside a company. In this context, image may serve both as a magnet to attract and retain the most promising outside contacts and as a spotlight to focus efforts, as Pharmacia has so well demonstrated.

Image, therefore, may help in the creative fusion between different, previously unrelated elements of knowledge: that is, in achieving what we call a synergistic technology use; bringing sparkling ideas together to start an innovative bonfire. Since image joins together rather than disengages disparate thoughts, it may help to focus the creative process in new directions. Thereby, it may provide a common bond between experts working in different areas of technology and help them to distill and communicate their own ideas. By putting different ideas into the same compartment of our Chinese box, we may promote interaction between them, yet retain their fundamental uniqueness.

Tour Agenturer, for instance, with an image of themselves as co-drivers racing against competitors to maintain and increase their lead, claimed that they put electrical and mechanical engineers in almost physical contact in the same room—with their desks together, facing each other—to promote the speed and flexibility which, as we noted on page 121, was vital to their business. Clearly putting each co-driver in his own car racing in different directions would have defeated their purpose, but in essence that is what their competitors were doing.

Another example of an image based marketing strategy is provided by Eco Tapeter, a leading Swedish wallpaper company. This company utilized an image of design, as layers of overlapping geometrical patterns, to combine visual variation with operational efficiency in producing wallpaper. It was thus possible to achieve both design and marketing flexibility with small batches of original designs; and low production costs by printing one pattern on top of another. For this purpose they employed an artist interested both in visual design and photography who worked closely in a team together with production people. Instead of the marketing people fighting the production people in a battle for design flexibility versus long run production, as is usually the case when explicit strategies divide the world, this image made possible the fusion of competing forces to a common purpose.

SUMMARY

In this chapter image management, the marketing component of the strategic creativity mix in our strategic management box, has been the focus of our interest. The traditional management view of marketing based on explicit marketing strategies and the management of market information relating to clearly perceived differences in market conditions, has been contrasted with the image management view emphasized in this book.

Image based marketing strategies are called implicit marketing strategies. They reflect a more wholistic, future oriented view of marketing, focusing on expectations and encompassing more total needs and possibilities than explicit strategies. By considering implicit strategies also we are better able to understand creative product and company development, compared to more traditional marketing models with a more analytical, contemporaneous perspective.

By the use of image management and implicit marketing strategies, companies may increase their marketing potential and their degrees of strategic freedom in product and company development. This attitude implies more freedom and creative possibilities for buyers in choosing and using products and services. Companies, as well as buyers, may benefit from this freedom by cooperating to find and develop new and better products and servics, as we saw in Chapter 4, when we discussed our other main component of the strategic creativity mix of a company, namely innovation management.

When dealing with radical product and company development, implicit marketing strategies are of fundamental importance and provide the basic strategic conditions for marketing success. More operational, explicit marketing strategies then need to be supplemented by implicit marketing strategies to provide a wide angled, but still focused, strategic view of the future. To deal only with explicit strategies leaves the company staring at a frozen picture of the past, while the future sweeps the company along at an ever increasing pace.

Generalization and discrimination are psychological mechanisms basic to our understanding of image marketing and image competition

7
Image Marketing and Image Competition—Some Empirical Data on the Psychological Management of Generalization and Discrimination

The theoretical foundation for the empirical results reported in this chapter,[1] is a model of image learning based on generalization and discrimination. This model was originally developed to study the implications of pricing for retail competition,[2] but the underlying mechanism is applicable to all types of image marketing, as should be evident from our discussion.

Both generalization and discrimination[3] may be viewed as general psychological mechanisms for influencing image and therefore are central to our understanding of image marketing and image competition. Transferring images from one level of analysis to another is called generalization, the direction may be from a more complex aggregate level to a more simple disaggregated level or vice versa. In the former case it is mainly a question of concluding, while in the latter case it is a question of learning what to conclude.

When concluding, the main risk is that of jumping to unjustified conclusions, for instance, assuming that a company with a hi-tech image necessarily has technologically advanced products. Such an image need not primarily be based on relevant evidence, relating to actual new products. It may reflect claims by a company to devote much effort and money to research or to be part of a hi-tech industry, without substantiating this in any directly observable way. When learning to conclude, on the other hand, the main risk lies in basing the learning on biased and nonrepresentative observations, such as using identical products in the assortments of competing firms to judge their overall price levels.

At the same time, it may be necessary for a company to achieve first a favorable image to be able to live up to it, not the other way around, as is usually assumed in traditional economic discussions of how business practices are or should be. Leif Lundblad, for instance, with little relevant manufacturing experience had to convince his potential customers that he could develop and produce a superior product, in order to gain the option and leeway to prove that he could do so, as we have seen in Chapter 3. Such image marketing is viewed as an important aspect of innovative entrepreneurship in our approach.

On the other hand, there is a pronounced need for image marketing even in more static marketing situations. Food retailers, for instance, need to convince their potential customers that they have an attractive price level in order to get them to their stores. At the same time it is a moot and almost metaphysical question what this really implies, since competing products in other stores often are not identical and therefore difficult or impossible to compare for quality. In addition to this, some stores are usually cheaper for one type of product, others for another, where meaningful comparisons may be made.

Each customer produces an idiosyncratic and temporary overall price level by the combinations of items actually bought in a store. If the retailer succeeds in attracting a larger number of customers to the store this will afford a better financial basis for maintaining low price for quality (there will be a large proportion of fixed costs); but actual prices will increasingly reflect the strategy for persuading buyers of their competitiveness, rather than some objective price reality which neither the retailer nor the customer knows how to accurately define and measure.

It is in practice almost impossible for both sellers and buyers in most real world situations to estimate relative price and quality implications in advance, with anywhere near the accuracy assumed by most economic and management theories. It is none the less highly important for both sellers and buyers that definite expectations exist as to the consequences of doing business, to introduce an element of choice in situations where otherwise no possibility for choice exists.

This means that image marketing becomes of major importance and actual prices are largely the result of this psychological interplay between sellers and buyers. This is true, owing to high informational complexity and noncomparability of competing offers, even in many relatively static situations, when products are well established on the market and buyers tend mainly to purchase items with which they are familiar. In more dynamic, uncertain situations, involving radically new products or services, the relative importance of image marketing and image competition may be expected to be even greater, and the consequences for ignoring the issue or dismissing it out of hand as unmanageable much graver.

In the rest of this chapter we shall illustrate the implications of generalization and discrimination for image marketing and image competition. This we shall do by using data from our studies of retail competition in the food market, focusing on price image and price evaluations and the implications of strategies for managing discrimination and generalization on both the company and product level.

This does not mean that price image need be the most important type of image influencing the outcome of marketing strategies. In retail pricing, price image clearly is important, but other types of images, such as quality images, also need to be considered. In the present chapter strategies for managing price image are used basically as an example of more general strategies for handling generalization and discrimination. This should be viewed against the background of our general thesis that image marketing is an important aspect of strategic management and decision making.

Our results clearly indicate that even in relatively stable business situations we need to consider image marketing and image competition in order to understand and evaluate company strategies and buyer behavior. In highly dynamic, evolving situations, the need is self evident; in these cases the future exists in and can be influenced by images, rather than by established facts.

GENERALIZATION AND DISCRIMINATION

To begin with, we may distinguish between different levels of analysis with regard to the psychological mechanism of image formation and change (Figure 7.1). In this book we are primarily interested in the product and company levels and the interrelationship between these two. We may, however,

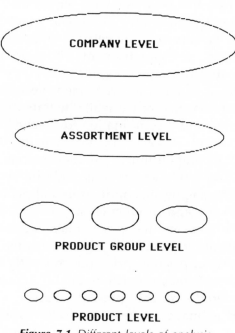

Figure 7.1 Different levels of analysis

also distinguish between other intermediate levels, for instance, the assortment level and product group level.

These levels are of interest both in the case of more static aspects of product and company development, such as pricing strategy[4] and more dynamic aspects such as technological and marketing strategies for finding and developing new products. In this chapter we are mainly concerned with the importance of image marketing and image competition for more static development, while in other chapters we have focused on the importance for more dynamic development, involving radical technological and market change.

The company level refers to the general type of enterprise a firm belongs to: it may be cooperatively or privately controlled, a distinction we found to be related to product development success in our study of Swedish food processing companies, presented in Chapter 10. From a price image point of view some buyers may believe, for ideological reasons, that cooperative firms and others that privately owned companies have lower prices, without basing this conclusion on any specific price information. Or buyers may believe, again without employing any specific price information, that more shabby stores are less expensive than more elegant ones. In either case this is a real issue confronting the companies and influencing their development possibilities.

The assortment level covers all products sold by a store and may be divided into various subdivisions; for instance, meat, dry goods or fruit and vegetables. The product level, which is our lowest level of analysis, refers to products viewed independently of each other.

Generalization is defined as taking place between different levels of analysis. A buyer may, for instance, generalize from the belief that cooperative stores are cheaper than private stores to thinking that a particular cooperative store is cheaper than a particular private store. This without having any information as to actual prices in these stores. Similarly he may generalize from the conception that the total assortment of a store is cheaper than that of another store, to the conception that a particular product group (meat) or product (pork chops) is cheaper. Obviously generalization can also take place in the opposite direction, for instance, from product level to assortment level, or assortment level to company level.

Comparisons on the same level of analysis are called discrimination. A buyer may discriminate on the company level by trying to compare one store with another, or on the product level by making comparisons with the closest substitutes sold by other stores. These comparisons may take place with regard to price, price changes or other information, such as whether or not a product is advertised. This means that there is no basis in our approach for assuming, as in economic theory, that lower prices or overall price levels always will lead to more favorable price evaluations and greater sales. Such an assumption is not consistent with our data and makes it impossible to understand both image marketing in general and the pricing strategies of companies and the price reaction of consumers in particular.

AN INTERVIEW STUDY OF PRICE IMAGE AND PRICE EVALUATIONS

To test if our model of learning, based on generalization and discrimination, was consistent with empirical data, an interview study[5] was carried out in 1968. It was based on a random sample of 60 households from a population of 508 in Solna, a suburb of Stockholm. They were all living close to the center of this community, where four food outlets belonging to different chains and an independent food market were located adjacent to each other.

Those interviewed could thus be assumed to be potential buyers of food items in these competing stores and it was easy for them, if they wanted to, to shop around and find price information on which to base their price images and price evaluations. Personal interviews, preceded by test interviews, were carried out from March 11 to April 12, with the member of each household chiefly responsible for food purchases. Each home interview covering 18 questions, took on the average 45 minutes and the response rate was 82%.

To begin with a filter question was used to check whether the persons interviewed thought that they could get more for their money by regularly purchasing in one store rather than in another. All respondents were of this opinion and were then asked to rank the five stores in declining order by price level. They then were asked to indicate how much they thought a purchase for 100 Swedish crowns in the cheapest firm would cost in the other ones (Table 7.1). They were also asked whether they had read or heard about any impartial investigations or consumer studies on food prices, to register possible outside influence on their price images and price evaluations. Of the 49 persons, 24 said they had and 25 that they had not.

We see that the most expensive store received an average rank of 1.3, the second 1.8, the third 3.3, the fourth 4.0 and the fifth 4.5. There was high agreement between individuals with regard to rank order, which makes it reasonable to use the average ranking to summarize the data. We also see that the persons interviewed believed that there were large differences in price level between the stores. Much greater than an impartial study published in the Swedish press of price levels for food stores in the Stockholm area in 1966 had arrived at, for stores belonging to the same chains as four of the stores we studied.

Our price image data thus indicates that the interviewees believed that there were large and consistent differences between the competing stores with regard to price image. Our data also indicate that buyers believed that their price

Table 7.1 Price image rankings of competing stores and estimates of average price levels

	Number of persons interviewed for each ranking from 1 (most expensive) to 5 (cheapest)					Average rank	Estimate of average price level (Swedish crowns)
	1	2	3	4	5		
Store							
A			5	13	31	4.5	101
B			12	23	14	4.0	103
C		3	31	12	3	3.3	107
D	14	31	4			1.8	114
E	35	13	1			1.3	118

images were accurate representations of reality, but tended to exaggerate differences in price levels compared to the results of the impartial study of food prices referred to above.

This supports our model of image competition, which assumes that buyers are price conscious in a subjective, psychological sense, but does not require that their estimates are based on realistic, objective calculations of actual price differences. More loyal customers, for instance, had significantly more favorable price images of their favorite store than had less loyal ones for the same store.

It is also interesting to note that 41 of the 49 respondents stated that they believed it was worthwhile to patronize several stores on the same shopping trip because of price differences, while eight did not believe that it was worth their effort. This may be due to the fact that the former were more apt to discriminate between the prices of different items, and the latter more apt to generalize from their overall price image when evaluating items.

At the same time, special prices were viewed with more suspicion than ordinary prices. Rather than infer that stores with many and frequent extra price reductions had a lower overall price level than competing stores, some buyers generalized in the other direction, and believed that such stores had a higher overall price level.

Our studies also point to the need for a more differentiated view of pricing strategies, than is usually employed in pricing studies. We found for instance that 27 persons thought that it is cheaper to make purchases in stores which often change their prices, while two believed it to be more expensive, and 20 could see no difference. This points to the hypothesis that flexibility of pricing in itself creates a tendency towards a more favorable price image, which may be due to the fact that price decreases tend to be promoted and price increases to be hidden. When asked whether certain stores change prices more than others, 40 believed this to be true and only nine did not think so.

To judge the extent to which buyers may have generalized from their price images on the company level to price evaluations on the product level, each person was asked to compare the prices of 16 products between the five stores.

For each store and product they were asked to indicate what price differences they believed to exist, if any. The price evaluations, that is, price rankings for products, were then compared with the price images, that is, the price level rankings shown in Table 7.1.

In our data we found a clear tendency for individuals to rank the prices for products in the same order as their price images for the companies selling them. This is consistent with the hypothesis, derived from our model of generalization and discrimination, that buyers often tend to generalize from their price images when evaluating specific products.

According to our model we should expect differences in the extent to which buyers generalize from price image or discriminate on the basis of specific price information, according to how comparable products are between stores and how frequently their prices had been advertised. Eight of the products studied were of the frequently advertised type, the others had been infrequently advertised during the weeks preceding the interviews.

We found the data for frequently advertised products more consistent than the data for the infrequently advertised ones, with a strong tendency for interviewees to generalize from their price images. This could be due to their having been frequently advertised or to some other factor which covaries with advertising. Such a factor could be product differentiation.

Indeed one of the main reasons for advertising certain products is probably that they are more differentiated, that is, more difficult to compare. Readers may be expected to infer from the fact that products are advertised that they are competitively priced, and this generalization effect is more likely to occur if discrimination is made more difficult by the fact that product differentiation is high. Among the frequently advertised group we find such products as meat, fish, fresh fruit and beer, where it is more difficult to compare price and quality between stores, while among the less frequently advertised group we find such products as butter, milk, eggs and flour, where it is easier to do so.

With regard to the less advertised group of products, we find our data consistent with the hypothesis that some individuals tend to generalize, while others are more likely to discriminate. To a large extent these products are almost identical between stores, and individuals who want to compare prices are well able to do so.

Consequently, the individuals who tend to discriminate between these products are probably better informed and behave more in accordance with what is expected of them in traditional economic theory. Our data indicates, however, that many individuals tend to generalize even in situations where it would be possible for them to discriminate on the basis of specific price information. In other situations product differentiation or lack of such information makes it difficult even for buyers who want to do so to discriminate. We therefore need a model of image marketing and image competition which deals with generalization and discrimination as factors that influence buyer response and which companies need to consider in forming their strategies.

RESULTS OF A PRICING EXPERIMENT

In order to test some crucial assumptions in our model of image marketing and image competition based on generalization and discrimination, a carefully controlled field experiment was devised and carried out.[6] In our model image transferal (generalization from the company to the product level) is an instantaneous effect, while image learning (generalization from the product level to the company level) requires repeated observations by buyers. The former type of generalization is consequently more amenable to experimental testing and the experiment reported on is therefore only concerned with generalization from the company to the product level.

For the purpose of the experiment an item was chosen for a temporary price reduction in a department store. Since only buyer reaction to differences in price information was to be investigated, all other factors which might influence buyer price evaluations were held constant as far as possible. The criteria for choice of the experimental item was that it should be the type of product normally sold by the department store in question, yet unique in the sense that the particular brand

and model had not previously been sold in the area. In other words, the item should be familiar enough to buyers to permit them to evaluate its approximate price level. They should have no specific price information for the chosen brand, however, such as having noticed it for sale previously at the store in question or at some other store.

This means that it should be the type of product where product differentiation—both in the psychological sense based on brand reputation perhaps, and in the functional sense based on variations in material and design—is relatively high. The price of the item, furthermore, should be relatively high to ensure deliberation on the part of customers before purchase, but not exceedingly so, in order to keep the length of the decision process for most customers within the time span of the experiment.

Based on the above criteria, men's shirts were chosen as the product category for the experiment and a specific brand of shirt was selected. The normal price for this shirt was set at 49.75 Swedish crowns and the reduced price in the experiment was 37 crowns. The same shirt in different sizes but only one color (blue) was used during the whole experiment.

The experiment was conducted in 1972 during four days chosen to be as comparable as possible with regard to sales climate, April 14–15 and April 21–22. Each day a different price sign was used which was the experimental stimulus (Table 7.2). On the first day the shirts were sold employing Sign A, which only stated the normal price and gave no other information. In our terminology only price level information was given. On the second day the price was reduced and Sign B was used, which in addition to the reduced price also gave the normal price. In this instance price level information was given both with regard to the normal and the reduced price, which of course also implicitly gave the price change. On the third day no further price reduction was carried out, but Sign C was used which gave the reduced price and stated that the normal price had been reduced but not how much. That is, both price level and price change information was given, but no information on the size of the reduction, either implicitly by giving the previous price or explicitly by stating

Table 7.2 Signs used in the pricing experiment

SIGN A

MEN'S
SHIRT
WASH AND WEAR
65% TERITAL
35% LINEN

49.75

SIGN B

MEN'S
SHIRT
WASH AND WEAR
65% TERITAL
35% LINEN
~~49.75~~
37.00

SIGN C

SPECIAL
OFFER

MEN'S
SHIRT
WASH AND WEAR
65% TERITAL
35% LINEN

37.00

SIGN D

MEN'S
SHIRT
WASH AND WEAR
65% TERITAL
35% LINEN

37.00

the price change. On the fourth day Sign D was used, which only stated the reduced price, without giving any information that the normal price had been lowered. That is, only price level information was given, the difference from Sign A being that it referred to the reduced, not to the normal price.

The following pricing hypotheses were formulated before the experiment based largely on the interview study summarized above.

H1:   The price images of customers with regard to the overall price level of a store do not change very much in the short run as a result of recent price experiences.

H2:   Special prices, that is temporarily reduced prices, are viewed as less representative of overall company price levels than normal prices.

H3:   Customers who experience difficulties in judging prices are more inclined to generalize from their price images of overall price levels to price evaluations of individual items than customers who find it easy to judge prices.

H4:   Customers who experience difficulty in judging prices are inclined to believe that prices are higher, compared to customers who find it easy to judge prices.

H5:   Knowledge of recent price changes influences price evaluations even when it is not possible to compare price levels.

Buyer reaction to price was studied by interviews according to a fixed questionnaire. Only customers indicating interest in the offer were interviewed to avoid forcing answers not related to real interest in the sales item. This interest was shown by their stopping at the display, handling the merchandise, asking questions and similar signs of being prospective customers. Since the intention was to test reactions to the specific experimental stimuli, that is the information contained in the signs, only spontaneously interested buyers were interviewed. Only those who were confronted with the item for the first time were included in the experiment, to avoid contamination from other possible effects not controlled for in the experiment.

Buyers were interviewed either when they left the site of the experiment without making a purchase or when they went to the cashier to buy the item. In both instances it was assumed that the initial price evaluation and the decision process whether or not to buy the item—the focus of the experiment—had been concluded. The total number of interviews carried out was 207 and the number per day and sign varied between 50 and 53. Non-response, normally a result of professed lack of time, was approximately 10% for all days.

In order to make the experiment as realistic as possible, salesmen were instructed to use normal sales procedures. No advertising outside the immediate sales area took place, which means that all price information was confined to the signs. Following test interviews 11 questions involving either fixed alternatives or an evaluative scale with 9 intervals were chosen for the experiment. In addition to background information to determine the initial decision and information states of respondents, information was collected on how they judged the price level of the specific offering (the shirt) and the overall price level of the company, that is the department store selling it.

The hypotheses were tested by assuming that responses were normally distributed and that intervals on the scales used were perceived by subjects as equal.

The first pricing hypothesis, H1, is of critical importance for our approach to image marketing. If the price images of overall price levels tend to change almost instantaneously as a result of recent exposure to price information, the learning mechanism assumed in our model, which assumes that such changes tend to take place rather slowly, would be invalid. This would then give support to the traditional economic approach to pricing, which is based on instantaneous buyer reactions. It would also imply that the stabilizing influence ascribed to overall price image in our model and the assumption that price image may have an independent influence on price evaluations at any specific moment regardless of the actual price information available for the item in question, would be inconsistent with the data.

This hypothesis was tested by comparing the price images of customers exposed to the various signs to see if the specific price information given for the shirts tended to influence buyer estimates of overall company price levels. Pairwise comparisons between the groups indicated that no such differences existed at the 5% level of significance between the average price images of customers exposed to different signs. Customers were asked to rank how expensive the store was on a nine interval scale from very high (1) to very low (9). The average price images for those exposed to Signs A–D and the *t*-values for pairwise comparisons between the different groups are given in Table 7.3.

The second pricing hypothesis H2 assumes that temporarily reduced prices are viewed as less representative of overall price levels than normal prices. This hypothesis was tested by investigating the average difference between overall price image and price evaluation for the shirt to find if it was significantly smaller for the group exposed to Sign A giving the normal price than for the groups exposed to the other signs, which in various ways indicated a special price. As with the evaluation of overall price levels, all subjects were asked to indicate how expensive they believed the shirt to be on a nine interval scale, ranging from very expensive (1)

Table 7.3 Average price images for groups exposed to the different signs

Group exposed to sign	Average price image
A	4.13
B	4.28
C	4.07
D	4.11
Pairwise comparisons	*t*-value ($n > 50$)
A–B	1.22
A–C	0.34
A–D	0.13
B–C	1.31
B–D	1.22
C–D	0.22

to very cheap (9). High numerical differences between price image and price evaluation may be taken as an indication that customers do not consider the price of a specific item as representative of the overall price level of a store.

In Table 7.4 we see that there was a significantly smaller average difference on the 5% level between price image and price evaluation for the group exposed to Sign A than for the other groups. This supports the hypothesis that the prices of specially reduced items are viewed as less representative of overall company price levels than ordinary prices.

The significance of this hypothesis for our model of price image learning based on generalization and discrimination, is that learning of price image is assumed to occur only when prices are viewed by buyers as representative for overall price levels. Against this background special prices may be seen as mainly having a short-run more instantaneous effect on sales and not as contributing very much to long-run sales by helping to create a more favorable price image. This hypothesis was suggested by our interview study on retail pricing, where as we noted in the previous section, buyers seemed to be suspicious of special prices and sometimes even concluded on the basis of such prices that overall company price levels were relatively high.

The third pricing hypothesis assumes that perceived difficulty in judging price leads to a greater tendency for buyers

Table 7.4 *Differences between price images and price evaluations for groups exposed to different signs*

Group exposed to sign	Average difference between price image and price evaluations
A	1.04
B	1.78
C	1.81
D	1.69
Pairwise comparisons	t-value ($n > 50$)
A–B	3.5
A–C	3.9
A–D	4.0

to generalize from price image. The subjects were asked to indicate on a nine interval scale how difficult they thought it was to evaluate the price of the shirt. The 25% of the prospective buyers who considered it most difficult according to this scale were grouped together as subjects finding it difficult to judge price and the 25% who considered it most easy were grouped together as subjects finding it easy to do so.

For each group the average difference between overall price image and price evaluation for the shirt was calculated. Those finding it difficult to judge prices tend to generalize more, according to our model, than those finding it easy to judge price. This in turn should lead to a closer correspondence between price image and price evaluation for the former group, that is, to a smaller average difference between price image and price evaluation.

In Table 7.5 we see that there is a significant difference between the two groups with regard to the correspondence between evaluations of the shirt and image for the store (5% level). Those who found it difficult to judge price evidently tended to rely more on their price image than those who found it easy to make these judgements. This confirms our hypothesis that generalization from price image tends to increase when price evaluations on the item level is viewed as difficult and is consistent with what we have assumed in our model of image formation and change based on generalization and discrimination.

The fourth pricing hypothesis, H4, states that individuals who find it difficult to judge price tend to have more negative

Table 7.5 *Differences between price image and price evaluations for subjects finding it easy or difficult to judge price*

Subjects finding it	Average difference between price image and price evaluations
Easy to judge price	1.97
Difficult to judge price	1.36

$t = 3.05$, $n > 50$.

price evaluations than those who find it easy to do so. The same grouping of subjects was used as in the testing of H3. As shown in Table 7.6, the average price evaluation for the shirt by the group of persons who found it difficult to evaluate its price was significantly more unfavorable than the average price evaluation by those who found it easy (5% level). The hypothesis that uncertainty with regard to price tends to create more negative evaluations was therefore confirmed.

A certain contamination of this result from the type of generalization evident in the testing of H3 cannot, however, be ruled out. The reason for this is that price images in the overall data tended to be more unfavorable than price evaluations.

Hypothesis H5 states that knowledge of recent price changes, independent of the actual price level before and after the change, tends to influence price evaluations. Since the only difference between Sign B and Sign D is that the former sign contains information of a recent change in price, this hypothesis may be tested by comparing the responses of those exposed to these two signs. In Table 7.7 we see that the average price evaluation differs significantly between those exposed to Sign B and Sign D. This indicates that knowledge of price change influences price evaluation. We may also assume that the greater product differentiation between the item and competing brands, the higher the tendency will be to evaluate price on the basis of price change alone, but we do not have data to test this, although it seems reasonable given our other results.

Table 7.6 *Price evaluations for subjects finding it easy to judge price compared to subjects finding it difficult*

Subjects finding it	Average price evaluation
Easy to judge price	6.02
Difficult to judge price	5.36

$t = 3.7$, $n > 50$.

Table 7.7 Price evaluations for subjects exposed to price change information compared to subjects only exposed to price level information

Subjects exposed to	Average price evaluation
Price change information (Sign B)	6.08
Only price level information (Sign D)	5.73

$t = 2.4, n > 50.$

With regard to sales results, Sign A sold 7 shirts, Sign B 17 shirts, Sign C 8 shirts and Sign D 8 shirts. Although the hypotheses tested in the experiment did not refer directly to sales, but to customer reaction to price, it is reasonable to assume that more favorable price evaluations tend to be related to greater sales. Purchase decisions, however, depend on many other factors besides price (amount of money available and perceived need) which were not controlled in the experiment, since it was directed towards testing the implications of our psychological model of image learning. It is therefore difficult to analyze the relationships between our price reaction data and sales and a tentative attempt to do so led to inconclusive results.

Our pricing experiment is consistent with our earlier explorative work on the psychological implications of pricing, reported on earlier in this chapter. It supports the theoretical results derived from our model of generalization and discrimination, that buyers, when it is difficult for them to discriminate, tend to generalize from their overall image. It also indicates that these images tend to be relatively stable and not subject to radical changes based on erratic observations.

This is consistent with our basic assumption that it is only when evaluations based on discrimination are viewed as representative of overall conditions that we can expect image to change. This points to the need for systematically considering how and when image learning and image change takes place, to make possible successive image marketing and image management.

SUMMARY

This chapter presents some empirical results in the context of price image and price evaluations in support of our general model of image formation and change based on generalization and discrimination. This shows the importance of image marketing and image competition in a relatively static development situation involving little technological and market innovation.

From this data it is clear that images influence buyer behavior in ways which may not be captured in traditional management models based on a more objective view of the economic realities facing buyers and sellers. We therefore need to consider the psychological interplay between images and evaluations even in these relatively static situations, and the need conceivably is much greater in more dynamic situations involving more radical product and company development. It is also clear from this data that we need to focus on both the product and company level of analysis, and on the interaction between these two levels, to understand buyer reaction to marketing strategies.

The dynamic management of marketing relationships is viewed as a creative learning process based on the interaction between buyers and sellers

8
Managing Marketing Relationships

In this chapter[1] we shall be concerned with one of the most important aspects of product and company development, namely how to manage marketing relationships. This is a subject which we have already dealt with to some extent in our previous discussion, but this chapter will tackle it more directly.

In traditional economic theory and marketing theory, buyer–seller relationships are mainly viewed as a direct function of the competitive mechanism.[2] Buyers are assumed to react to and be passive users and consumers of what is offered on the market place, rather than interact with producers to develop new and better products and processes. Producers and sellers are assumed to know what buyers want, and to compete with each other to satisfy given and well-defined buyer needs. At each moment prevailing technological and market conditions are therefore assumed to coordinate transactions between buyers and sellers. In this relatively static framework there is no need for innovations to create and handle radical change or images to guide ventures into the unknown.

To deal with innovative product and company development we therefore need to extend this framework to consider dynamic interaction and knowledge development on the part of both buyers and sellers.[3] Actively exploring and taking advantage of long-run and open development patterns and possibilities (image and innovation management) then becomes a key requirement for achieving satisfactory long-term marketing relationships.

In our approach the dynamic management of marketing relationships is viewed as a creative learning process, based on the interaction between buyers and sellers. If successful, this will lead either to more favorable company images and a strengthening of existing ties to established customers, or to the establishment of favorable psychological and economic relationships with new customers.

If dynamic interaction dominates the marketing relationship, we speak of a pronounced holding strategy; companies may maintain and further strengthen holding strategies, for instance, by trading information[4] with and using business partners for developing and marketing new products or processes to fit their specific technological and market needs. If more static interaction dominates the relationship, we call this a pronounced competitive strategy. Companies then use their technological and marketing strategies primarily to outdo their competitors to gain a larger market share for existing products.

Extreme holding strategies thus lead to dynamic, bilateral monopoly situations, where it is in the interest of both parties to develop, integrate and improve their technologies and know-how.

In the case of more pronounced competitive strategies, on the other hand, it is less likely that customers will benefit from cooperative relationships with producers and suppliers. The emphasis then is less on satisfying specific needs than on catering to a wider, more anonymous market. The incentives for customers to take part in such interaction may therefore be expected to be less than in the case of more pronounced holding strategies, since they cannot expect such careful attendance to their individual needs.

In practice, strategies for managing marketing relations almost always are a mixture of competitive and holding elements and companies therefore need a strategic marketing mix which balances these two components (Figure 8.1).

Our approach therefore is to assume that both competitive and holding relationships determine the outcome of company

Figure 8.1 *Strategic marketing mix as a balance between competitive action and buyer–seller interaction*

strategies, and that the relative importance in each situation must be determined empirically given the overall strategic situation. Companies in given development situations may choose different strategic marketing mixes. By appropriate strategic management they may also succeed in various ways, if they have or can develop the necessary resources and technologies. In our view, how companies carry out their strategies may be more important than what strategies they choose, and it is therefore important to focus on the implications of different strategic choices.

VERTICAL AND HORIZONTAL COMPLEXITY IN MARKETING RELATIONSHIPS

All learning processes are basically a question of ascertaining the types and degrees of complexity which are exhibited by the phenomena, and the stability of the underlying conditions. In the case of marketing relationships it appears to be important to distinguish between two types of complexity, horizontal and vertical, since they have different implications for marketing strategy (Figure 8.2). The degree of vertical complexity in our approach is used to refer to the average complexity in the relationships between a seller and each individual buyer. The degree of horizontal complexity refers to the complexity confronting a seller because different buyers have different requirements. We may call the former intra-firm complexity and the latter inter-firm complexity, if we keep in mind that these complexities are due to both buyer and seller characteristics. It is the fit between economically

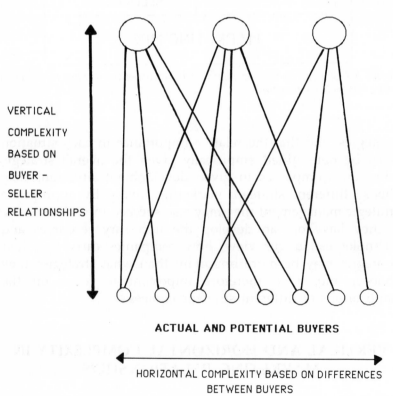

COMPETING SELLERS

VERTICAL
COMPLEXITY
BASED ON
BUYER –
SELLER
RELATIONSHIPS

ACTUAL AND POTENTIAL BUYERS

HORIZONTAL COMPLEXITY BASED ON DIFFERENCES
BETWEEN BUYERS

Figure 8.2 *Vertical and horizontal complexity*

significant buyer needs and seller offerings which determine both.

Traditional micro economic theory does not consider vertical complexity; instead, horizontal complexity is given priority in determining the optimal marketing strategy of a firm. This means that there are assumed to be no economically or technically significant restrictions on doing business between individual sellers or buyers. Instead they may momentarily start or stop doing business with each other at any time, the only determining factor being the quality adjusted prices of comparable competing products and, in more modern versions, how well informed the parties are of alternative possibilities.

In practice this is a highly limiting assumption, particularly in the case of industrial marketing, where high vertical complexity and mutual adjustment between buying and selling firms over long periods often lead to low mobility in buyer–seller relationships and stable networks of buyers and sellers. In consumer marketing the assumption is usually less unrealistic, but even in these situations there are often ties between buyers and sellers which make the distinction between vertical and horizontal complexity useful for conceptualizing and handling marketing strategy.

FACTORS AFFECTING VERTICAL AND HORIZONTAL COMPLEXITY

In this section a number of factors will be given which may be expected to influence the degree of vertical or horizontal complexity in marketing relationships (Figure 8.3).

At first, greater complexity in use, that is, a greater number of distinctive uses for a given product or product category by individual buyers, will tend to lead to greater vertical complexity. It also leads to greater scope for innovation, for instance, joint product development between buyers and sellers. If a customer uses a product in many different ways a seller has a number of options in differentiating an offer to fit the needs of this specific buyer, which together may make the customer more dependent on buying from that firm.

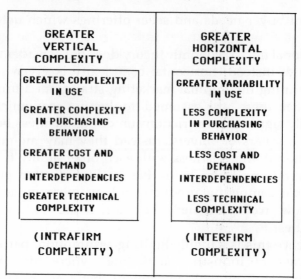

GREATER VERTICAL COMPLEXITY	GREATER HORIZONTAL COMPLEXITY
GREATER COMPLEXITY IN USE	GREATER VARIABILITY IN USE
GREATER COMPLEXITY IN PURCHASING BEHAVIOR	LESS COMPLEXITY IN PURCHASING BEHAVIOR
GREATER COST AND DEMAND INTERDEPENDENCIES	LESS COST AND DEMAND INTERDEPENDENCIES
GREATER TECHNICAL COMPLEXITY	LESS TECHNICAL COMPLEXITY
(INTRAFIRM COMPLEXITY)	(INTERFIRM COMPLEXITY)

Figure 8.3 Factors influencing the degree of vertical and horizontal complexity in marketing relationships

Greater variability in use, on the other hand, between different buyers will lead to greater horizontal complexity, and a greater need to cater to common needs in technological and marketing development.

In paper manufacturing, for instance, a chemical company may cater to the needs of a specific buyer by adapting along a number of company specific dimensions, such as paper format and strength, thereby increasing the degreee of vertical complexity in the relationship. Or the company may cater to a wide range of requirements without adapting the offer to any specific buyer. In the latter case the horizontal complexity between different buyers is stressed and it is hoped that many of them will find the offer competitively attractive, even though it has not been tailored to their specific needs.

In our data the paper chemical system, Compozyl, is a good example. It was when Eka Nobell recognized the inherent vertical complexity in their product, viewed as a customer specific solution, that they were able to successfully differentiate and market it. They had viewed it formerly as a general concept catering to the horizontal complexity of an abstract market, which was not as willing to pay for it in this capacity.

The number and combinations of different products which individual buyers purchase from a firm will also influence the degree of complexity in marketing relationships. A large number of different products frequently bought by a buyer from a given firm will lead to a high degree of vertical complexity in relationships. On the other hand, when different buyers infrequently purchase quite different products in small quantities from various firms, the degree of horizontal complexity for this reason will tend to be high. In the former case it is easier for sellers to adapt to specific buyer needs in purchasing patterns and behavior, while in the latter case it is more difficult.

The greater are the cost and demand interdependencies between the products sold by a firm, the more pronounced these relationships will tend to be. Such interdependencies make it necessary for the selling firm to consider its assortment as a whole, rather than individual products, in determining marketing strategy. This increases the complexity vertically, when the number of interrelated products purchased by an individual customer increases; and horizontally, when different customers buy different combinations of related products from a given firm.

In convenience goods retailing, where it is usually too much trouble to buy each item from a different outlet, the degree of vertical complexity between buyers and sellers is typically quite high. It tends to be lower in the case of specialty goods, where it is usually more worthwhile to shop around. Similarly, the degree of vertical complexity tends to be higher in industrial marketing, with, in general, larger and more frequent purchase needs for typical items, than in consumer marketing, with by and large smaller and less frequent purchases by each buyer. For this reason the possibilities for innovative interaction between buyers and sellers in general probably is greater in industrial marketing than it is in consumer marketing.

Another factor affecting the complexity of marketing relationships is the technological complexity of the products or processes. The more components involved and the more qualified each component, the greater the degree of vertical complexity will tend to be. If technical requirements vary between customers, on the other hand, the level of horizontal complexity will increase.

This points to a marketing strategy whereby companies may strike a balance between achieving a high level of vertical complexity and benefiting from the horizontal complexity of the market. By using standard components and technologies and combining them to buyer specific applications, companies may achieve both a differentiated product and large scale benefits in production and sales. This strategy is often used by manufacturing companies, such as Asea and Atlas Copco in our data.

In this case the innovative potential is reduced since neither sellers nor buyers have strong knowledge or control of the basic technologies involved. This limits independent company innovation and joint development with customers to systems applications, rather than encouraging radical technological change. At the same time, however, it makes it possible to combine close customer relations with a wide market appeal, but it does not usually provide the company with a leading competitive edge, since competitors have access to the same basic technologies. Some companies, however, such as Inter Innovation, have been able to develop their own standard components and thereby achieve a stronger competitive situation by using this strategy.

The strongest instances of vertical complexity are usually the result of joint ownership, either mergers or cooperative ventures. Manufacturers may, as in the case of SCA the leading Swedish wood and paper company, sell a very large part of their primary production to their own processing companies; vertical integration may then lead to mutual adaptation in production and marketing between the subsidiaries. A more innovative way to achieve a high degree of vertical complexity is establishing joint companies with buyers to develop radically new products and processes. In our data we find such a venture between ASEA and the Swedish State Railway company to develop high energy locomotives and another between Ericson and the Swedish State Telephone Company to develop telecommunications.

IDENTIFIABILITY OF MARKETING RELATIONSHIPS

A main requirement for successful learning with regard to marketing relationships and marketing strategy is identifiability of the crucial underlying factors. The first step in achieving identifiability consists in establishing the basic units of analysis (Figure 8.4). Ideally, these units should be as independent from each other as possible with regard to the relationships analyzed, to permit separate analysis of how each unit reacts to changes in the relevant conditions. In marketing situations characterized by a high degree of vertical complexity this means that a high level of vertical aggregation is desirable in establishing our basic units of analysis. To achieve this the buying firm as a whole, rather than individual products or transactions, should be used as our basic unit. Thereby a high degree of intra-unit rather than inter-unit complexity will characterize the marketing relationships and permit more clear cut conclusions. We need to stress the

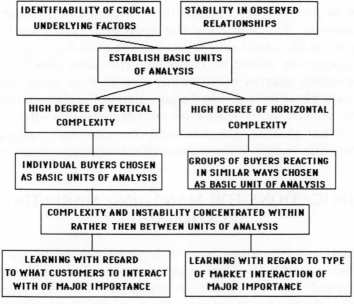

Figure 8.4 *Requirements for successful learning with regard to marketing relationships*

organizational aspects[5] in managing marketing relationships, such as how to organize buying and selling centers and coordinate their activities.

In situations characterized by a high degree of horizontal complexity, on the other hand, a high level of horizontal aggregation is desirable in establishing the basic units of analysis. This means that groups of buyers, reacting in a similar way to a given type of offer, should be treated as an analytical unit in determining the market strategy of the firm. Since products may be defined as offerings catering to similar buyer needs this basically means using single products as a basis for market segmentation,[6] which is the basic approach to market strategy in marketing theory.

But identifiability in itself is not sufficient for successful strategic learning. Instead, it should be viewed as a necessary condition. Since the term successful learning should apply to learning about future conditions likely to occur, some stability in the observed marketing relationships is necessary for such learning to take place. In other words, the firm needs to learn about the most stable elements in its marketing environment—as a basis for establishing its main strategy—and must then adapt to the resulting instabilities which follow the use of this strategy. By identifying the appropriate basic units of analysis, as discussed above, this process of strategic learning and adaptation should be facilitated. The main complexities and possible sources of instability will then be of an intra-unit nature and by individual adaptation to the characteristics of the chosen units—firms or market segments—the firm should be able to stabilize and develop its marketing relationships, which is the essence of marketing management.

IMPLICATIONS FOR MANAGING MARKETING RELATIONSHIPS

In marketing situations with a high degree of horizontal complexity and a low degree of vertical complexity, such as the typical case of consumer marketing, learning should initially take place with regard to the type of market interaction that is most suitable. The chosen type of interaction will then largely determine what specific individual customers a firm receives.

By selling through mail order, for instance, a firm will reach one group of potential customers and by selling in specialty stores another. Likewise, in the case of prestige type goods, the firm often can decide its market segment by the price it sets and the arguments it uses in its advertising and sales promotion. In this type of marketing the main strategic choice concerns what type of market interaction to use. Individual customers are usually not identified in advance and any adaptation to specific customer demands takes place afterwards. The most stable element in marketing strategy in this case is the type of market interaction—price, advertising and other devices—and the least stable the specific customers received. The conditions of the offer are set in advance, not negotiated, and this in turn determines whom the buyers will be.

With regard to marketing situations characterized by a high degree of vertical complexity and a low degree of horizontal complexity, such as the typical industrial marketing situation, it follows that strategic learning should primarily take place with regard to which specific customers to interact with.[7] When this important strategic choice has been made, and the potential customers identified, adaptation should take place with regard to the type of interaction best suited for each individual customer.

In other words, the most stable element in the marketing strategy now should be the set of intended customers, and instability should be mainly limited to relationships with these customers. Although this is not the strategic planning process normally advocated in the marketing literature, it is common practice in industry. One reason for this could be the overconcern in the marketing literature with consumer marketing and the relative neglect of industrial marketing.

In our former marketing situation the characteristics of given single products and their possibility of satisfying partial needs for groups of individually unidentified customers are of primary interest. In our later marketing situation more total needs of identified individual customers and the possibility of the firm satisfying these needs are the focus of interest.

TWO BASIC MARKETING STRATEGIES

As a result of the preceding discussion we may distinguish between two basic marketing strategies. The first, which we may call a *competitive strategy*, is the type of strategy which is extensively analyzed in micro economic theory and in traditional marketing theory. The second, which we may call a *holding strategy*, is until recently very little dealt with in the literature (Figure 8.5).

Both are ideal strategies in the sense that they are theoretical abstractions for the purpose of highlighting tendencies which are more or less present in actual situations. That is, a combination of these extreme strategies—what we call the strategic marketing mix—emphasizing one of the components but not to the exclusion of the other, is most likely to be evident in a real marketing situation. For the purpose of theoretical discussion it is, however, better to start with the extreme instances, which are most illuminating, and subsequently to modify the conclusions in empirical applications, than to do it the other way around.

Competitive strategies, thus, as we have indicated above, involve *market selection of customers*. That is, the selling firm is assumed to set its price and quality and its level of promotion, without considering the effects on individual customers. Overall market response is estimated on the basis of market potential and the overall attractiveness of the firm's offer in relation to the offers of competing firms. This strategy emphasizes substitutability between the offers of competing firms and assumes that firms basically use marketing to counteract competitive action.

Strategic learning in this case means learning about competitive behavior and how buyers respond to differences in product offers between firms. Oligopoly theory[8] from Cournot to more recent days is concerned with company efforts to adapt to this type of market situation, mainly by avoiding open competition. Chamberlin's concept of product differentiation is another attempt in economic theory to deal with this problem by assuming that companies may create limited monopoly situations which diminish the need for learning about and reacting to competitive action.[9]

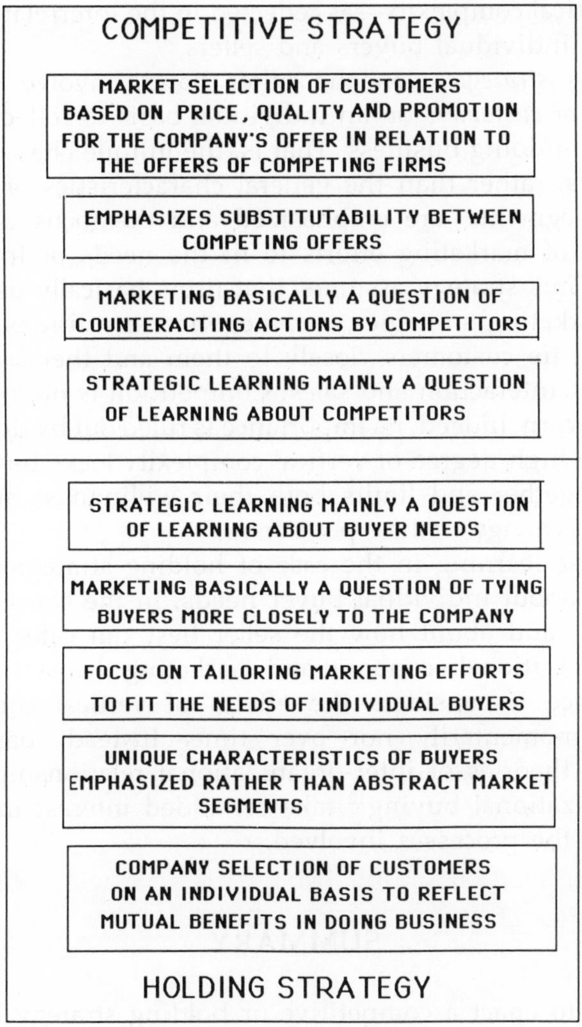

COMPETITIVE STRATEGY

MARKET SELECTION OF CUSTOMERS
BASED ON PRICE, QUALITY AND PROMOTION
FOR THE COMPANY'S OFFER IN RELATION TO
THE OFFERS OF COMPETING FIRMS

EMPHASIZES SUBSTITUTABILITY BETWEEN
COMPETING OFFERS

MARKETING BASICALLY A QUESTION OF
COUNTERACTING ACTIONS BY COMPETITORS

STRATEGIC LEARNING MAINLY A QUESTION
OF LEARNING ABOUT COMPETITORS

STRATEGIC LEARNING MAINLY A QUESTION
OF LEARNING ABOUT BUYER NEEDS

MARKETING BASICALLY A QUESTION OF TYING
BUYERS MORE CLOSELY TO THE COMPANY

FOCUS ON TAILORING MARKETING EFFORTS
TO FIT THE NEEDS OF INDIVIDUAL BUYERS

UNIQUE CHARACTERISTICS OF BUYERS
EMPHASIZED RATHER THAN ABSTRACT MARKET
SEGMENTS

COMPANY SELECTION OF CUSTOMERS
ON AN INDIVIDUAL BASIS TO REFLECT
MUTUAL BENEFITS IN DOING BUSINESS

HOLDING STRATEGY

Figure 8.5 Marketing strategy box

In both cases, as in the mainstream of economic and marketing theory, it is competition between sellers, not the interaction between individual buyers and sellers, which is assumed to determine the success or failure of a marketing strategy. This type of reasoning is mainly applicable to analyzing the effects of horizontal complexity—as reflected in the competitive relationships prevailing on a market—rather than vertical complexity—as reflected in the interrelationships between individual buyers and sellers.

Holding strategies, on the other hand, involve *company selection of customers* on an individual basis to reflect mutual benefits in doing business. That is, the unique characteristics of buyers, rather than the general characteristics of abstract market segments, are emphasized and the focus is on the tailoring of marketing efforts to fit the needs of individual buyers. This strategy assumes that firms basically determine their marketing strategies, and negotiate conditions of their offers, to tie customers closely to them and thereby ensure long term interaction and sales. Competition is no longer the main concern. Indeed, its importance is ruled out by definition, since the high degree of vertical complexity locks buyers and sellers together and limits both their willingness and their ability to change trading partners.

Strategic learning in the case of holding strategies means learning about individual buyer needs, in the short and the long run; and about how the seller best can cater to these needs. Traditional economic and marketing theory is of little help, since it considers the effects of vertical complexity neither momentarily nor over time. Instead, bargaining theory,[10] theories of inter-organizational relationships[11] and of organizational buying[12] take on added interest in understanding the processes involved.

SUMMARY

In order to enact a competitive or holding strategy the firm has recourse to various action parameters. In competitive strategies more indirect action is necessary, since individual buyers are usually not identified in advance, and desirable, since a large number of prospects need to be contacted to ensure success. In holding strategies more direct action is called for, to facilitate interaction with known customers, and it is feasible, since the number of prospective customers considered is relatively small, each customer accounting for a substantial segment of a firm's business.

Competitive strategies concentrate on reaching large numbers of customers at low cost and dealing with customers is subordinate to achieving short-run profit. The identity of the customer is less important than are the terms of the offer. Mass media advertising is therefore often used to attract anonymous customers to open stores, where the transaction usually takes place without much interaction between buyer and seller. Prices are set in advance to reflect overall market conditions, rather than negotiated to reflect individual demand.

There is not much scope when using competitive strategies for joint product development between buyers and sellers, since each hardly knows the other, and has little knowledge of the other's specific needs. Also, there is limited opportunity for specific attention to be paid to individual buyer needs, since the main concern is to attract a wide range of potential customers. Competitive strategies concentrate on finding out what customers think about already developed products, as a basis for sales promotion. While more positional companies by definition use competitive strategies basically to maintain their market positions, more innovative companies mainly use them to develop new business.

Holding strategies, on the other hand, concentrate on establishing and maintaining close relationships and business dealings with a selective group of important customers. Direct, personal selling, takes precedence over mass promotion, such as mass media advertising. Flexible, individually negotiated prices are used to facilitate interaction with and adaptation to individual buyer needs, rather than to generate sales. While prices in competitive strategies are active determinants of sales, in holding strategies they may be viewed mainly as accounting figures, which show how successful companies have been in their business activities.

Since holding strategies are based on and encourage intensive interaction with and adaptation to specific buyers needs they are likely to lead to joint development of products and processes, which, as we have seen in Chapter 3 may often be expected to lead to innovative product and company development. Our data contains many such examples of successful cooperation between buyers and sellers.

In Chapter 9 the framework presented in this chapter will be used as a basis for measuring and evaluating marketing strategies in Swedish paper companies.

*Companies need to achieve a
constructive balance between
competitive and holding elements in
their strategic marketing mixes*

9
Balancing Competitive Action and Buyer–Seller Interaction—Marketing Strategies for Swedish Paper Companies

As we have noted in Chapter 8, two schools of marketing thought are evident today. One traditional, emphasizing competition and cooperation between sellers, and one recent, stressing the role of interaction and cooperation between sellers and buyers.

The former line of thought still dominates the academic view of marketing in the US, where it perhaps is most applicable. This is a result of the higher degree of competition often confronting American companies in their home markets, compared to the domestic market situations in many other countries. In Western Europe, for instance, where the newer interactive approaches to analyzing and managing marketing relationships have largely been developed and applied.

There is, however, always the danger of going from one extreme to another. The fact that many marketing situations, particularly in industrial marketing, show strong elements of buyer interaction and cooperation, does not mean that we can neglect the other main component of marketing strategy, active competition between firms fighting for a market share. With regard to large Swedish multinational companies, for instance, there is usually strong competition on the world market. This is as necessary to consider as the buyer–seller relationships which have been neglected in the past but which are the center of attention in interaction approaches to marketing.

In this chapter[1] the framework presented in Chapter 8, distinguishing between competitive strategies and holding strategies, is used to study marketing strategies in Swedish companies manufacturing and selling newsprint paper. The main theme in our approach is that companies need to achieve a constructive balance between competitive action and buyer–seller interaction in their strategic marketing mixes. If we wish to achieve a generally applicable framework for studying marketing strategy we then need to distinguish between what, in our approach, is called horizontal and vertical complexity.

As defined in Chapter 8, horizontal complexity depends on the interrelationships between sellers competing on the same markets, while vertical complexity depends on the interrelationships between sellers and buyers. The only active agents in traditional economic theory are sellers, and horizontal complexity therefore is implicitly assumed to be the major predeterminant for and result of marketing strategy. The more recent interaction approaches to marketing, on the other hand, are mainly concerned with the interrelationships between buyers and sellers, which in our approach is reflected in the degree of vertical complexity.

Even when buyer–seller interaction is the main factor influencing market success, sellers usually compete with other sellers as well as interacting with buyers. This makes both competitive action and buyer–seller interaction crucial marketing variables. The term interaction includes both negotiations and agreements with external parties and vertical and horizontal integration of external functions into the company.[2]

Our framework assumes that companies balance competitive and holding elements in their realized marketing strategies. Competitive strategies, as we have seen in Chapter 8, depend on the market mechanism for the selection of buyers for the offering of a company. The selling firm is assumed to set the price and quality of its offers and its level of sales promotion (for example, advertising) without directly considering the responses of identified, individual buyers. Instead of being buyer specific, this is a mass marketing approach. Overall market response is estimated on the basis of market potential and the attractiveness of the firm's offering in relation to the offerings of competing firms.

Competitive marketing strategies thus assume a high degree of substitutability between the offerings of competing firms and the action taken is that companies set their marketing strategies to counteract competitive action. With this type of strategy the main marketing problem is to learn about competitive behavior and the aggregate response of buyers to the offers of different sellers in order to counteract competitive action.

In this case it is competition between sellers, not interaction between individual buyers and sellers, which is assumed to determine the success or failure of marketing efforts. This reasoning is mainly applicable to analyzing the effects of horizontal complexity on the adverse relationships between competing companies, rather than the effects of vertical complexity on the beneficial interrelationships between individual sellers and buyers.

Holding strategies, on the other hand, involve company selection of customers on an individual basis. The unique characteristics of buyers, rather than the general characteristics of market segments, are emphasized, and adaptation of the marketing efforts of the firm to fit the needs of individual buyers and tie them more firmly to the company are the crucial marketing variables.

The main marketing concern with regard to holding strategies is learning about individual buyer needs, both in the short and long run, and catering to these needs. Traditional economic and marketing theory are of little help, since by definition they exclude holding strategies. A new marketing approach is needed, which draws heavily on contributions from other disciplines, such as bargaining theory and inter-organizational relations.

In order to enact a competitive or holding strategy a firm has recourse to different action parameters. In competitive strategies, indirect action is necessary, since individual buyers are usually not identified in advance; and desirable, since a large number of prospects need to be contacted to ensure success. In holding strategies more direct action is called for, to facilitate interaction with known customers; and feasible, since the number of prospective customers is usually relatively small and each customer accounts for a substantial portion of the company's business.

Competitive strategies, therefore, concentrate on reaching large numbers of customers at low cost, and dealing with customers is subordinate to achieving short term profit. The identity of the customer is less important than the terms of the offer, and prices are set in advance to reflect overall market conditions, rather than negotiated to consider individual demand. Mass media advertising is often used to attract anonymous customers and transactions take place without much interaction between sellers and buyers.

Holding strategies, on the other hand, concentrate on establishing and maintaining business with a number of important customers. Direct selling, for instance by sales representatives, and flexible, individually negotiated prices are used to facilitate interaction and individual transactions are carried out with the intention of establishing and maintaining continued long term dealings with customers.

Both competitive strategies and holding strategies are ideal strategies in the sense that they are theoretical abstractions for the purpose of highlighting tendencies which are more or less present in actual marketing conditions. In other words, combinations of these ideal strategies, emphasizing one of the components, but not to the exclusion of the other, are likely to be reflected in most real world marketing situations. These combinations are called the strategic marketing mixes of the companies. For the purpose of empirical applications the question of making the dimensions of these marketing mixes operational and considering their joint effects then becomes the central problem.

EMPIRICAL BACKGROUND

Within the research program upon which this book is based, a number of studies of marketing strategies have been carried out among leading Swedish wood and paper processing companies.[3] One of these studies,[4] dealing with marketing strategies for newsprint paper, will be summarized in this chapter, as an example of how the approach may be used in empirical studies. The objective is to measure the degree of competitive versus holding strategies—the strategic marketing mixes—employed by the companies and to try to relate these strategic marketing mixes to differences in market and commercial success.

Paper for making newspapers is one of the largest product groups in the Swedish wood and paper industry, which in turn is one of the key industries in Sweden. In 1980 the export of this type of paper from Sweden was 3 billion Swedish crowns. The forest sector supplied the largest contribution, generating a net amount of 22 billion Swedish crowns for the Swedish economy.

In Sweden there are four companies manufacturing and selling newsprint paper, all of them in the private sector. These companies are Holmens Bruk, Hylte Bruk, Stora Kopparbergs Bergslags AB and Svenska Cellulosa AB. All these companies are included in our study, based on personal interviews with leading company executives and other data collected in connection with the interviews.

In spite of the importance of the wood and paper industry for the Swedish economy, very few studies of marketing strategies for companies in this sector have been carried out. Except for the studies in the research program referred to in this paper, no published studies have been found, in our review of the literature,[5] which try to relate marketing strategies in wood and paper companies to market and commercial success.

This product group is particularly interesting from the point of view of developing and applying an approach to marketing strategy which considers both competition and cooperation. Newsprint paper is a highly standardized commodity which makes it susceptible as a product to traditional competition, for example, with regard to price. There is, however, considerable technical product differentiation, particularly with regard to paper weight and strength, which tends to modify the degree of outright competition between sellers. At the same time, the buyer–seller structure, with a small number of large buyers and sellers, has led to numerous agreements between buyers and sellers, with regard to, for instance, delivery contracts and prices.

The market situation with regard to Swedish manufacturers and sellers of newsprint paper is interesting from the point of view of applying our framework for analyzing marketing strategies. The companies have considerable choice, particularly in the long run but to a lesser extent also in the short run, as to how much they want to use competitive versus holding elements in their strategic marketing mixes.

In other words, it is not a priori clear from product, production and demand characteristics, what strategic marketing mix it is optimal to employ. The balance between competitive action and buyer–seller interaction in the choice of marketing mix, is therefore a real issue to the companies concerned, or at least it should be judging from our results. This is evident from the fact that different companies have chosen different mixes of these basic strategic variables in their historical strategies, which makes it meaningful and interesting to try to relate differences in strategic marketing mix to differences in market and commercial success.

From our interviews it seems clear that the more successful companies at least are intuitively aware of and try to consider the need for establishing a balance between competitive action and buyer–seller interaction, in their strategic marketing mixes. At the same time the lack of an appropriate model of marketing strategy for describing and formulating the issues involved, makes it difficult for them to analyze these factors and consider them together in their realized strategies. This points to the need for developing an operational framework of the type proposed in this paper.

STRATEGIC DIMENSIONS

In our analysis a number of dimensions are used to measure the degree of competitive action versus buyer–seller interaction in the marketing mixes of the companies studied. These are the degree of product differentiation, buyer characteristics, the degree of vertical integration, production technology and product and technology development. These dimensions have been derived both from established economic theory, our own thinking with regard to the implications of our framework and our early explorative interviews with company and industry representatives.

Our first dimension, product differentiation, refers to how well adapted the product of a company is to individual customer needs, in other words, how specific the product design is from the point of view of the buyer. A high degree of holding strategy usually both requires and leads to a high degree of product differentiation. By adapting to specific buyer needs a company ties these customers more tightly to its products, and makes it more difficult to pursue a highly competitive mass marketing strategy.

A *priori* price setting, for instance, which is assumed in traditional marketing models, becomes less necessary and more difficult to employ when the degree of product differentiation is high. General price setting tends to be replaced by individual price negotiations and price contracts, the final conditions of which are often not fully determined until later on.

With respect to product differentiation, the differences between our four companies is relatively small. As mentioned above, newsprint paper is a relatively standardized product, and the latitude for customer specific product differentiation is fairly small. It is primarily by offering different paper weights and widths that companies can differentiate their offerings. One of the companies used this possibility considerably more than the others, which all had about the same degree of product differentiation in this respect.

Another important point is the extent to which companies offer complementary products, since product differentiation in our framework refers to the total assortment and not only to individual products. This affects a company's ability to cater more specifically to the needs of individual customers.

Again, we do not find this to be a highly differentiating factor for the product group we are interested in; but one company offered a complementary product, which we take as evidence of a holding strategy with regard to product differentiation.

Our second dimension, buyer characteristics, differs among the different companies with regard to the degree of competitive versus holding element in marketing strategies more than our first dimension, product differentiation. It is also more complex, since we found it necessary to use three separate indicators to estimate it.

The first is the proportion of established customers, the second the relative proportion of company sales which the largest customers accounted for, and the third the proportion of sales going to geographically closer customers, by which we mean customers in Western Europe. The thinking behind this is that companies usually have tighter relationships, that is, more of a holding strategy, with big, established customers closer to home than with small or faraway ones.

Our third dimension, the degree of vertical integration, is almost by definition linked to the degree of competitive versus holding strategy. To the extent that a company controls its own sales to subsidiaries, or directs its own suppliers, it has a captive output or input market, which we view as an indication of a holding element in its strategic marketing mix.

In this respect we have extended the concept of marketing strategy to include purchasing strategy, which means our concept more totally portrays the overall business strategy of the company. Our other dimensions also extend the range of strategic activities considered beyond what is normally included in the term marketing strategy. This, then, makes it more valid for us to try to relate marketing strategy to market and commercial success for the companies concerned.

Our fourth dimension of strategic marketing mix is the production technology of the company. Of interest here is, to begin with, flexibility in switching between different products in the product range of a company, where higher flexibility should make it easier to pursue a competitive strategy. An example of this is flexibility in making paper with different weights. This did not differentiate between the different companies, however, which all had the technological capacity to make such switches easily, but none of them had made much use of this possibility.

Another aspect of production flexibility appeared to have been of greater importance. This was the possibility of accepting small, spontaneous orders, which we found to be related to the number and sizes of paper machines a company has. A larger number of smaller machines makes a company more flexible in accepting small *ad hoc* orders, which makes it easier for it to pursue a more competitive strategy. A smaller number of larger machines leads to economies of scale, and for this reason makes a higher degree of holding strategy more attractive and more feasible.

Our fourth and final dimension of marketing strategy is product and technology development. By buyer specific product and technology development, preferably in joint projects together with customers, a company can make customers more dependent on its products and technologies, and thus achieve more of a holding strategy. By more general product and technology development, on the other hand, it can facilitate a more competitive strategy by improving the general features of the product or by lowering its production costs.

It is this latter type of product and technology development which was most common among the companies studied, but one of them had a more consumer specific orientation in its development activities. This company, therefore, was classified as having a more pronounced holding strategy, while the rest were classified as showing the same degree of competitive strategy with regard to product and technology development.

STRATEGIC MARKETING PROFILES

All the companies were ranked along each dimension with regard to the degree of competitive versus holding element. The resulting profiles showing their strategic marketing mixes—based primarily on the company interviews and supplementary written material—are shown in Figure 9.1. We see that, with the exception of Company A, the companies are quite consistent in their marketing strategies. In other words, they tend to show the same relative degree of competitive versus holding tendencies along the different dimensions. Whether or not this makes the analysis more reliable and valid is an open question, but at least it makes it more interesting.

We see that Company B had the most pronounced holding strategy and represents a category of its own. Only along one dimension, production technology, do we find that another company, namely A, shows a higher degree of holding strategy and only along one dimension, product differentiation, does another company, D, show the same degree of holding strategy.

Companies C and D show very consistent, and fairly similar profiles, with D exhibiting somewhat more of a holding tendency, particularly with regard to product differentiation. Company A, finally, has the most inconsistent profile, but

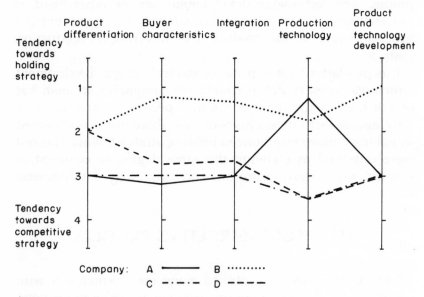

Figure 9.1 *Marketing strategy profiles for the companies studied based on rankings along the different dimensions*

apart from the dimension production technology, it does not differ much from Company C. While Company B shows a strong holding tendency in its overall strategy, Company C, and to a somewhat lesser extent Companies A and D, have a relatively strong tendency towards an overall competitive strategy.

STRATEGIC OUTCOME

We shall now try to relate the marketing mixes of the different companies to market and commercial success. In this type of analysis it is of course necessary to use an extended time period. We shall therefore look at sales volume and profitability for the different companies from 1968 to 1980 and discuss these diagrams in relation to marketing strategy.

Figure 9.2 shows how production in the companies studied varied over this period which we can use as a good estimator also of sales, since newsprint paper is usually delivered quickly to buyers. We see that Company A drastically increased its production during the period. The marketing strategy dimension which most clearly distinguishes Company A from the other companies is that it has a very strong holding element with regard to production technology. Compared to them it has a small number of large paper machines, which has probably led to much better scale economies during the period and evidently also made it possible to increase production and sales.

Among the other companies, C has been most successful and D least successful from a volume point of view. For these companies the most competitively oriented strategic mix thus appears to have been associated with the highest production and sales, but the differences between these companies is much less than between Company A and the rest.

We collected data also on changes in market share for the different companies, both for Western Europe (Figure 9.3) and for the rest of the world (Figure 9.4). We see from Figure 9.3 that all Swedish companies increased their market shares somewhat on what is in essence their home market, Western Europe. As we might expect from the data on total production

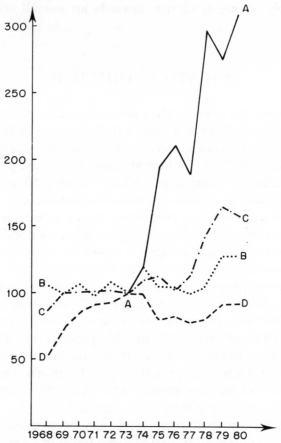

Figure 9.2 Volume production for the companies during the period

increases, Company A and Company C show the fastest growths in market share in Western Europe.

It is somewhat surprising that the growth rate was not even greater for Company A, with its great increase in total production volume, which evidently means that the Company sold a large proportion of its added production outside Western Europe. This is also evident from Figure 9.4 which shows a very rapid growth in market share for Company A

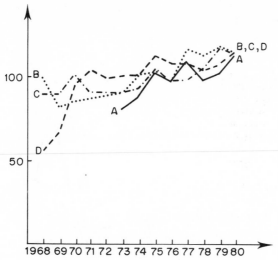

Figure 9.3 *Percentage change in market share—Western Europe*

in this area from 1976 to 1979. By and large, all Swedish companies increased their market shares considerably outside Western Europe during the period, which shows that Swedish companies were very competitive on the world market after 1976.

From Figure 9.3 and 9.4 we also see that the fluctuations in market share were much more pronounced outside Western Europe with an increase in amplitude over a period of time. This indicates a strong and growing emphasis by companies during the period on more competitive marketing strategies for distant markets.

Company C, with the most competitively oriented strategic marketing mix, according to Figure 9.1, shows the greatest fluctuations in market share. Furthermore, this company had by far the lowest proportion of established customers, only about 75%, while the other companies had figures close to 100%. This is also consistent with their highly competitive overall marketing mix.

We may note also that Company A showed a rapid increase in market share outside Western Europe, without significantly decreasing its share of established customers. While it is more natural to conceptualize and implement a competitively oriented strategic marketing mix—particularly with regard to

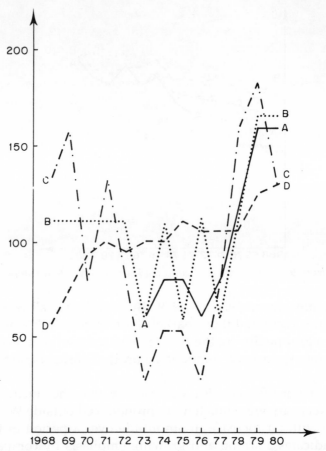

Figure 9.4 Percentage change in market share outside Western Europe

buyer relationships—on distant markets, Company A shows that it was possible to achieve a strong element of holding strategy towards new customers outside Western Europe.

It is also interesting to note the great increase in market share outside Western Europe after 1978 for Company B, with its very pronounced overall holding strategy. This would seem to indicate that the company about this time changed its emphasis to a more competitive strategy for distant markets. This was confirmed by company representatives, who said that a strategic decision had been made around 1978 to compete more aggressively on faraway markets.

For the period as a whole, two companies show a marked improvement in market share outside Western Europe, Company A and Company D. Both these companies had a high proportion of established customers, so that there existed a strong holding strategy in this respect. However, both companies had a large number of small and intermediate-sized customers, which as such may be taken as an indication of a more competitive strategy and market success on more distant marginal markets.

With regard to distribution system, Companies A and D both show a relatively high degree of competitive strategy. Company D, for instance, used agents for 20% of its sales, which is a high figure for this type of product. In other words, the two companies, as Figure 9.1 shows, appear to have used relatively competitive marketing strategies during the period, a policy which seems to reflect a greater interest than the other companies in selling to distant markets.

The ultimate measure of strategic success is profitability. While it is impossible to isolate the effects of marketing strategy on profitability, production and sales volume, it is still of interest to look at the development of these outcomes in relation to marketing strategy.

We must then also keep in mind that we do not have any data on changes in strategy for the companies during the period. Our data reflects some kind of average strategy for the period, with probably some bias towards more recent time. Our interviews do indicate, however, that the strategic dimensions we have measured have been relatively stable during the time period. This probably is due to the fact that they are quite basic strategic factors, which companies do not, and cannot, change radically on short notice.

With due consideration for what has been said above, we can now look at the relative changes in profitability for different companies, which are shown in Figure 9.5. These figures have been obtained from the companies, and as far as possible made comparable by carrying out adjustments. The analysis is complicated by the fact that there were only three companies in the business until 1973, which makes necessary the use of two scales in the diagram. For reasons of confidentiality and comparability the analysis is based on

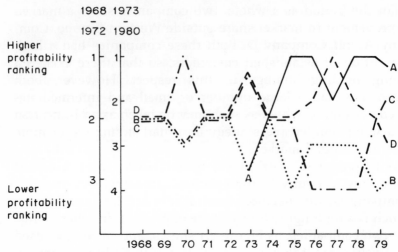

Figure 9.5 Relative profitability for the companies during the period

rankings of the companies with regard to their relative profitability, rather than taking absolute measures.

We see that, despite its understandably low profitability during its initial year of operation, 1973, Company A has the most favorable average profitability ranking among the companies (1.43) and by and large the most positive development over the period. We may compare this with our earlier conclusion, that A had a strong competitive element in its marketing mix, with the exception of production technology, where it had the most pronounced holding strategy. A combination of scale economies in production and a flexible sales and distribution strategy, particularly evident on distant markets, has evidently contributed to A's success. As we noted above, Company A has also been able to achieve a relatively high number of established customers in the highly competitive market outside Western Europe.

Company B, on the other hand, has the lowest profitability ranking for the period (3.28), and a fairly even, but steadily declining trend. This may be compared with the fact that Company B had the most pronounced overall holding strategy, with a strong holding tendency for all the studied dimensions.

This may be taken either as an indication that an extreme holding strategy is difficult to employ profitably in the type of market situation studied, or that other factors have been more conclusive in determining profitability. Our conclusion is that a higher degree of marketing flexibility, for instance with regard to distribution and sales, would have been preferable from a profitability point of view.

Company C, with the most competitive strategic marketing mix, had the most uneven profitability development, and also a relatively low average ranking for the period as a whole (3.0), but with a drastic improvement from 1978 to 1980. For this company the relatively low proportion of established customers and the high percentage of sales obtained via competitive sales channels, probably has contributed to the uneven profitability during the period. For Company C only 35% of sales went through its own sales subsidiaries, while for Company A the figure was about 85% and for Company B about 60%.

Company D, finally, with a relatively strong competitive emphasis in its strategic marketing mix, had the second most favorable average profitability ranking for the period, but a highly unfavorable development from 1977–1980.

We do not find any clear relationships between strategic marketing mix, as measured in the present study, and the level and development of profitability over time. This is hardly surprising, since both the level of profitability and its change over time depends on many factors, not measured in our analysis. The companies, for instance, have quite different costs situations, with regard both to raw material and production costs.

This said, it still is interesting to look at the data and make some observations. There is, for instance, no support in our data for the general conclusion that pronounced and consistent strategies focusing on either competitive or holding elements are to be preferred from a sales or profitability point of view. Since traditional marketing theory tends to favour competitive strategies and interaction theories holding strategies, either approach would appear to be too extreme and too general to be adequate for formulating and implementing actual marketing strategies in marketing situations such as the one we have described.

SUMMARY

There would appear to be a need for a balanced, situationally determined view of marketing strategy, which focuses on a larger number of dimensions than are normally considered in the marketing and strategic management literature. Earlier in the book we introduced a framework for the balanced analysis of competitive and holding relationships; the strategic marketing mix of a company. In this chapter we have further discussed this model and suggested a number of operational dimensions for measuring and evaluating marketing strategies against the background of an empirical application of an analysis of a study of Swedish paper companies.

*The same basic strategic factors
appear to be related to product
development success in the food
processing industry as in more hi-tech
industries*

10
Product Development Strategies for Swedish Food Processing Companies

This chapter[1] presents and discusses the main results of a study of technological and marketing strategies for product and company development in 20 major Swedish food processing companies. While the emphasis is on how companies develop new products, data were also collected with regard to overall company strategies and consumer outcome. This enables us to view product development in a wide and integrated context. In the product development literature[2] the interrelationships between company and product development and the effects of different strategies on buyer satisfaction and welfare are seldom systematically dealt with.

The overall approach to strategic management in this book deals with both technological and marketing strategies for product and company development. Food processing usually is a very low-tech business involving very conservative companies and customers. At the same time, the same basic strategic factors appear to be related to product development success in food processing as in more hi-tech industries. Companies realizing this may succeed by using innovative technological and marketing strategies to benefit both themselves and buyers who are alert to new possibilities the better to satisfy their needs.

DESIGN OF THE STUDY

1thin the research program summarized in this book, in
1979 personal interviews were carried out with leading
company representatives for 20 major Swedish food processing
companies. Since our approach includes both company and
product policies, strategies and outcomes, these interviews
were held with a wide range of executives, company directors,
R & D and marketing people, directly concerned with product
and company development issues.

To make possible an evaluation of the results of realized
company strategies on sales, profits and consumer outcome,
specific detailed data was collected for 121 new food products
which had been developed and marketed by the companies
during the 10-year period 1969–1979. These products were
chosen by company executives to be representative of their
overall product development during the period, to give as
balanced and valid a picture as possible of their realized
strategies. The sample included dairy and fat products, cereals,
meat and fish, fruit and vegetables, as the main groups.

A large part of the most innovative new food products
developed in Sweden during the period—such as *lätt och
lagom*, a new dietary fat—are included, as well as more normal
examples of product development involving less radical
change, such as new bread varieties. Since new product
development in the food area is often linked to packaging,
such developments were also included in our study. The
interviews were supplemented with written material and
consumer interviews to gain a more complete picture of
factors related to new product success.

NEW PRODUCT SUCCESS

As mentioned above, our main measure of technological
success for new products is the level of technological innovation. This is defined as how successful companies have
been in solving the critical technical problems in specific
product development situations. If the level is high, this

indicates that the companies have been very creative in their technological efforts. A high level of technological innovation usually makes it easier to achieve patent protection, know-how advantages and market strength, based on unique knowledge and a strong market position.

In our studies, the level of technological innovation is directly estimated by interviewing company executives who have been personally involved in developing the new products studied and in assessing their market potential. A scale from 1 to 5 is used with higher values indicating a greater level of technological success in overcoming the crucial development issues.

In most instances, two experienced interviewers estimated the level of technological innovation based on interview data in comparison with other interviews. If the assessments were not the same, average values were used, unless additional efforts to gain more information from other sources resolved the differences.

Supplementary data were obtained by more indirect measures of the level of technological innovation, concerning patent protection and development time. Our studies show that radically new products, demanding a high level of creativity in solving the critical technical development problems, usually take longer to develop than other products.

Market success for new products is measured in the food processing study, as in our other studies, by the competitive situation for a product when it is introduced on the market. The more unique a product is judged to be from a buyer point of view, in comparison with the closest competing products on the market, the greater the market success. As in the case of technological success, market success was independently estimated by each interviewer, based on information from respondents with marketing experience of the new products studied. Again a scale from 1 to 5 was used with higher values indicating greater market success.

Commercial success, finally, was measured by the estimated profit level of a new product, again as judged by knowledge-able company executives. For products which had been on the market long enough to make such estimates meaningful, a scale from 1 to 5 was used. A product was either judged to be a big commercial success (5), a small success (4), break-even (3), a small failure (2) or a big failure (1).

COMPANY ANALYSIS

The number of companies in different product groups and their average size and research intensity are given in Table 10.1. The largest number of companies (6) have meat- and fish-based products as their dominant product group, while companies with milk- and fat-based products are the second largest group (5) followed by companies with other food products (4), cereal-based products (3) and vegetable- and fruit-based products (2).

The average research intensity ranges from a high rate of 0.96% of sales for companies with mainly milk- and fat-based products to a low rate of 0.27% for predominantly cereal-based companies. The average company size, measured by sales, varies from 1192 million Swedish crowns for the milk- and fat-based companies to 245 million for the meat- and fish-based companies. All these figures are averages for the ten-year period 1969–1978.

If we look at Table 10.2, we see that on the average companies with predominantly milk- and fat-based products

Table 10.1 Company size and research intensity for dominant product groups

Dominant product groups	Number of companies	Average company size (millions Swedish crowns)	Average research intensity (%)
Cereal-based products	3	583	0.27
Meat- and fish-based products	6	245	0.73
Milk- and fat-based products	5	1192	0.96
Vegetable- and fruit-based products	2	525	0.55
Other food products, e.g. soups, spices, sauces	4	331	1.18

Table 10.2 Product development outcome for companies in different product groups

Dominant product groups	Number of companies	Technological success	Market success	Commercial success
Cereal-based products	3	2.1	3.3	2.9
Meat- and fish-based products	6	2.4	3.5	3.5
Milk- and fat-based products	5	2.7	3.6	3.6
Vegetable- and fruit-based products	2	2.4	3.2	3.4
Other food products	4	2.3	3.4	3.2

had been technologically most successful (2.7), followed by companies with meat- and fish-based and vegetable- and fruit-based products (both 2.4), other food products (2.3) and cereal-based products (2.1).

With regard to market success we also find that companies with milk- and fat-based products were most successful (3.6), followed by companies with meat- and fish-based products (3.5), other food products (3.2), cereal-based products (3.3) and vegetable- and fruit-based products (3.4). In the case of commercial success, we again find that companies with milk- and fat-based products were most successful (3.6), followed by companies with meat- and fish-based products (3.5), vegetable- and fruit-based products (3.4), other food products (3.2) and cereal-based products (2.9).

The relationships between size and new product success are given in Table 10.3. We see that the largest food companies appear to have been slightly more successful in their technological strategies than the middle-sized companies, which in turn seem to have been somewhat more successful than the smallest ones. The average level of technological innovation for new products diminishes from 2.5 to 2.4 to 2.3, when the size level of the companies goes down.

With regard to market success we find that all sizes of companies have succeeded in finding relatively unique new products but the largest companies have been most successful

Table 10.3 Company size in relation to technological, market and commercial success for 120 products from 20 Swedish food processing companies

Size group	Number of companies	Technological success	Market success	Commercial success
Largest companies	6	2.5	3.7	3.4
Middle-sized companies	8	2.4	3.4	3.3
Smallest companies	6	2.3	3.3	3.3

Company size measured by average annual sales during the ten-year period 1969–1978.
Higher numbers indicate higher technological, market and commercial success.
Technological success is measured by the level of technological innovation.
Market success is measured by the market situation at product introduction.
Commercial success is measured by estimated profitability for new products.

(3.7) followed by the middle-sized ones (3.4) and the smallest ones (3.3). With regard to commercial success the largest companies appear to have been slightly more successful (3.4) than the middle-sized and smallest ones (both 3.3).

With regard to research intensity measured by R & D expenditures in relation to sales, we found that the more research intensive companies had achieved a higher level of technological success (2.7) than the less research intensive ones (2.4 and 2.3) (Table 10.4). This is what we would expect,

Table 10.4 Research intensity in relation to technological, market and commercial success for 121 products in 20 Swedish food processing companies

Research intensity	Number of companies	Technological success	Market success	Commercial success
High	6	2.7	3.5	3.4
Intermediate	8	2.4	3.4	3.3
Low	6	2.3	3.5	3.3

Research intensity measured by average annual expenditure on R & D in relation to average annual sales.
Higher numbers indicate higher technological, market and commercial success.
Technological success is measured by the level of technological innovation.
Market success is measured by the market situation at product introduction.

if companies are reasonably successful in their R & D and our measure of technological success is valid.

With regard to market success, however, there are no consistent differences related to research intensity. The most research intensive and the least research intensive companies show the same degree of market success (3.5), with the companies in between showing a slightly lower success rate (3.4).

This is in line with our general impression from the interviews that high research intensity was not usually associated with any stronger efforts to develop new markets or technologies than was low research intensity; but the most research intensive companies appeared to give even greater priority to their established markets and technologies than did the less research intensive. With regard to commercial outcome, the more research intensive companies were slightly more successful (3.4), compared to the less research intensive groups of companies, which both showed the same success rate (3.3).

Our conclusion with regard to research intensity is that even the more research intensive companies were satisfied with the opportunities for new products within their established markets and technologies, and viewed exploiting such opportunities as more attractive than venturing into new areas. In other words, there seems to be a lack of highly innovative companies in our data, in spite of the fact that it includes most of the food processing companies in Sweden that carry out substantial R & D. All the food processing companies studied appeared to be quite positional companies, which confirms our general impression that this is a conservative industry which does not favor change.

Another company variable which we have focused on in our study is ownership (Table 10.5). In Sweden both private and cooperative ownership are well represented in the food processing industry, which makes it interesting to see if this is associated with differences in success.

To begin with, we looked at differences between cooperative and private companies and then extended the analysis to different types of cooperative and private companies. Seven of the companies were classified as cooperatively controlled

Table 10.5 Ownership in relation to technological, market and commercial success for 120 products from 20 Swedish food processing companies

Ownership	Number of companies	Technological success	Market success	Commercial success
Consumer cooperatives	3	2.5	3.3	3.5
Producer cooperatives	4	2.5	3.6	3.5
All cooperatives	7	**2.5**	**3.5**	**3.5**
Swedish dominated private companies	7	2.3	3.5	3.3
Foreign dominated private companies	6	2.5	3.4	3.2
All private companies	13	**2.4**	**3.4**	**3.3**

Higher numbers indicate higher technological, market and commercial success.
Technological success is measured by the level of technological innovation.
Market success is measured by the market situation at product introduction.
Commercial success is measured by the estimated profitability for new products.

and 13 as privately controlled, while three of the cooperative companies were consumer cooperatives and four producer cooperatives. Seven of the Swedish companies were classified as Swedish controlled and six as foreign controlled.

In this analysis we found that the cooperative companies as a group had been slightly more successful technologically and in the market in developing new products than had the private companies (2.5 versus 2.4 and 3.5 versus 3.4). They had also been more successful commercially (3.5 versus 3.3).

When comparing producer cooperatives with consumer cooperatives we found that the former had been more successful from a marketing point of view (3.6 versus 3.3), while there was no difference from a technological or commercial point of view. Looking at the two types of private companies we found that the Swedish dominated private companies had been slightly more successful from a market (3.5 versus 3.4) and a commercial point of view (3.3 versus 3.2), while the foreign dominated companies had been more successful from a technological point of view (2.5 versus 2.3).

TECHNOLOGICAL STRATEGY

Based on the results of our earlier studies, we focused on two main dimensions of technological strategy in our study of food processing companies. The first is technology use and the second technology orientation.

As we have noted in Chapter 4, technology use refers to the extent to which companies work within established technologies to find and develop new products, or to try to combine different technologies to achieve more radical breakthroughs. Working within established technologies is called isolated technology use, while combining different technologies is called synergistic technology use. A technology is viewed as a relatively well defined and delimited area of technical knowledge, usually the basis for educational and professional specialization.

Synergistic technology use is interdisciplinary and makes necessary the bridging of information and communication gaps between different specialists and specialized areas of knowledge. Isolated technology use is intradisciplinary and may more easily be carried out by isolated individuals and companies without going outside their established areas of specialization.

Our analysis (Table 10.6) shows that for the food processing companies studied, synergistic technology use was clearly related to greater technological (2.9 versus 2.0) and market success (3.8 versus 3.3) compared to isolated technology use, and also to somewhat greater commercial success (3.4 versus 3.3). For the Swedish food processing companies it thus appears to have been a successful strategy to expand, rather than concentrate, technological knowledge to find and develop new food products successfully.

With regard to technology orientation external versus internal orientation, as we have noted before, refers to the extent to which companies stress their internal compared to their external research environment in looking for and developing new products. The more a company relies on its own knowledge and competence in idea generation and technical product development, the more internal its R & D orientation is. The more it depends on outside aid and assistance for these purposes—for instance by cooperating with universities, consultants and other companies—the more externally oriented its technological orientation is.

Table 10.6 shows, as in the case of synergistic technology use, that external technological orientation was associated with greater technological (2.7 versus 2.4) and market success (3.5 versus 3.4), than internal orientation. With regard to commercial success, however, an internal orientation was associated with greater profitability than an external orientation (3.4 versus 3.1).

It thus appears that it had been more profitable for the food companies to stress their own competence in product development, while utilizing the outside research environment evidently led to more unique new products from a technological and market point of view.

One reason for this could be the conservative demand situation which, according to our interviews, is highly characteristic for the consumer food market. Customers, by and large, are not very willing to try unfamiliar food products.

Table 10.6 Technology use, technology orientation and marketing orientation in relation to technological market and commercial success for 121 products from 20 Swedish food processing companies

	Number of new products	Technological success	Market success	Commercial success
Synergistic technology use	54	2.9	3.8	3.4
Isolated technology use	67	2.0	3.3	3.3
External orientation	27	2.7	3.5	3.1
Internal orientation	94	2.4	3.4	3.4
Diversified marketing	45	2.4	3.6	3.0
Concentrated marketing	76	2.5	3.4	3.5

Higher numbers indicate higher technological, market and commercial success.
Technological success is measured by the level of technological innovation.
Market success is measured by the market situation at product introduction.
Commercial success is measured by the estimated profitability for new products.

Companies can take advantage of this by developing new food products similar to their old ones, for which they enjoy high customer confidence and for which they probably often have a special in-house R & D competence. This shows the importance of image marketing for new food products. It also helps to explain why external orientation seems to be less common and less successful in developing new food products, than in most other product groups we have studied.

MARKETING STRATEGY

In our analysis of factors related to success for new food products we distinguish between two main marketing strategies. The first, concentrated marketing, means that a new product fits into a company's existing product groups and also is mainly directed towards the needs of existing customers. The second, diversified marketing, means that a new product either falls outside existing product groups or is mainly directed towards new customer groups.

Table 10.6 shows that a concentrated marketing strategy was associated with somewhat greater technological success than a diversified marketing strategy for the food products studied (2.5 versus 2.4). A diversified marketing strategy, on the other hand, was associated with somewhat greater market success (3.6 versus 3.4). With regard to commercial success, a concentrated strategy was clearly associated with greater success than a diversified strategy (3.5 versus 3.0).

It thus appears to have been more profitable for the food companies studied to develop new products similar to their existing ones, directed towards the needs of existing customers, than to diversify into radically new products and markets. The implications of marketing strategy for technological and market success is less clear from our data.

CONSUMER OUTCOME

In our study we also tried to assess consumer outcomes of the companies' product development strategies, based on our interview data (Table 10.7). Five aspects of consumer outcome,

Table 10.7 Consumer outcomes for 121 products from 20 Swedish food processing companies

Consumer outcome	Number of products in each category				
	Price	Taste	Convenience	Nutritional	Medical
Favorable	20 (16%)	40 (33%)	49 (40%)	31 (16%)	17 (14%)
Neutral	94 (78%)	74 (61%)	70 (58%)	87 (72%)	104 (86%)
Unfavorable	7 (6%)	7 (6%)	2 (2%)	3 (2%)	0 (0%)

price, convenience, taste, nutritional and medical value were analyzed.

Price outcome refers to whether or not a new product at market introduction had a higher or lower price than the closest competing products on the market. Our results indicate that price competition between new products and existing products had not been very intense. A majority of the new products (78%) had about the same price as the existing closest substitutes, considerably fewer (16%) a lower price, and very few (6%) a higher price.

This is not surprising, since one important reason why companies develop new products is to avoid intense price competition. This they can do by making them more attractive to buyers than existing products, and therefore less price sensitive. From a consumer point of view this means that product development during the period evidently had not led to very many new food products with either a higher or a lower price than comparable products on the market.

The second consumer variable, convenience, refers to whether or not new products are easier to prepare, handle or store compared to the closest competing products on the market. Our data indicate that convenience is an important aspect of consumer outcome for new food products. Almost half the products (40%) were judged to be superior to competing products from a convenience point of view and almost none (2%) inferior.

With regard to the third consumer outcome variable, taste, about one third (33%) of the new food products were judged to be more attractive to consumers than other comparable products on the market and only a few (6%) were judged to be less attractive. After convenience, better taste was the most frequently mentioned consumer attribute of new food products.

Our fourth consumer outcome variable, nutritional value was assessed on the basis of fat, fibre, protein and sugar content. From this point of view about one-fourth of the new products were judged to be beneficial from a consumer point of view and very few (2%) detrimental.

Considering our fifth consumer outcome variable, better medical value, we found that this was attributed to a relatively small proportion of the new products (14%) which were directly intended for medical treatment.

We may now sum up our analysis of the consumer outcome of product development, as viewed by the companies themselves. We see that the most common type of consumer benefit attributed to new products compared to the closest existing substitutes on the market was convenience. Somewhat less frequently mentioned was better taste and nutritional value, while a lower price or higher medical value was seen as characterizing only a small number of the new products studied.

Since the results are not particularly favorable from a company point of view, and are as far as possible based on measurable qualities, there is little reason to believe that company representatives intentionally gave misleading information as to what they believed were the consumer implications of the new product studies. Further support for the above conclusions was also arrived at by carrying out direct consumer interviews, which by and large led to similar results.

SUMMARY

Our study of product development strategies for Swedish food processing companies has both theoretical and empirical implications. It has influenced the general framework presented in this book and has also led to some insights as to specific conditions prevailing in the food processing industry. Since most of our other studies refer to industrial goods, it is useful as an application of the framework to reflect conditions in the consumer market.

It is somewhat surprising that the results of this study in many respects are quite similar to the results of our early study, summarized in Chapter 4, of research and technology intensive companies, specializing, for instance, in pharmaceutical drugs, industrial electronics, and industrial chemicals.

This early study concentrated on technological strategies for product development. As in our study of food processing companies it showed that more open strategies emphasizing synergistic technology use and external technological orientation, were clearly associated with greater technological success in finding and developing new products than were the more closed strategies which stressed isolated technology use and internal orientation. It would appear that these findings apply not only to hi-tech, research intensive industries, but also have relevance for food processing, a very low-tech industry.

From this we may conclude that there is a large underutilized technological potential in the food industry, at least in Sweden, of which creative companies probably could take advantage. Our data indicate that by using more innovative development strategies food processing companies should be able to achieve nutritionally better, gastronomically more appealing and commercially more profitable new food products. To realize this potential they need to use more open and flexible technological and marketing strategies and entrepreneurship to develop, link together and exploit technological and market possibilities.

With regard to the relationship between company size and product development success our study of Swedish food processing companies suggests that larger companies were more successful than smaller ones. This in contrast to our study of mechanical engineering companies described in Chapter 5, which clearly showed, by employing other measures of success, that smaller companies were much more successful than larger ones in finding and developing new products.

*In our study of pulp and paper
companies we again find support for
the conclusion that open technological
and marketing strategies tend to be
associated with greater technological
and market success in finding and
developing new products*

11
Product Development Strategies for Swedish Pulp and Paper Companies

In this chapter,[1] product development strategies for four leading Swedish pulp and paper companies are described and analyzed by using the same research methodology as in our other studies. Pulp and paper manufacturing is a very low research and technology intensive industry, the products of which reflect industrial use more closely than final consumer demand. We therefore may use product development in pulp and paper companies as an example of low-tech industrial product development. It is interesting to compare the strategies of these companies both with the strategies of more research and technology intensive companies manufacturing and marketing industrial goods, and with other low-tech companies emphasizing consumer rather than producer goods. The former category is represented in our data by, for instance, industrial electronics and chemical companies and the latter by food processing companies.

RESEARCH METHOD

Basically the same approach was employed in our study of pulp and paper companies, as in our other studies of product development strategies, described in Chapters 4 and 10. In each company, leading executives responsible for product and company development were personally interviewed and data was collected on both expressed overall policy and specific new products developed during a ten-year period, 1974–1984. To qualify as new products some degree of technological and marketing novelty was required, based on development activities pursued by the company.

Company representatives were asked to give a representative sample of new products to use as a basis for our evaluation of product development strategies and new product success. For each product, specific data was collected covering a wide range of marketing and technological factors.

Using this method it is possible to analyze both company specific and product specific factors related to technological, marketing and commercial success, as we have described more fully in earlier chapters. Since the number of companies in our studies quite naturally is much smaller than the number of products, and since companies tend not to consistently develop only one type of product, the results of the company analysis generally are less clean cut and more difficult to draw conclusions from, than the product analysis; previous chapters therefore have emphasized the product level of analysis. In this chapter, since the number of companies and of new products is relatively small, it is possible for us to deal in more detail with both levels of analysis. The results of the product analysis give specific information on how companies should develop and market new products. The results of the company analysis tell us about the settings in which more or less successful product development has taken place.

COMPANY DESCRIPTIONS

In this section the four pulp and paper companies and their overall policies and strategies will be presented. Company A had about 8000 employees in 1982 and approximately 500 million $US in sales. Its product mix was mainly pulp, cardboard, paper sacks, chemicals, lumber and electricity. Its overall policy was to concentrate existing product lines to achieve large scale cost benefits. Its international strategy was to add value to raw material by processing abroad in daughter companies. Company A believed this would give better market contact and technical adaptation to foreign markets, compared to direct export. In our terminology, Company A tended to employ a pronounced holding strategy with R & D and production technology mainly aimed at process innovation and existing products and customers.

Company B had about 10 000 employees in 1982 and sales of about 600 million $US. Its product mix was mainly pulp, fine paper, lumber, chemicals and electricity. In its overall development policy it stressed diversification of existing product lines. To achieve this it was trying to change its emphasis from mainly process innovation, as in the case of Company A, to more innovation in product design. In our terminology, Company B tended to have a strong competitive emphasis in its marketing strategy with its technological strategy more directed towards new products and customers than did Company A.

Company C had about 6200 employees in 1982 and sales of about 450 million US dollars. Its product mix was predominantly pulp, craft liner, journal paper, lumber, electricity and paper machines. Its overall policy was to concentrate on its existing product lines with wood and electricity as its strategic base. It emphasized both biological and technical product innovation and diversified mainly by acquisitions, which are not included in our study. From the point of view of our approach, Company C, like Company A, had employed a pronounced holding strategy in its marketing, with R & D and production technology largely geared towards existing products and customers.

Company D, finally, had about 630 employees and 45 million dollars in sales in 1982. Its product mix was more concentrated than the other companies, and consisted mainly of pulp, craft liner and cardboard. Its overall development policy was to diversify within the limits imposed by its own raw material (pulp). Company C stressed production flexibility and market segmentation to increase the value added to its basic product. From our point of view it had a stronger competitive emphasis in its marketing strategy than the other companies, with its

R & D and production technology more linked to product rather than process innovation and to new customers.

STRATEGIC ANALYSIS ON THE COMPANY LEVEL

In Tables 11.1–11.5 the product development strategies for companies A–D are summarized. It is interesting to compare these realized strategies, based on actual new products, with the policy statements given in the previous section.

In Table 11.5, which summarizes Tables 11.1–11.4, we see that Company A had the most open marketing strategy (3.7) with Company C following (3.5). Companies B and D show the most closed marketing strategies (both 3.0). The more a company develops radically new products, outside its existing product lines, and sells these products to new customers, the more open and diversified its marketing strategy is. The more products that are variations of existing products and sold to existing customers, the more closed and concentrated its marketing strategy is.

Products which are radically new and sold to new customers are called competitive product innovations, and assigned the value 5 on a scale 1–5, with higher values indicating more open marketing strategies. Products which are variations of existing products sold to new market segments are called competitive product modifications and products which are radically new and sold to existing segments are called holding product innovations. Both these types of new products are viewed as intermediate on our scale from most open to most closed marketing strategies and given the value 3. Products which are variations of existing products sold to existing customers are called holding product modifications and are viewed as indicating the most closed marketing strategies on our scale, with the value 1.

If we compare Tables 11.1 to 11.4 with this discussion of overall company development policies, we see that realized strategy based on developed and marketed new products is quite consistent with stated policy.

The stated policy of Companies A and C was predominantly of a holding nature. Five of their seven new products were

Table 11.1 Product development in Company A

Type of innovation	Marketing strategy	Market success	Technological strategy	Technological success	Development time	Commercial success	Buyer outcome
A1 General process and general product	Competitive product innovation 5	High 4	Internal and isolated 1	Medium 3	2 years	Profitable 4	Price advantage
A2 Specific process and general product	Holding product innovation 3	High 4	Internal and isolated 1	High 4	10 years	Very profitable 5	Price and quality advantage
A3 Specific process and specific product	Holding product innovation 3	High 4	External and isolated 3	High 4	7 years	Profitable 4	Price and quality advantage
Average	3.7	4.0	1.7	3.7	6.3 years	4.3	

Higher values indicate more open strategies and greater success.

Table 11.2 Product development in Company B

Type of innovation	Marketing strategy	Market success	Technological strategy	Technological success	Development time	Commercial success	Buyer outcome
B1 Specific process and general product	Competitive product modification 3	Low 2	Internal and isolated 1	Low 2	1 year	Profitable 4	Price advantage
B2 General process and general product	Holding product modification 1	Medium 3	Internal and isolated 1	Low 2	1/2 year	Profitable 4	Quality advantage
B3 General process and general product	Competitive product modification 3	High 4	Internal and isolated 1	Low 2	1/2 year	Profitable 4	Price and quality advantage
B4 Specific process and specific product	Competitive product innovation 5	Medium 3	Internal and isolated 1	Low 2	2 years	Loss 2	Price advantage
Average	3.0	3.0	1.0	2.0	1.0 years	3.5	

Higher values indicate more open strategies and greater success.

Table 11.3 Product development in Company C

Type of innovation	Marketing strategy	Market success	Technological strategy	Technological success	Development time	Commercial success	Buyer outcome
C1 General process and general product	Competitive product innovation 5	Medium 3	Internal and isolated 1	Medium 3	6 years	Profitable 4	Price and quality advantage
C2 Specific process and general product	Holding product innovation 3	High 4	Internal and isolated 5	High 4	10 years	Break-even 3	Price and quality advantage
C3 Specific process and specific product	Holding product innovation 3	High 4	External and synergistic 5	High 4	2 years	Profitable 4	Price advantage
C4 Specific process and specific product	Holding product innovation 3	High 4	Internal and isolated 1	Low 2	2 years	Break-even 3	Quality advantage
Average	3.5	3.8	3.0	3.3	5.0 years	3.5	

Higher values indicate more open strategies and greater success.

Table 11.4 Product development in Company D

Type of innovation	Marketing strategy	Market success	Technological strategy	Technological success	Development time	Commercial success	Buyer outcome
D1 General product and specific process	Competitive product modification 3	Medium 3	External and isolated 3	Medium 3	1 year	Profitable 4	Price and quality advantage
D2 Specific process and specific product	Competitive product modification 3	High 4	External and isolated 3	Low 2	1 year	Break-even 3	Price and quality advantage
D3 Specific process and specific product	Holding product innovation 3	Medium 3	External and synergistic 5	High 4	2 years	Profitable 4	Quality advantage
Average	3.0	3.7	3.5	3.0	1.3 years	3.3	

Higher values indicate more open strategies and greater success.

Table 11.5 Company strategies and outcomes

Company	Marketing strategy	Market success	Technological strategy	Technological success	Commercial success
A	3.7	4.0	1.7	3.7	4.3
B	3.0	3.0	1.0	2.0	3.5
C	3.5	3.8	3.0	3.3	3.5
D	3.0	3.3	3.7	3.0	3.3

Higher values indicate more open strategies and greater success.

classified as holding product innovations; that is, radically new products mainly directed at tying existing customers closer to the company.

The stated policies of Companies B and D were more competitive. Five of their seven new products were classified as competitive product modifications or innovations; that is, new products that are mainly aimed at capturing new market segments.

In Table 11.5 we further see that more open marketing strategies tend to be associated with greater market success, that is, a higher level of market innovation, than more closed marketing strategies. Since the level of market innovation is measured by the competitive situation for a new product at the time of its market introduction, the more unique a product is from the buyer's point of view, compared to the closest competing product, the greater is the level of market innovation.

We see that Company A had the most open marketing strategy and also the highest level of market success (4.0), while Company C had the second most open marketing strategy and also the second highest level of market success (3.8). We also see that the most open marketing strategy is associated with the greatest commercial success (4.3).

Turning to technology strategy, synergistic technology use (combining technologies) and external technology orientation (cooperation with the outside research environment) are defined as indicating more open strategies. Isolated technology use (working within established technologies) and internal technological orientation (emphasizing the company's own competence) are seen as indicating more closed strategies.

The most closed strategy associated with a new product (internal orientation and isolated technology use) is given the value 1 and the most open strategy (external orientation and synergistic technology use) the value 5. The two intermediate strategies (internal orientation and synergistic technology use and external orientation and isolated technology use) are each given the value 3.

Table 11.5 shows that Company D has the most open technological strategy (3.7), but only the third highest level of technological success (3.0), measured by the level of technological innovation. Remember this refers to the degree of creativity required of the company in technical product development. Company A with the second most closed technological strategy (1.7) had the highest level of technological success (3.7) and Company B with the most closed technological strategy (1.7) the lowest level of technological success (2.0). Company C with the second most open strategy (3.0) also had the second highest level of technological success (3.3).

With the major exception of Company A, more open technological strategies on the company level therefore seem to be linked to greater technological success. The exception is notable, however, since in this case a relatively closed strategy was technologically more successful than more open ones.

Except for Company D we also see that internal orientation and isolated technology use, as well as external orientation and synergistic technology use, tend to go together. In this company we find the combination external orientation and isolated technology use for two of the three new products.

Looking at commercial success for different technological strategies on the company level, we see that Company A, with the second most closed technological strategy, had been most successful. As we have noted above, Company A had the most open marketing strategy and also the greatest market and technological success. Company D with the most open technological strategy had the lowest level of commercial success (3.3), but the differences compared to Companies B and C are small.

If we look at the average development time for new products in the companies, the differences are striking between

Companies A and C on the one hand and Companies B and D on the other (Tables 11.1–11.4). The former companies have long average development times (6.3 and 5.0 years) while the latter have very short development times (about 1 year). The companies with longer development times have higher levels of market and technological success, which is what we should expect if more innovative change takes longer time and our measures are valid. We may note also that the company with the longest average development time for its new products, Company A, was commercially most successful. Company C, however, with the second longest development time, was more successful than one of the companies with a shorter development time, Company D and as successful as the other one, Company B.

With regard to buyer outcome the differences between companies are not very clear (Tables 11.1–11.4). In all companies except D, price advantages to buyers as a result of product development are more common than quality advantages, while in Company D quality advantages are more frequent. This is surprising, since product development is often seen as a way to avoid intense price competition. This does not appear to have been the case in the Swedish pulp and paper companies. Instead product development seems to have led to a greater tendency to compete with price, which is the opposite of what we found in our study of food processing companies.

STRATEGIC ANALYSIS ON THE PRODUCT LEVEL

In this section we will give the results of our analysis of product development success on the product level. Only the 14 new products for which complete data are available are included. To begin with a distinction is made between specific and general process and product innovations. A specific process innovation mainly affects the production of a given product, while a general process innovation may influence a number of quite different products, at least from a buyer/ user point of view.

A specific product innovation is directed towards a narrow market segment, while a general product innovation is aimed

Table 11.6 Strategies and outcomes for different product types

Type of innovation	Number of products	Market success	Technological success	Commercial success	Buyer outcome
Specific product and specific process	6	3.7	3.0	3.3	2 price 2 quality 12 price and quality
General product and general process	4	3.5	2.5	4.0	1 price 1 quality 2 price and quality
Specific process and general product	4	3.3	3.3	4.0	1 price 3 price and quality

Higher values indicate greater success.

at a broader market. A company in its product development strategy may thus choose to be more specific or more general in its technological and marketing efforts, and to emphasize production process or product design in its development activities. It is therefore of interest to try to relate this to differences in success.

In Table 11.6 we see that six of the new products are classified as being both specific product and process innovations. Four of the products are classified as both general product and process innovations, while four are classified as specific process and general product innovations.

We find the highest level of technological success for the specific process and general product innovations (3.3), and also for market success (3.3).With regard to commercial success the general product and process innovations and the specific process and general product innovations are most successful (both 4.0).

In Table 11.7 we see the outcomes for each of our two dimensions of technological strategy. Synergistic technology use is associated with a far higher level of technological success (4.0) than isolated technology use (2.6) and also with a somewhat higher level of market success (3.7 compared to 3.5). There is no difference in commercial success, however, between the two types of technology use (3.7 for both). External orientation is clearly associated with both greater technological success (3.5 versus 2.5) and greater market success (3.7 versus 3.4) than internal orientation. Again there is no difference in commercial success between the two types of technological orientation (3.7 for both).

Table 11.7 Outcomes of technological strategies along single dimensions

Technological strategy	Number of products	Technological success	Market success	Commercial success
External	6	3.5	3.7	3.7
Internal	8	2.5	3.4	3.7
Synergistic	3	4.0	3.7	3.7
Isolated	11	2.6	3.5	3.7

Higher values indicate greater success.

Table 11.8 shows the outcomes for the different combinations of technology orientation and technology use. We see that most of the new products are the result of internal orientation and isolated technology use. External orientation and synergistic technology use is as common as external orientation and isolated technology use. None of the products however is the result of both internal orientation and synergistic technology use.

We find by far the highest level of technological success (4.0) for external orientation and synergistic technology use. The level of market success is the same for the two strategies involving external orientation (3.7) and somewhat higher than for internal orientation and isolated technology use (3.4). Just as when we look at each factor independently, we find no difference in commercial success for the different technological strategies.

Tables 11.9 and 11.10 give the outcomes for the different dimensions of marketing strategy, viewed in isolation. In Table 11.9 we see that competitive and holding strategies each account for the same number of new products, while product innovation is almost twice as common as product modification.

We find the highest level of technological success for holding strategies (3.4), followed by product innovation (3.3). With regard to market success, these same two marketing strategy

Table 11.8 Outcomes of technological strategies along combined dimensions

Technological strategy	Number of products	Technological success	Market success	Commercial success
External and synergistic	3	4.0	3.7	3.7
External and isolated	3	3.0	3.7	3.7
Internal and synergistic	0			
Internal and isolated	8	2.5	3.4	3.7

Higher values indicate greater success.

Table 11.9 Outcomes of marketing strategies along single dimensions

Marketing strategy	Number of products	Market success	Technological success	Commercial success
Competitive	7	3.3	2.4	3.6
Holding	7	3.7	3.4	3.9
Product innovation	9	3.7	3.3	3.7
Product modification	5	3.2	2.2	3.8

Higher values indicate greater success.

Table 11.10 Outcomes of marketing strategies along combined dimensions

Marketing strategy	Number of products	Market success	Technological success	Commercial success
Competitive product innovation	3	3.3	2.7	3.3
Competitive product modification	4	3.9	2.3	3.8
Holding product innovation	6	3.8	3.7	3.8
Holding product modification	1	3.0	2.0	4.0

Higher values indicate greater success.

dimensions are associated with the highest levels of success (3.7 for both). As in the case of technological strategies we find fairly small differences in commercial success, although the outcome for competitive strategies is least favorable (3.6).

In Table 11.10 we see that the marketing strategy combining holding with product innovation, that is, innovating to keep existing customers, is more frequent and also associated with the highest levels of technological and market success (3.7 and 3.8). Competitive product innovation, innovating mainly to attract new customers, shows the second highest level of technological success (2.7) and the third highest level of market success (3.3). Holding product modification, adjusting products primarily to keep old customers, is associated with both the lowest level of technological success (2.0) and the lowest level of market success (3.0), but this group contains only one new product. With regard to commercial success, competitive product innovation is least successful (3.3) and holding product modification most successful (4.0).

Table 11.11 gives the development times for different new products in relation to our measures of success. We see that both the level of technological success and of market success increases with development time. The differences are especially pronounced in the case of technological success, which we may take as an indication of high validity for our measurement of the level of technological innovation. With regard to commercial success the longest development time is associated with the highest value (4.0) but the shortest time has a higher value than the intermediate one (3.4 versus 3.8).

Table 11.12, finally, gives the buyer outcome for new products in relation to our strategy dimensions. We see that the combination of price and quality advantage is most frequent, while price advantage alone is somewhat more frequent than merely a quality advantage. We furthermore find a higher level of both technological and market success for the new products associated with the most frequent type of buyer outcome (3.1 and 3.7). This outcome is also associated with a somewhat greater commercial success than quality

Table 11.11 Development time and outcomes for different products

Development time	Number of products	Technological success	Market success	Commercial success
Less than 2 years	5	2.2	3.2	3.8
2–5 years	5	3.0	3.6	3.4
6–10 years	4	3.8	3.8	4.0

Higher values indicate greater success.

Table 11.12 *Buyer outcomes for different products and strategies*

Buyer outcome	Number of products	Technological success	Market success	Commercial success	Dominant marketing and technological strategy
Price	4	2.8	3.3	3.5	Competitive product innovation. Internal and isolated.
Quality	3	2.7	3.3	3.7	Holding product innovation. Internal and isolated.
Price and quality	7	3.1	3.7	3.9	Competitive product modification. External and isolated and internal and isolated.

Higher values indicate greater success.

advantage alone (3.9), which in turn is somewhat higher in commercial success than price advantage alone (3.7 versus 3.5).

With regard to marketing strategy, price advantage as a buyer outcome is mainly associated with competitive product innovation, while quality innovation is mainly associated with holding product innovation. This is consistent with the assumption that quality advantages are mainly used to tie customers closer to the company and price advantages to attract new customers. When new products are characterized by both price and quality advantages to buyers, holding product innovation and competitive product modification are used equally, and more frequently than other strategies.

If we relate technological strategy to buyer outcomes, we find that internal orientation and isolated technology use are most common in the case of both price advantage and quality advantage as single attributes of new products. For new products characterized by both price and quality advantage to buyers, external orientation in combination with isolated technology use and internal orientation together with isolated technology use are both as frequent.

SUMMARY

In this chapter, product development strategies for four Swedish pulp and paper companies have been discussed in more detail than was possible, when giving the results of our more extensive study of product development strategies in Swedish food processing companies in Chapter 10. In particular, the relationship between policy and realized strategy and between company and product development has been examined in this chapter. As in most of our other studies we find support for the general conclusion that more open technological and marketing strategies tend to be associated with greater success in finding and developing new products than more closed strategies.

A favorable company culture and climate is viewed as one of the firm's most important development resources

12

Managing Culture and Climate—A Case Study of a Leading Swedish Chemical Company

In this chapter,[1] technological and market innovation is seen as the result of the interaction between strategy and structure, with organizational culture and climate viewed as important intervening variables (Figure 12.1). Structure leads to stability and continuity, while strategy is necessary to achieve innovative direction and radical change.

Producing and marketing mature products for established markets may, for instance, be carried out successfully with a highly positional orientation, while developing and marketing new products demands a more innovative orientation. Although this is usually not dealt with much in the management literature, our results strongly indicate that companies need explicitly and systematically to recognize and manage culture and climate to succeed in product and company development.

As we have noted in Chapter 2, companies emphasizing stability and the status quo are called more positional companies, while companies stressing innovative strategies and the need for more radical change are called more

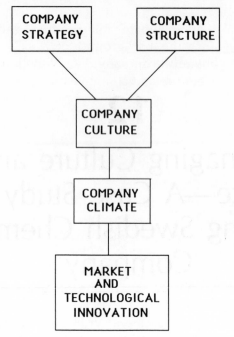

Figure 12.1 Company culture and climate as intervening variables

innovative companies. In relatively stable environments a strong positional orientation and an emphasis on short run efficiency are conducive to company success.

In more dynamic and changing environments a strong innovative orientation is necessary. In our framework structure thus refers to both more tangible aspects of companies such as production facilities and products and more intangible aspects such as organization structure.

Our approach allows structure to determine strategy, in the case of highly positional companies; and strategy to determine structure, in the case of highly innovative companies.

Thus we are in agreement with most economic and sociological writers that structure may influence strategy[2] and with writers on strategic management[3] that strategic change may lead to structural change. In our approach, the relationship between structure and strategy depends on the type of company development, positional or innovative, so that either structure or strategy may be the leading factor.

In this chapter we shall focus on the management of company culture and climate for product and company development against the background of a case study of a leading Swedish chemical company, Eka Nobell. In this study strategy, structure, culture and climate were assessed by using interviews and psychological measurements, both on the individual and company level.[4] For this purpose both psychological tests and personal interviews were used. Altogether, more than 50 persons were interviewed one or more times with each interview lasting 1–2 hours. Questionnaires were administered to 124 persons and in addition to this group, interviews were held to present and discuss preliminary results.

Strategy and structure in this study was assessed by interviews with top management in Eka, both on the company and divisional level. Organization structure was further measured by a questionnaire containing about thirty statements. The 142 respondents, almost all the employees in the divisions, stated their agreement with these statements on a scale from 0 to 3, with 0 signifying very little agreement and 3 very much. Some of the results of main interest to our present discussion are given in Table 12.1.

Goal clarity refers to the extent to which members feel they have been informed about the strategy, plans and intentions of their division. Formalization means the extent to which rules and formal procedures govern decision-making. Pre-planning refers to the degree to which decisions are set ahead

Table 12.1 Some dimensions of organization structure in the various divisions

	B	VP	TS	PK
Goal clarity	2.1	1.8	1.6	1.6
Formalization	0.8	0.8	0.9	0.8
Pre-planning	1.8	1.8	1.1	1.0
Role clarity	2.2	2.0	1.4	1.5
Strict routines	1.3	1.5	0.8	0.8

Higher values indicate higher loadings on the factors on a scale from 0 to 3.

of time and followed in practice. Role clarity refers to how precisely employees feel that their functions have been clearly delineated and set out by top management. Strict routines means how closely formal rules and procedures are followed.

Since high loadings on all these factors may be assumed to reduce innovative potential by leaving less room for radical change and decentralized initiative, and to promote stability by clearly stating in advance what decisions should be taken, we may use them to indicate to what extent organization structure is conducive to innovative or positional development.

CULTURE AND CLIMATE AS DEVELOPMENT FACTORS

In our framework, a favorable company culture and climate for achieving creativity and innovation is viewed as one of the firm's most important development resources. A difference between our approach and most other attempts to understand product and company development is that we explicitly consider and measure culture and climate as factors which may inhibit or promote structural stability and strategic change.

Since some cultures and climates may be assumed to better reflect the development needs of more positional companies and others of more innovative companies, we may use our distinction between different types of companies to study the management of culture and climate under more or less stable conditions. In the study on which this chapter is based, differences in culture and climate between various divisions in Eka Nobell were related to development requirements and performance in developing and marketing new products.

Company culture[5] is defined as the values, norms, beliefs and assumptions embraced by members (Figure 12.2). In our study, culture was measured by a content analysis based on an open questionnaire where the 142 respondents were able to use their own words to describe how they perceived prevailing conditions. Almost all Eka employees in the various divisions are included in this sample, both top managers and subordinates.

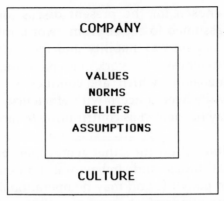

Figure 12.2 *Company culture box*

A number of themes emerged, which were used to classify the cultures in the different divisions. In this chapter responses to one of the questions: 'What motto would you use to describe the underlying philosophy and striving in your division?', will be used to characterize the cultures, since they seem best to display the aspects that interest us. The number of times each theme was touched upon in the answers from each division are given in Table 12.2.

Table 12.2 *Number of times in each division that various themes occurred in response to the question, What was the basic philosophy of the division?*

	B	VP	TS	PK
Risk-taking	3	6	5	12
Quality	3	2	3	2
Competitiveness	—	3	—	4
Efficiency	2	3	2	—
Profit	9	5	13	—
Survival	7	—	—	—
Work enjoyment	2	7	9	1
Hard work	1	1	1	7
Market and customer orientation	2	2	5	1

The themes chosen for the present discussion are factors which may be assumed to either promote or inhibit creativity and change as opposed to stability and the status quo. Risk taking, competitiveness and work enjoyment may be viewed as cultural dimensions which are conducive to innovative performance, while over-concern with efficiency, profitability, and survival may be viewed as contributing to more positional behavior.

Company climate,[6] on the other hand, may be defined as the feelings, attitudes and behavioral tendencies, which characterize company life and may be operationally measured through the perceptions of its members. While culture is more normative and stable, climate thus is more descriptive and changeable. Climate thus may be seen as the way culture is expressed at each point of time, and by trying to change culture, company leaders may hope to influence climate, which is more directly related to company behavior.

In our study, climate has been measured by a previously developed questionnaire[7] given to the same people as the culture questions. The respondents were asked to state on a four point scale from 0 to 3 for 77 questions whether they believed a statement to apply or not. The measuring instrument has proved to possess good reliability and validity in differentiating between more and less innovative organizations. By using factor analysis of the correlations a number of dimensions of climate have been operationally determined,

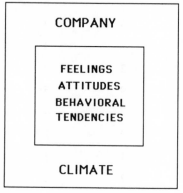

Figure 12.3 Company climate box

high values for which may be assumed to be positively correlated with creativity and change. These dimensions are challenge, idea support, richness in ideas, liveliness, playfulness, debate, conflicts, trust, freedom to initiate, harmony, achievement motivation and risk taking (Table 12.3).

CASE DESCRIPTION

Until the beginning of the 1970s Eka, or Eka kemi as it was then called, was a highly positional company. Its business consisted in the efficient production and distribution of basic chemicals, and the company had been in this line of business since 1895. During the 1960s profitability in the dominant product line, chlorine/alkali, diminished after being high during the 1950s. The situation was made worse by the greater environmental demands made by the authorities, which threatened a closedown of the established factories.

Table 12.3 Some dimensions of climate in the various divisions

	B	VP	TS	PK
Challenge	1.8	2.1	2.2	2.1
Idea support	1.7	2.0	2.1	2.0
Richness of ideas	1.6	1.9	2.2	2.6
Liveliness	1.3	1.7	2.1	1.9
Playfulness	1.3	1.7	2.0	1.8
Debate	0.9	1.0	1.4	1.8
Conflict	0.9	0.3	0.4	1.3
Trust	1.6	1.8	1.8	1.1
Freedom	1.8	2.0	2.3	2.1
Peaceful working conditions	1.7	1.8	1.8	1.7
Achievement orientation	1.6	2.0	2.0	1.9
Risk-taking	0.9	1.4	1.9	2.4

Higher values indicate higher loadings on the factors on a scale from 0 to 3.

A necessary reorientation towards new products and markets was difficult to achieve with the existing personnel and organization structure which had little innovative potential. To become a more innovative company a more flexible, market oriented organization and some renewal of personnel was needed.

After top management had decided to change direction, a number of structural changes were carried out to allow for a more innovative strategy. To begin with a product organization was implemented around 1970. This was followed by divisionalization in the early 1980s to facilitate technological renewal and market adaptation. By changing the mix of technologies and markets in the different divisions, a clearer distinction was achieved between them with regard to innovative potential.

This made it possible to increase the technological and marketing development efforts in the more innovative divisions without this leading to disturbances in the more positional ones. Since the divisions to a large extent utilized the same basic technologies, a problem with this divisionalization was how to handle these interdependencies from a development point of view. This made necessary formal or informal cross-divisional project groups to integrate joint technology needs.

With regard to culture and climate there were great differences between divisions, which became a major focus of our research. We assumed that these would be related to differences in innovative potential and performance. If so, there was a need to promote such cultures and climates in the various divisions that they could function well in their basic capacities. Some culture and climate aspects are well suited for achieving stability and efficiency, while others are more likely to be associated with creativity and innovative change. A major research question, which we addressed, is to identify these factors and relate them to positional and innovative performance.

After this general description of the company we shall now describe in more detail the strategies, structures, cultures and climates in the different divisions. It is quite clear that the strategic ambition of top management since the early 1970s had been to make the company more innovative by increasing its innovative potential. At the same time it was easier to achieve this goal in some divisions than in others and this influenced the strategies pursued by divisional leaders.

To find out about these strategies personal interviews were carried out with top management in all divisions. Structure, culture and climate were measured by both company interviews at all levels of the organization and psychological measurements and questionnaires administered to almost all employees. At the same time, information on product development was collected as a measure of innovative performance. These data were supplemented by other information such as internal documents and sales material.

We shall begin with the most positional division both with regard to structure and strategy, the B-Division. Basically, its business is to make caustic soda and chlorine by electrolyzing dissolved salt. This process also leads to hydrogen gas which is used to make hydrogen peroxide. The chlorine is sold by a company owned by all Swedish producers of this product. It is mainly delivered to the Swedish Cellulose industry where it is used for bleaching chemical pulp. The caustic soda is also sold to the same jointly owned company and largely used for bleaching; but also for making soap, water purification and other industrial uses. A large part of the production is sold to the other divisions and further refined by them.

The B-Division thus almost entirely manufactures standard products and essentially no product development to find new products is carried out. Little active marketing to final consumers is pursued. Instead, the joint sales company acts as an intermediary between the division and the final market for much of what is produced. The rest of the production sold outside the company is sold on more competitive terms with some active marketing and customer adaptation.

In the absence of product development and active marketing, rationalization of production to achieve cost reduction and greater efficiency is the main possibility to increase profitability. Most caustic soda is sold in Sweden at profitable prices, since transportation costs for importing this commodity are high.

The B-division thus shows the most positional orientation with regard to products, mainly selling established standard commodities. Its organization structure and sales organization are in line with this orientation. Production processes are large scale and highly specialized and most sales go to established sales outlets and customers. More emphasis is placed on pre-planning than is the case for most of the other divisions, and there is a clear view of the goal. Role definition also is clear, so that most people know quite well what they are expected to do. Somewhat surprising is that formalization, as in all the other divisions, is fairly low, but the extent to which existing rules are strictly followed is relatively wide. The emphasis in this division is on stable operations; the leadership largely recognizes this requirement. The head of the division has an authoritarian, production oriented leadership style using distinct orders to achieve planned results.

The culture and climate of the B-Division also reflect its highly positional orientation. The culture, that is the basic values, norms, beliefs and assumptions, expressed by the people in the B-Division, is dominated by a felt need for profit and survival. This is viewed as much more important than risk taking and enjoying work for its own sake. Efficiency and quality are viewed as important, but competitiveness is not seen as an important requirement to achieve success. This culture reflects positional values such as security, disciplined work and even complacency, which help to explain why the climate is not very exciting and unlikely to lead to strong innovative efforts.

The climate, that is, the psychological mix of feelings and attitudes which affect day-to-day organizational behavior, is viewed by subordinates in the B-Division as low key, with some underlying, unresolved conflicts. It is perceived as less challenging, risk-encouraging and playful, than in any other division. It is not seen as very achievement oriented, lively or supportive of new ideas. Debate is not common and the freedom to take initiatives in decision making is viewed as low. Conflict is fairly high and trust relatively low, compared to most of the other divisions.

Obviously this is not a very creative climate but one which promotes stability and faith in the existing way of doing things. As long as the B-Division is seen as a stable backbone in the company and is successful in doing what it has always done, its culture and climate may be quite conducive to achieving its goals. If it is met by demands to become more innovative and creative, as was the case in the 1970s and early 1980s, problems will arise because of its prevailing attitudes and basic values and assumptions.

The VP-Division is the division in Eka which, after the B-Division, appears to be most positional in its strategy and structure. The main product of this division is hydrogen peroxide. The basic raw material used is hydrogen, delivered from the B-Division, which is oxidized by using air. Most of this product is sold to the paper industry, where it is used for bleaching chemical and mechanical pulp and return paper. It is also used for purification processes and internally to produce other chemicals for the detergency industry.

Most of the development efforts in the VP-Division are directed towards solving customer problems, and technical service is one of its main ways of competing. The division has a high level of competence in bleaching chemistry, which is used to develop new products in cooperation with customers, for instance, highly bleached mechanical pulp, raffinated pulp and other high yield types of pulp.

In addition, the division has been able to use its competence to develop new products for different markets. One successful example is Ekarox, which is a derivative of hydrogen peroxide used for chemical purification processes, for instance in the steel and food industry. Most of its development work has been carried out internally in the division in cooperation with customers, and little use has been made of experts from other divisions or outside the company.

The reason seems to have been a positional tendency in the company to remain within its basic area of technology, bleaching, and not to try to combine this knowledge in a more innovative fashion with other technologies, for instance mechanical engineering, to find new products. The company thus has tried to become more innovative primarily by finding new applications for existing technology, rather than by developing new technologies.

In line with its relatively positional strategy the company has developed a structure which, as in the case of the B-Division, is more suited for promoting stability than change. It employs large scale and highly specialized production processes. Following the B-Division, it comes second as regards goal clarity, and places a strong emphasis on pre-planning and strict routines. It is also second as regards role clarity.

Its divisional leadership, however, is less authoritarian than in the B-Division. It is divided between three different leaders, each responsible for a clearly defined area. One is responsible for general production and process development, another for technical marketing towards the cellulosa industry and the third for technical marketing towards other markets as well as administrative development and control. Both productive and administrative stability are given top priority by all three leaders, although a certain degree of innovative entrepreneurship is permitted.

As may be expected when a fairly positional type of business tries to develop in a somewhat more innovative direction, we find fairly strong elements of risk-taking and competitiveness in the expressed culture. Work enjoyment is emphasized quite strongly and the need to be profitable is downplayed somewhat. The need for efficiency, however, is stated more frequently than in any other division. The culture thus seems to be fairly favorable for promoting creativity and change, but the restraints on going too far from the established business are quite strong.

With regard to climate, it is rich in challenge, idea support, trust and the need for achievement, and fairly rich in wealth of ideas, risk taking and freedom; all of which are factors which may be viewed as creativity promoting. It is also fairly rich in playfulness, but not in debate or conflict, and seems to stress the need for harmony more than any other division.

The climate in the VP-Division seems to be a dual one, in some ways promoting, but in other ways inhibiting creativity and innovation. This may reflect both a dissonance between innovative ambitions and perceived innovative potential and some indecisiveness in strategic leadership as to how much support should be given to promoting creativity and change. Culture and climate are somewhat incompatible and display a need for more consistency if either positional or innovative tendencies are to be given priority.

Our third division, the TS-Division, seems to have been more ambitious in trying to become more innovative than the VP-Division, and also succeeded better in this respect, in spite of the fact that it to a large extent produces standard products. Its main business is producing meta silicate and perborate for the detergency and cleaning industry, but it has also developed radically new products based on its silicate technology.

In Eka the TS-Division had been given responsibility for R & D in silicate technology. The division has actively cooperated with other divisions to find new products. Compared to the VP-Division the TS-Division sells most of its products under intense competition, with little customer specific adaptation, technical service and consultation.

Among the new products the TS-Division has developed we may mention Bindzil, a binding medium for carpets. The idea for this new product is related to the idea for Compozil, the paper chemical system which the TS-Division pioneered together with the VP-Division and which subsequently has been spun off to a new division, the PK-Division. Bindzil is technologically and in the market quite a new product. It was developed together with customers and a textile research institute. Another new product developed by the TS-division, Meta 5, was not as new from a technological standpoint and less unique on the market, but commercially very successful.

The TS-Division is relatively innovative in its strategy and performance, and this is reflected in its structure. It has more flexible production facilities and organizational procedures than the VP- and B-Divisions. It has, for instance, used flexible project teams to promote product development. Its organization structure is also characterized by less goal clarity, pre-planning and strict routines, than these other divisions. This is understandable, given its more searching and innovative strategy and greater emphasis on R & D, the results of which of course are difficult to perceive clearly in advance for use as a basis for detailed planning. There is less role clarity, that is greater ambiguity in perceived roles in the TS-Division than in the B- and VP-Divisions which could both facilitate and be the result of innovative change.

With regard to culture, the TS-Division is very strong on work enjoyment and market and customer orientation. It is also characterized by a relatively high preference for risk taking, but surprisingly enough competitiveness is not emphasized, despite the fact that it is working under tougher market conditions than the B- and VP-Divisions. It shows a very strong concern for profit, even stronger than in the case of the B-Division. This could be due to its taking a longer run view of profit, consistent with an innovative orientation, but it is not possible to judge this from the data. The fact that its culture is not as strong in emphasizing efficiency suggests such an interpretation. This seems more appropriate for a culture favoring innovation than does a focus on short run profitability.

The TS-Division does not seem to have a very strong culture for facilitating creativity and change. To achieve its relatively ambitious innovative strategy, it appears that a somewhat more supportive culture in this respect would have been desirable.

The climate of the TS-Division, on the other hand, seems more creative and favorable to innovation than does the culture. It has the highest value of all divisions for challenge, idea support, liveliness, playfulness and freedom to initiate. It has the second highest for richness of ideas, debate, peaceful working conditions, achievement orientation and risk taking. Together with the VP-Division it is highest in trust; it is second lowest in conflict after the VP-Division.

It would appear that the climate of the TS-Division is the most favorable for creativity and innovation in Eka, but looking at its results it is clear that it has not been able to live up to its potential to the same extent as the PK-Division, which we shall next present. Since actually innovating usually leads to substantial debate, conflict, disharmony and lack of trust, it is not surprising that the PK-Division—the performance of which has been most innovative—scores higher in these respects than the TS-Division. This division thus appears to have been less successful in realizing the innovative potential in its climate than it has in creating it.

The final division in Eka is the PK-Division. Since this, as we have noted above, is a relatively new division, formed to develop a new program of paper chemicals, Compozil, it is not surprising that our data shows it to be the most innovative division. Its origin was a joint research project carried out by the VP-Division and TS-Division with which it still has close ties.

The PK-Division is a good example of how external influences may lead to radical changes in an established line of business. The person who had been division head from the start to the time of our interviews came from the paper industry, where the main potential customers for Compozil were to be found. To begin with he was a consultant to Eka and a member of the joint divisional new product team that started to develop the new concept. Initially, this team had been formed to develop a new binding medium together with a customer firm. This effort was not successful and instead the interest turned to the development of new paper chemicals.

A number of coincidences led to Compozil. Shortly after Eka had started a pilot plant for silicic acid and wanted to find more applications for this product, Eka obtained an agency for a chemical which could be used for producing cationic starch to be used in making paper. Together with an expert consultant on silicic acid a number of ideas for using this starch in the paper industry were conceived. After a number of failures in the test production of paper by using the new ideas, the project group arrived at an application for filling fine paper, which was patented.

By combining cationic starch with silicic acid and other chemicals it proved possible to obtain a superior 'superfilled' fine paper, with a high content of substitutes for wood fibers. These substitutes are cheaper and therefore the process leads to cost reductions, but also to a higher quality paper in many respects, such as retention, dry strength, formation and drainage, compared to other methods for saving fiber.

The resulting paper chemical system, Compozil, was a new concept in the industry with potential for improving paper quality and lowering cost. It was, however, marketed too soon, which led to a number of disappointments. The potential market was overestimated as was the willingness of prospects to adopt the new process. It was initially not sufficiently adapted to market needs and a number of technical problems remained to be solved.

The division then changed its marketing strategy for Compozil and began to focus on customer specific applications and selling know-how, rather than on marketing the general process. This was more successful and soon a substantial and growing number of paper mills were using the chemical system. Some customers had even used the process to develop their own new products, such as a low weight bible paper and a better paper for pocket books.

The strategy and structure of the PK-Division are well in line with its highly innovative orientation. It has been very flexible in responding to customer demand and actively involved in persuading and training them to use its new concept for papermaking.

Its organization structure is characterized by poor clarity of goals and little pre-planning, which may be viewed as both the result of and facilitating factors for a creative, entrepreneurial style of decision-making, focusing more on action-based experimentation and learning than on advance planning. The PK-Division also has poor role clarity; that is, the employees are often uncertain as to what is expected of them, which is not surprising in a creative organization requiring a lot of self initiative.

The leadership style of the division head is entrepreneurial. He is highly intuitive, takes rapid decisions, is willing to take great risks and to experiment. He is a visionary activist who displays many of the qualities of creative leadership: flexibility, willingness to reconsider and tolerance of ambiguity. This leads to a high innovative potential in the division, but also to uncertainty and anxiety in less creative individuals.

At the same time the leader is non-authoritarian, listens to his staff, supports their ideas and initiatives and delegates responsibility for carrying out major decisions. His leadership is highly dynamic and displays both the positive and negative sides of promoting creative change.

This is as far as we can get in EKA from administrative stability and positional behavior and in the PK-Division these tendencies are encouraged by the Managing Director of EKA, who is aware of the need for this type of organized anarchy to achieve radical innovation.

When we look at the culture and climate of the PK-Division we find that the prevailing values and attitudes are also clearly related to a creative, entrepreneurial way of doing business. Risk taking is found as a cultural theme much more often than in the other divisions and together with competitiveness dominates the culture. Efficiency and profit are not stressed, which follows from the innovative focus of the division. Profits are a positional factor related to the present, while innovative organizations are future oriented and need not show immediate profit as long as they can maintain credibility as the money makers of tomorrow. Surprisingly enough, quality and customer orientation are not stressed either as basic values. Evidently the preoccupation with creativity and change is so strong that it dominates most cultural factors directly linked to performance, which are stressed in more positional business organizations.

PK's climate is richer than in any other division on risk taking, richness of ideas, debate and conflict. It is also quite rich in challenge, idea support, liveliness, playfulness and freedom. All these climate values are what might be expected in a highly creative and entrepreneurial organization. It is surprising, however, that the climate is not richer in achievement orientation. The very low value for peaceful working conditions is, on the other hand, understandable. Creativity and radical change are not very often linked to tranquility. For the low degree of trust displayed, it is more difficult to judge the implications. On the one hand, dynamic conditions may easily lead to a lack of trust between individuals, but on the other hand, creative organizations must learn to fight this tendency in order to perform well.

Compared to the TS-Division, the PK-Division shows somewhat lower values on some climatic dimensions, such as challenge, idea support, liveliness, playfulness and freedom. But the PK-Division is much better at creative performance.

This points to the conclusion that the TS-Division has not been utilizing its creative potential to the same extent as the PK-Division; this has not been necessary, given its more positional strategy. At the same time, it has been able to avoid many of the negative aspects of innovative performance such as conflicts and a certain lack of trust.

SUMMARY AND IMPLICATIONS

We may now compare the different divisions along a scale from most positional to most innovative with regard to strategy, structure, culture, climate and performance. As we have seen from the discussions, all the divisions seem to have a relatively good fit between these variables; that is, structures, cultures and climates that seem conducive to achieving the type of performance their strategies demand.

B	VP	TS	PK

Most positional   Most innovative

The B-Division has a clearly expressed positional strategy which has been realized in its business activities. Its major objective is to produce basic chemicals in a safe and efficient way and thereby create a basis for more innovative activities in other divisions. It has not been expected to do R & D on its own and has essentially lived up to this expectation. Its production and organization structure are well adapted for this purpose as well as its strategic leadership style stressing stability and predictability. Its culture and climate also show clear stability promoting elements emphasizing efficiency and control.

The VP-Division has a somewhat more innovative strategy, but essentially concentrates its efforts to a well-defined area of technology—based on hydrogen peroxide—and established markets. The main marketing efforts are directed towards strengthening its ties to existing customers by helping them to solve their technical problems. The production and organization structures are well adapted to this purpose.

While it displays more flexibility than in the B-Division, this division still is basically geared towards achieving stability in production and sales. Its culture and climate seem somewhat more creativity-inducing and it has been able to develop a number of successful new product applications within its established area of technological competence. Its culture and climate, while somewhat more change oriented than in the B-Division, seems much more to reflect the need for stability than for change. Its leadership, while less authoritarian than in the B-Division, appears to stress administrative efficiency rather than the need for innovation.

The TS-Division seems to be more mixed in its basic orientation than the other divisions. It displays relatively strong positional tendencies related to its established products, but also quite strong innovative efforts to develop new products and find new markets. It has been quite active and open in its search for and development of new areas of technology. Its structure has been more flexible and innovation permitting than in the VP-Division and its strategic leadership more aimed at actively promoting innovation.

The culture and climate of the TS-Division seem even more innovative than its strategy, structure and performance, and therefore may to some extent be viewed as an unrealized potential. They stress the positive aspects of creativity and change, such as freedom and playfulness, but there is less awareness of the negative aspects.

The PK-Division, finally, has been most innovative, which is not surprising since it is a recently established venture division. It has had no production of its own, which has made it possible for it to concentrate on its development activities. Since its leadership is highly entrepreneurial, focusing on new possibilities and rapid adaptation to action based learning, change has clearly been the policy of this division. This is also reflected in the flexible, somewhat ambiguous organization structure and highly challenging and risk-willing culture and exciting, but also stress-producing climate. In this division we clearly see both the positive and negative aspects of highly innovative performance, and the Managing Director of Eka has been aware of this and taken a calculated risk in promoting its activities.

Our study shows the need to consider not only technological and marketing strategies if we want to understand and influence company innovation. We also need to measure and to evaluate the effects of culture, climate and leadership styles. In the case of Eka, the ambition of top management was first to try to make all divisions more innovative, by changing their strategies. Our data show that this is probably not feasible if we cannot also change structure, culture, climate and strategic leadership, so that together they reinforce and make possible a more innovative total orientation and a more innovative performance.

By realizing that culture and climate are difficult to change in established organizational units, top management may then choose the more realistic course of letting more positional units basically maintain and strengthen their established activities.

Innovative efforts can instead be concentrated in established, more innovative units, if these exist, or in new organizational units with strong innovative potential. If these are built up based on entrepreneurial leadership, creative culture and climate and more flexible structures, the likelihood of achieving successful innovation is probably much greater than if attempts are made to force existing positional units to become more innovative.

There is a great need for a more balanced and comprehensive view of company innovation. The partial views usually presented in the management literature are unsatisfactory. Such a panoramic view will not permit simple conclusions and generalizations. It must be based on detailed studies of innovation in different types of companies. This research must consider the need for strategic management (to consider technological and market needs); organizational design (to allow for flexibility and change); and the management of culture and climate (to promote creativity and innovation). For this purpose, we must combine the thinking and techniques of management theory and practice with psychological theory and measurement to gain a more complete understanding of and basis for the influencing of company innovation.

*Knowledge development is the key to
the future*

13
A General Framework for Product and Company Development

In this chapter[1] a general framework for product and company development will be presented. The main components of this framework are a strategy development box and a knowledge development box. The strategy box illustrates the basic idea that companies may use different development strategies to succeed under different technological and market conditions. It also shows how companies with more closed and positional development strategies may achieve more open innovative strategies and more unique products from a technological and market point of view.

The knowledge development box is based on the interaction between product and company development, rather than on either one of these perspectives. It illustrates how companies can become more innovative by using more open strategies and transforming the resulting technological and marketing possibilities into new products, processes and marketable know-how.[2] They may do this by increasing their innovative potential in many ways and by creatively utilizing this potential, as we have discussed in more detail earlier in this book.

Innovative success is seen as dependent on the evolvement and generation of new knowledge and opportunities. More

255

so, than on the utilization of existing information to design the company and predesign offers to satisfy well defined market needs, which is the traditional economic management approach to product and company development.

THE STRATEGY DEVELOPMENT BOX

Our strategy development box is based on two main dimensions, the degree of technological innovation and the degree of market innovation for what the company has to offer to customers (Figure 13.1). To begin with we shall use the term

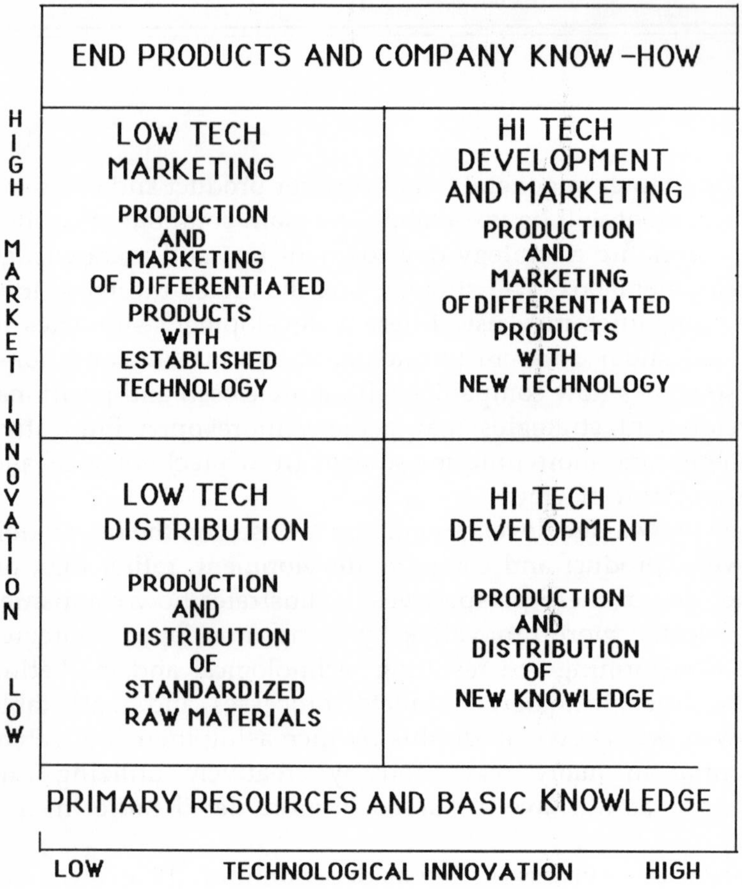

END PRODUCTS AND COMPANY KNOW-HOW

	LOW TECH MARKETING PRODUCTION AND MARKETING OF DIFFERENTIATED PRODUCTS WITH ESTABLISHED TECHNOLOGY	HI TECH DEVELOPMENT AND MARKETING PRODUCTION AND MARKETING OF DIFFERENTIATED PRODUCTS WITH NEW TECHNOLOGY
	LOW TECH DISTRIBUTION PRODUCTION AND DISTRIBUTION OF STANDARDIZED RAW MATERIALS	HI TECH DEVELOPMENT PRODUCTION AND DISTRIBUTION OF NEW KNOWLEDGE

HIGH MARKET INNOVATION LOW (left vertical axis)

PRIMARY RESOURCES AND BASIC KNOWLEDGE

LOW   TECHNOLOGICAL INNOVATION   HIGH

Figure 13.1 The strategy development box

product, as we have done earlier in this book, to refer to this output, but we must remember that the term product then refers to anything that may produce revenue. Later on in our knowledge development box we shall give a general definition of what we mean by the output of a company, but for our present purpose the above definition is sufficient.

Examples of products with a low level of both technological and market innovation, as we have defined these terms in Chapter 4, are, for instance, standardized raw materials, such as iron, steel, wood and wheat. With regard to this type of product, efficient production and distribution is the main concern of management. Prices tend to be highly competitive and overproduction often leads to surpluses, as we see in the agricultural area today. Supply and demand situations on the open market are usually erratic and difficult to predict. This often leads to efforts by companies to control sales, for instance, by using holding strategies, as we have seen in Chapter 9 in our discussion of marketing strategies in Swedish paper companies.

To obtain greater sales and profits, market and technological upgrading of products is usually viewed as desirable by companies dependent on products with low degrees of technological and market innovation. To achieve this objective and become more innovative, such companies need, however, to open up their marketing, organization and technological strategies. This, then, also requires that they increase their innovative potential by designing and implementing a more creative culture and climate and more flexible forms of production and distribution. This presents formidable obstacles to change for most positional companies. Swedish Farm and Forest Cooperatives, producing and distributing basic food and wood products, are examples of companies which rely on products with a low level of market and technological innovation for most of their business.

One way for these companies to achieve a competitive advantage is to try to increase their level of market innovation, without significantly increasing the level of technological innovation. This is the most common way in which positional companies try to improve their financial situation and the main route to success outlined in the marketing literature.

Essentially this type of low-tech marketing strategy requires companies to become more market oriented by differentiating and positioning their products to achieve competitive advantages. Thereby these companies, if successful in their efforts, may achieve more of a holding strategy and find market niches where their products are viewed as superior to competing ones.

Research intensity is in general very low in this type of company and mainly limited to perfecting existing technologies, rather than developing new ones. Technological strategies are usually very closed and based on in-house development and established knowledge, examples of what in this book are called isolated technology use and internal orientation. As we have seen in Chapters 10 and 11, this type of low-tech development strategy is almost the only strategy pursued by Swedish food processing companies, and the main development strategy for companies in the Swedish forest industry.

A more radical and innovative development strategy, on the other hand, implies achieving a high level of both technological and market innovation for new products. This strategy involves both high risk and high possibilities for growth and profit. It demands, as we have seen before, highly open and flexible technological, organization and marketing strategies and high research intensity to generate new knowledge.

Some companies in this hi-tech category devote upwards of 20% of sales to R & D while low-tech companies often spend less than 1%. Strategic ventures with buyers, universities, other firms or inventors are often used to achieve synergistic technology use and external orientation in development activities, as we have noted in Chapter 4. Company organization is very flexible and project based and both culture and climate challenging and risk rewarding.

By using this type of strategy several companies in our data, such as Pharmacia and Perstorp, have historically been able to change their products mix, to include many more products with a high level of technological and market innovation. Essentially this has meant going from basic chemicals for established uses to fine chemicals and chemical diagnosis for new applications. The result has been a strong and steady growth in sales and profits during the 1970s and 1980s.

Many less innovative companies with problems today should be able to achieve successful innovative growth by employing similar development strategies. Positional agroindustrial companies could for instance change in the direction of innovative pharmaceutical companies, either by emphasizing the medical value of food products or by utilizing their processes and raw materials for developing substances also for medical use. In our data we find several companies who are pursuing these possibilities, either alone or in cooperation with established pharmaceutical companies.

Pharmacia for instance finds the basic source for its eye operation substance, Healon, in rooster combs. This is supplied by a farmer/entrepreneur who has helped to breed a suitable stock of roosters with giant combs. This entrepreneur also uses eggs to produce antibodies for medical use and is actively involved in research to develop this technology in a venture company.

In our strategy development box we also find companies whose products are characterized by a high level of technological innovation, but a low level of market innovation. Usually they are independent inventors or research organizations, such as universities. Sometimes established companies have project groups or venture departments looking for new ideas without any obvious market applications, but this is not common even in companies that could afford to explore such possibilities.

New ideas and basic research are of dominating importance for this type of hi-tech development strategy, which is usually largely publicly funded to provide new knowledge for society as a whole. At the same time innovative companies are usually highly aware of the importance of this type of knowledge development for finding and developing radically new implicit technologies of commercial importance for their own business. The most successful hi-tech companies in our data have, as we have noted before, actively used external image marketing and creative and flexible ways to organize their relationships with the outside environment to attract and exploit radical new knowledge developed outside the company.

Areas such as medical diagnosis and genetic engineering

are examples today of basic research, which most companies usually cannot and do not want to carry out on their own. At the same time keeping up with and integrating the results of such research in their own development efforts is essential, if technological leadership is to be achieved and maintained in knowledge intensive industries.

Strategic ventures between companies and independent or university based researchers then become of major importance for finding new products in the outskirts of and intersections between existing areas of knowledge, as we have stressed many times before in this book. Inventors are other sources of new ideas which are difficult to incorporate in existing companies.

The potential for profit and growth can be great, however, as we have seen in Chapter 3, if entrepreneurs or intrapreneurs are present to project and transform the ideas into the top right segment of our strategic development box, characterized by products with high levels of both technological and market innovation. This then involves both building a creative culture and climate and a flexible organization and requires open strategies for developing, producing and marketing the new products.

THE KNOWLEDGE DEVELOPMENT BOX

In this section we shall set our framework for product and company development in a more general context to summarize and extend some of the main ideas. As we have argued before, it is more meaningful from a strategic management point of view to regard successful new products as the result of, rather than the reason for innovative company development. Trying to develop new products in companies without innovative potential is like angling in a lake without fish. Technological and market knowledge, competent personnel and leadership, a creative culture and climate and technological and marketing strategies for transforming this innovative potential to achieve successful company and product development are the main strategic issues focused on in our approach.

Exactly what new products will be the result is of less interest, the main requirement is that they are successful. This means that traditional models for product development and management are of limited interest from a strategic management point of view. They require that we identify in advance the specific characteristics of new products we are interested in. This is not possible in highly innovative situations when we do not know what products will emerge, but can create favourable conditions for their appearance.

Knowledge development is the key to the future. Although we cannot read what is written tomorrow we can gather experience and try to visualize and influence what will happen. Innovative companies are like artists in the sense that they do not only reflect the present, but also help to determine the future.

We can summarize the above in what we may call the knowledge development box (Figure 13.2). This illustrates how companies may choose either a relatively closed and

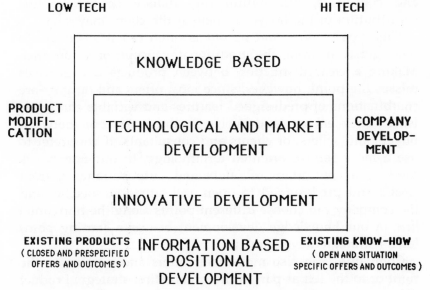

Figure 13.2 The knowledge development box

static, information based development pattern, what we have called a positional strategy, or a more open and dynamic, knowledge based innovative strategy.

Instead of focusing on products, the knowledge development box views the results of company development in terms of marketable offers and output. The horizontal dimension in the diagram shows how closed and predesigned or open and situation specific these offers are. To the far left we find the type of offer and output assumed in traditional economic theory, that is standardized products the characteristics of which are predetermined and the same for all customers.

To the far right we find open, situation specific offers and outputs, related to company know-how, the final design of which are determined in interaction with customers or clients. The basic design is usually, but not always set in advance, but the precise way in which a company contributes to customer satisfaction depends on the specific requirements of individual buyers and the ways in which companies can fulfill these requirements. If an individual, for instance, uses a lawyer to make a contract, the overall design of the professional work is given by legal and commercial practice and consensus, but within this framework the specific contribution of the lawyer to benefit the client may vary.

This type of offer and output is often called a service[3] to distinguish it from the traditional concept of a product. Making a clear distinction between products and services misses the point, however, since most offers and outputs are combinations of predesigned features and variable character-istics. They emerge and evolve in the interaction between buyers and sellers, or clients and consultants, if we prefer to use a more service oriented terminology. In our framework there is a continuum of offers and outputs ranging from closed and predesigned to open and situation specific, and the company can choose different points along the horizontal line in our knowledge development box as a starting point for its strategic development.

Companies can also move their offers and outputs to the right or to the left as part of their marketing strategy. Product differentiation, for instance, in this framework means moving from the far left towards the right, by making offers and outputs more open and better adapted to specific buyers or market segments. At the same time, companies with offers and outputs far to the right can make them more closed and predesigned, to achieve better planning and efficiency in carrying out business.

An example of this is McDonald's success in turning a more open situation specific offer and output into a more closed and predesigned one by specifying in detail what a hamburger is and what the customer can demand in terms of extra benefits. Thereby McDonald's has achieved better economy in preparing and marketing its meals, while the customer has given up his right to choose in order to gain a lower price.

Moving sideways in the knowledge development box is a positional strategy in our framework. Companies try to do better what they already are doing, and there is no radical technological or market innovation involved. Essentially, this is a question of using marketing to focus the existing business of a company to achieve more efficient production and distribution.

There is little need with this type of strategy for basic research to develop new technologies, and therefore more closed technological strategies based on internal orientation and isolated technology use are usually quite appropriate. In this case, management is mainly directed towards refining existing knowledge and the primary development requirement is for information about given conditions. A highly creative company climate and culture and an entrepreneurial leadership style can then generate frustration, rather than enthusiasm, and should be avoided if the company is not willing to commit itself to a more innovative strategy.

At the same time companies employing highly positional development strategies can be quite successful if strategic conditions remain stable and they are able to control their markets, as our studies of food processing companies and pulp and paper companies in Chapters 9–11 show.

The vertical dimension in our knowledge development box refers to strategic management, which means the extent to which companies employ innovative strategies for developing new technologies and markets. In contrast to the operational management of existing resources and knowledge, which the horizontal dimension denotes, the vertical dimension is concerned with the generation and utilization of radically new knowledge.

The traditional management approach to product development essentially means that companies try to move almost directly upwards in our diagram, by improving existing products. This may involve substantial R & D efforts and radical technological change, but as long as the basic design and market characteristics of the product are retained, we shall call this product modification, rather than new product development. Product modification is the major type of product development in established companies and one of the main strategic issues in this book, as we have seen for instance in Chapter 4.

Open technological and marketing strategies and creative and flexible company culture, climate and organization, may be expected to lead to products and services with high degrees of technological and market innovation. The desirable degree of openness and the need for creativity and flexibility is reduced, however, when companies mainly want to improve their existing offers, and can do so by more closed, internal and concentrated development of their existing areas of competence. The need for new knowledge and external orientation is less in these situations, than when companies want to develop radically new technologies and markets, but new technological combinations are still desirable to build and maintain technological leadership within the companies' established fields.

The most radical and innovative development strategies are shown in our knowledge development box by diagonal development patterns. Companies which move from the lower left to the upper right, for instance, emphasize knowledge development in the company as a whole and if successful are able both to develop products and services with high degrees of technological and market innovation (that is which are highly unique both from a technological and market point of view) and also satisfy the specific technological needs of individual customers. They then become providers of high technology both in hardware and software, and consultants as well as sellers of traditional products.

Exactly what new product they will succeed in developing depends on their own knowledge development, as well as on the support they can gain from the environment. External orientation—development help from outside experts such as universities, other companies and qualified buyers—becomes of crucial importance for achieving and maintaining technological and market leadership. In some instances the borderline, from a development point of view, between a company and its outside environment becomes so difficult to maintain that joint ventures for developing and marketing new products and technologies are organized as separate companies.

The need for creative climates, cultures and entrepreneurial leadership is obvious in this type of company, but not easy to achieve, as we have seen in Chapter 12. Recruitment is used as one of the means to broaden the knowledge base and increase the innovative potential. Flexible project groups are used to fuse creative contributions together and make possible creative leadership.

The main concern of strategic management in this type of company is to develop the overall knowledge and competence of its personnel and use internal and external marketing to focus this knowledge. There is also a great need to eliminate technical and organizational restrictions on using these resources creatively, and to provide entrepreneurial leadership to break down existing barriers and point the way to the desired future; in this case product development is company development, and company development is knowledge development. Companies which realize this are better able to innovate; that is, create the future, rather than adapt to present conditions, which tomorrow may no longer exist.

SUMMARY OF MAIN IDEAS

In this final section the main ideas in our approach to strategic management and strategies for product and company development will be summarized.

- Strategic management means managing the future.

- Realized strategy is the actual evolving pattern of decisions and activities. In strategic management we need to be more concerned with actual results (realized strategy) than with policy issues (intended strategy).

- We need to consider both company strategy and product strategy—and the interaction between the two—in strategic management.

- Company strategy should deal more with the configuration and orientation of an enterprise than with its marketable results. The more innovative a company is, or wants to be, the more necessary this becomes.

- Product strategy should deal both with existing products and the possibility of finding new products. The balance between these types of activities reflects how innovative the intended product strategy of a company is.

- Image management and innovation management are basic strategic mechanisms for realizing the future.

- Image and innovation are challenging terms—they challenge our imagination and way of doing things.

- Images—visions and ideas—are our guides when venturing into the unknown. They are also implicit promises which companies make to obtain development resources.

- Innovation is the creation of the future—the process of bringing new ideas into use. It is the generation, acceptance and implementation of new ideas, processes and products.

- Image and innovation are closely linked to creativity and entrepreneurship—the elusive but decisive ability to break out of existing patterns of thought and behavior. The entrepreneur is seen as a visionary activist enacting strategy by directly influencing strategic conditions and outcomes.

- Image management is closely related to marketing strategy and innovation management to technological strategy.

- Marketing is viewed as the activities that relate an organization successfully to its environment. It is mainly concerned with relationship management and the focusing and integration of internal and external opportunities. Marketing strategies may be more open and diversified, stressing products and customers, or more closed and concentrated, emphasizing new products and customer groups.

- Technology means knowledge that is potentially useful for product and company development, although the immediate implications may not be clear. This stresses the open possibilities implied by knowledge, rather than the closed applications we may call techniques. Open aspects of technological strategy stressed in our approach are combining existing technologies in new ways and strategic ventures (cooperation with, for instance, customers, other companies, universities or outside inventors) to broaden the technological base of a company. This requires organizational flexibility both within a company and in relation to its external environment.

- Hi-tech companies are defined as innovative companies which use open and offensive technological and marketing strategies to achieve high levels of market and technological innovation; that is, unique new products from a technological and market point of view.

- Low-tech companies are defined as positional companies which use closed and defensive technological and marketing strategies to maintain competitive advantages with existing products and technologies.

- Company culture and climate are viewed as crucial links between intended and realized strategy. Challenging, creative cultures and climates are necessary for the successful implementation of innovative strategies.

Notes

NOTES TO CHAPTER 1

1 Boulding, 1956.
2 What in this book is called static image management is often discussed in the literature in relation to corporate image, for instance in the context of corporate communication and corporate advertising. Bernstein, 1984. A static concept of image management (concerned with buyer perceptions) is also used in the consumer marketing literature, for instance when dealing with product positioning. See Wind, 1982, Chapter 4.
3 Schon, 1967, p. 132. Similarly Shackle, a highly unconventional economic theorist, speaks of the 'pleasure of the imagination' and 'enjoyment by anticipation' as what decision makers want to maximize, 1958, p. 41f. He suggests that the intensity of a decision-maker's enjoyment will be greater the more brilliant the success he can visualize as the outcome of his decision.
4 *cf.* Normann, 1977, p. 97.
5 Drucker, 1985, p. 17.
6 Schumpeter, 1934, p. 91.
7 Schumpeter, 1934, p. 89.
8 In Sweden, Chalmers University in Gothenburg has been particularly active in innovation research and promoting innovation, leading for instance to university spinoffs in new areas of technology. Innovation research has also been carried out, in addition to the research reported on in this book, for instance in Lund at the Science Policy Research department. In Denmark, The Technological Institute at Tostrup has been a center of management research and teaching in creativity and product development for many years. (See Arleth, 1981, and Graversen and Trolle, 1983). In England, The Science Policy Research Unit at the University of Sussex has a long

tradition of carrying out innovation research and Manchester Business School has provided facilities for creativity and innovation research for many years. In the US, Stanford University, for instance, has given a course 'Creativity in Business' since the early 1980s (Ray and Meyers, 1989). The Center for Creative Leadership, Greensboro and the Center for Studies in Creativity, Buffalo, are examples of American organizations doing research on and giving courses in creativity. At Babson College in Massachusetts there is a center for entrepreneurial studies. Many technical universities in the US, such as MIT, give courses on the management of technology and similar courses are given by universities in other countries, for instance in Scandinavia.

9   See, for instance, Chandler, 1962; Rumelt, 1975; and Miles and Snow, 1978.

10   Miles and Snow, 1978, p. 282.

11   See Nyström 1970, p. 50; Minztberg, 1976, p. 2; and Quinn, 1980, p. 9f, for this view of realized strategy as a pattern in a stream of decisions.

12   The term Scandinavian approach to management is used in this book to refer to the management literature by writers with Swedish, Norwegian or Danish as their basic language. It includes the writing in Finland by people with Swedish as their first language. Some typical examples of the Scandinavian approach to management, within the area of interest of this book, are Nyström, 1970; Sandkull, 1970; Rhenman, 1973; Valdelin 1974; Brodin, 1976; Holt, 1977; Melin, 1977; Normann, 1977; Gadde, 1978; Arndt, 1979; Brege, 1979; Granstrand, 1979; Nyström, 1979a; Vedin, 1980; Edvardsson, 1981; Hägg and Johansson, 1982; Hammarkvist, Håkansson and Mattsson, 1982; Håkansson, 1982; Sjölander, 1983; Arndt and Friman, 1983; Brunsson, 1985; Grönroos, 1985; Grönroos and Gummesson, 1985; Kristensen, 1985; Sveiby and Risling, 1986; Benndorf, 1987; Brege and Brandes, 1987; Ekvall, Arvonen and Nyström, 1987; Åhgren, 1987; Edvardsson and Gummesson, 1988; Liljegren, 1988; Lindell, 1988.

13   This empirical work is reported in Nyström, 1977a, 1979a, 1979b, 1979c, 1980, 1985a, 1985b, 1985c, 1986; Nyström and Edvardsson, 1978, 1980a b, 1982, 1986; Edvardsson, 1981; Nyström and Åhgren, 1983, 1984; Nyström, Hellström and Åhgren, 1986; Åhgren, 1987; Ekvall, Nyström and Waldenström, 1983; Ekvall, Arvonen and Nyström, 1987; Nyström and Willén, 1987; Lagerström and Nyström, 1987; Edvardsson, Edvinsson and Nyström, 1988.

14   Nyström, 1970 and Nyström, Tamsons and Thams, 1975.

NOTES TO CHAPTER 2

1 Glazer and Strauss, 1967, provide a methodological framework for empirically grounded theory development.

2 Kerin and Peterson, 1980, give a number of perspectives on strategic marketing management.

3 Little, 1981, deals with the strategic management of technology.

4 Tushman and Moore, 1982, contains a large number of articles on innovation management. Managing technological innovation is dealt with in Twiss, 1974.

5 The basic model distinguishing between positional and innovative companies as ideal categories was first presented in a Swedish article (Nyström, 1971). The ideas were further developed in a broad organizational context in a Swedish book on company creativity and innovation (Nyström, 1974b). A revised and expanded version of this book was later published in English (Nyström, 1979a). See also Nyström, 1983. The distinction between positional and innovative companies has subsequently been used by, for instance, Vedin, 1980; Parker, 1982; Johne, 1985; and Ekvall, Arvonen and Nyström, 1987; as a basis for empirical studies of company innovation.

6 Leavitt, 1986. His book deals with a number of issues relating to corporate pathfinders, viewed as visionary managers using imaginative strategies to shape the future of their companies.

7 Burns and Stalker, 1961, p. 96ff.

8 Kanter, 1983. This book deals with the need for an American corporate renaissance and change masters (corporate entrepreneurs) to achieve such a transformation.

9 Kanter, 1983, p. 28.

10 Kanter, 1983, p. 27.

11 See, for instance, Lawrence and Lorsch, 1967; Khandvalla, 1977; and Pfeffer, 1978.

12 For concept of psychological positioning see Ries and Trout, 1981.

13 Smith, 1956, is the classical reference for this distinction.

14 Porter, 1980, p. 35. In a later book (Porter, 1985) he extends his basically static framework to consider, for instance, technology strategy and interrelationships among business units.

15 Utterback and Abernathy, 1975, discuss product and process changes over the product life cycle.

16 Riggs, 1983, p. 1.

17 Gupta, Ray and Wilemon, 1985, deals with R & D and marketing dialogue in hi-tech firms, based on an empirical study of more than 200 R & D and marketing managers.

18   Shanklin and Ryans, Jr, 1984, stress technological and market change in their book on marketing high technology.
19   Gupta, Ray and Wilemon, 1985, p. 290.
20   Gupta, Ray and Wilemon, 1985, p. 289.
21   Originally technological strategy was the focus of our empirical studies of strategies for product and company development. Later studies have emphasized marketing strategies and the strategic relationship between technology and marketing.
22   Nyström, 1970, p. 50.
23   See, for instance, Glueck, 1972; and Wind, 1982.
24   Nyström, 1970, p. 50.
25   Nyström, 1970.
26   Mintzberg, 1972, p. 2.
27   Nyström, 1979a, p. 7.
28   See, for instance, Thompson, Strickland and Fulmer, 1987, for a variety of articles on strategic management.
29   Kerin and Peterson, 1980, contains a number of articles on strategic marketing.
30   Brown and Oxenfeldt, 1972, p. 3.
31   Thompson, 1969, p. 5.
32   Myers and Marquis, 1969, p. 1.
33   Crawford, 1983, p. 44.
34   Weick, 1969, deals with the process of organization and how organization emerges. His view of the 'enacted environment' is consistent with our view of company creativity and innovation and entrepreneurship as learning by doing. Galbraith and Nathanson, 1978, discuss organizational processes for implementing strategy and the relationships between strategy and structure without, however, considering company culture and climate.
35   cf. Schein, 1984.
36   Payne and Pugh, 1976, discusses the concept and measurement of organizational climate.
37   Hughes, 1978, p. 3.
38   See Speckman and Johnston, 1986, for a conceptual approach to relationship management, viewed as the handling of the selling and buying interface of a company.
39   Abel and Hammond, 1979. This book presents and discusses three formal approaches to strategic market planning, portfolio analysis, market attractiveness—business position analysis and PIMS (the use of pooled business experience). Portfolio analysis is used to refer to the Boston Consulting Group model.
40   Abel and Hammond, 1979, p. 173ff; see also Day, 1977.
41   This term was first used in Nyström, 1977c.

42 Nyström, 1970, p. 119ff.
43 *cf.* Salancik and Porac, 1986, p. 76, 'We believe that people understand complex causal structures well because they distill meaning holistically rather than as a mass of bivariate associations.'
44 Skinner, 1982, p. 464.
45 See Blake, 1978, p. 16, for this view of R & D strategy.
46 For the generally accepted view of marketing see, for instance, Cox, Alderson and Shapiro, 1964; and Hunt, 1976.
47 See, for instance, Hippel, 1978, on the importance of customer ideas for successful new industrial products.
48 Hippel, 1976, shows the dominant role of users in the scientific instrument industry.
49 See Nyström, 1979a, p. 73.
50 Nyström, 1979a, p. 74.

NOTES TO CHAPTER 3

1 This chapter is mainly based on Nyström, 1979a, 1985a, 1987, 1988a; and Ekvall, Nyström and Waldenström-Lindblad, 1983.
2 For some discussions of different definitions of the word entrepreneur see Casson, 1982; Hyrenius, 1983; Davidsson, 1989; and Cohen, 1989.
3 Kirzner, whose definition of entrepreneurship is not very radical, nevertheless states that, 'the orthodox theory of the firm completely ignores the very possibility of and need for entrepreneurship' (1973–84). Similarly, Casson states that there is, 'no established economic theory of the entrepreneur' and that, 'almost all the social sciences have a theory of the entrepreneur, except economics' (1982–9).
4 Schumpeter, 1934. Among Scandinavian economists Dahmén, 1970, 1982, has been the leading advocate of Schumpeterian ideas.
5 Klein, 1977, p. 29.
6 Kirzner, 1973, p. 29.
7 Casson, 1982, discusses the role of the entrepreneur in economic theory.
8 See Peters and Waterman, 1982, for their view on how a number of large American companies appear to have increased their organizational potential for innovation. Their work is largely based on the Seven S framework, used by the management consulting firm, McKinsey & Co. The seven variables are structure, strategy, skills, staff, style, systems and shared values.

9   Kanter, 1983, focuses on how 'change masters' have achieved innovative organizational change.

10 Hickman and Silva, 1984, emphasize the need for creative leadership and insight in managing change.

11 Drucker, 1985, describes six main sources for innovation, the unexpected, incongruities, process need, industry and market structures, demographics, changes in perception, and new knowledge.

12 For an overview of the general creativity literature, see Andersson, 1959; Taylor and Barron, 1963; Cropley, 1967; Vernon, 1970; and Isaksen, 1987. Organizational creativity is dealt with in Steiner, 1965; and Crosby, 1968. An early highly stimulating book on the creative process is Koestler, 1964. Popularly written and pragmatic books concerned with creativity include de Bono, 1971; Adams, 1979; Parnes, 1981; Miller, 1987; and Ray and Myers, 1986. In Sweden, interesting research on creativity has been carried out by Ekvall, 1972, 1988.

13 May, 1959, p. 55, states that the subject of creativity was generally avoided in academic psychology during the first half of this century as 'unscientific, mysterious, disturbing and too corruptive of the scientific training of graduate students'.

14 Bolton, 1972, discusses different views of thinking in psychological theory.

15 Rokeach, 1960, provides a broad coverage of issues related to dogmatic thinking and closed belief systems.

16 Wertheimer, 1959, one of the founders of the gestalt approach to psychology, presents a wholistic view of 'productive', that is creative thinking, based partly on studies of Einstein's thought processes.

17 Bruner, 1965, p. 112, speaks about the 'smashability of a theory', the extent to which it is corrigible or incorrigible.

18 See Nyström, 1974a, for a discussion of the role of intuition for decision making.

19 Rogers, 1959.

20 A famous discussion of the creative process is Poincaré, 1913. See also Wallas, 1926, for his often-cited model of the different stages.

21 Drucker, 1985, p. 17.

22 Knight, 1921, views profit as the entrepreneur's reward for accepting uncertainty. This is consistent with our approach, which, however, focuses more on the handling than on the acceptance of uncertainty. Kay, 1979, p. 17, states that, 'uncertainty is the dominant consideration in analysis of the innovative process, and that it is the influence and implications of uncertainty for decisionmaking that have to be focused on in constructing models of innovation'.

23 See Pinchot, 1985; and Duncan, Ginter, Rucks and Jacobs, 1988.

NOTES TO CHAPTER 4

1 Most of the concepts and ideas in this chapter originate in the exploratory research summarized in Nyström, 1979a. In Sweden early research on technology management, based on R & D strategies and the organization of R & D in a number of large Swedish companies, has also been carried out by Granstrand, 1979. He concludes that 'R & D policies were generally vague and loosely connected to corporate policies, as were considerations of patterns of technological development and sources of innovation' (p. 162). This points to the need for an operational framework for empirically measuring and evaluating actual patterns of technological change and relating these to overall product and company development as a guide for strategic management. Working towards such a framework is our overall research objective.

2 In Sweden, industrial technological development has been studied with interesting results by a number of researchers using a network approach. See Håkansson and Laage-Hellman, 1984; Håkansson, 1987; Hägg and Johansson, 1982. Like us, they stress cooperation strategies and the need for companies to interact widely with their outside environment in managing innovation and developing new products. They use the term extrovert/introvert strategy to refer to our dimension external/internal orientation, but do not consider our other main dimension of technological strategy, technology use. Neither do they try to measure directly the strategy or to relate strategic dimensions to innovative performance, which is one of our main objectives. Instead, their work is essentially descriptive, rather than normative, and mainly based on case study data to illustrate the reasoning rather than evaluate the outcome of strategic choice.

3 See Langrisch, Gibbons, Evans and Jevons, 1972, p. 6, Uhlmann, 1977, p. 23; and Zaltman, Duncan and Holbek, 1973, p. 7.

4 Utterback, 1977.

5 Bhalla, 1987, p. 170, presents a model of technological development, distinguishing between existing, key and emerging technologies.

6 See Nyström, 1979a, Chapter 3.

7 Vedin, 1980, p. 96.

8 Vedin, 1980, p. 88.

9 See for instance Pessimier, 1966. Wind, 1982, gives an overview of models and formal techniques for product screening and program evaluation, such as Risk-Return Analysis, PERT (Program Evaluation and Review) and CPM (Critical Path Method). Little, 1974, states that only 17 out of 436 new products he had studied had been initiated by a formal market research study.

NOTES TO CHAPTER 5

1 This chapter is based on Nyström and Edvardsson, 1978 and 1980b.
2 Achilladelis, Jervis and Robertson, 1971.
3 Langrish, Gibbons, Evans and Jevons, 1972.
4 Gerstenfeld, 1977.
5 Utterback, Allen, Holloman and Sirbu, 1976.
6 Hippel, 1976.
7 See for instance Jewkes, Sawers and Stillerman, 1958; Lindström, 1972; Freeman, 1974; and Davidsson, 1989.

NOTES TO CHAPTER 6

1 The basic ideas in this chapter have their origin in Nyström, 1970, 1985d and 1988b.
2 Our view of the role of image for organizational decision making is similar to that employed by Mitchell, Rediker and Beach, 1986, in their outline for a new descriptive theory of decision making, which they call image theory. This approach assumes that decision makers have images of themselves, their pasts, their presents, and their futures. They mostly look at the paths that are open to them in terms of how well they fit these images and they adopt those paths that are congruent with the images and reject those that are incongruent (p. 296).
3 See Alderson, 1969, p. 2.
4 Hughes, 1978, is typical of this approach to marketing management.
5 Green, 1964, discusses the usefulness of information measures in marketing. See also Hogarth, 1980, p. 53ff.
6 See Cohen and Cyert, 1965, for a summary of traditional and newer approaches to the economic theory of the firm.
7 Katona, 1969, deals with the contribution of psychology to consumer analysis in economic theory.
8 See Hill and Hlavacek, 1972; Burgelman, 1985; and Bart, 1988.
9 Nyström, 1970, p. 111 ff.
10 The role of image for service marketing is emphasized in Onkvisit and Shaw, 1989. See also Normann, 1983, Chapter 8, and Grönroos, 1985, p. 40 ff.
11 See Gummesson, 1977, for a discussion of marketing professional services, such as consulting.
12 Nyström, 1985.
13 For the marketing mix concept see Borden, 1969.
14 See McCarthy, 1960, for the 4 Ps model of marketing.

NOTES TO CHAPTER 7

1 This chapter is mainly based on Nyström, 1970; and Nyström, Tamsons and Thams, 1979. The former reference contains a much more detailed discussion of the issues dealt with in this chapter, and many more references to the relevant literature.

2 The treatments of retail pricing most similar to our approach are Holdren, 1960, and Nelson and Preston, 1966. Neither of these approaches deal systematically with psychological management and the role of image in influencing behavior.

3 Generalization is not used by us in the special psychological sense of stimulus or response generalization. The former term refers to the fact that a given response can be elicited to some degree by a range of similar stimuli. The latter applies to the fact that the same stimulus can be shown to produce a range of responses. As we use the term, generalization refers to the generalization from one cognitive element or structure to another, which is in some sense subjectively related. Discrimination is used to refer to distinguishing between different cognitive elements to achieve a more detailed level of analysis. It is not used in the socio-economic sense of treating individuals differently, implied for instance by the term price discrimination.

4 See Oxenfeldt, 1975, for a broad treatment of pricing.

5 Nyström, 1970, Chapter 8.

6 Nyström, Tamsons and Thams, 1979.

NOTES TO CHAPTER 8

1 This chapter is mainly based on Nyström, 1977b, where the distinction between horizontal and vertical complexity and competitive versus holding strategies was first presented. These ideas have been empirically tested in a number of studies of the wood and paper industry in Sweden (Nyström and Åhgren, 1983, 1984; Nyström, Hellström and Åhgren, 1986).

2 See for instance, Porter, 1980.

3 In Sweden, the importance of looking at buyer–seller interaction as a basis for understanding marketing relationships has been stressed by a number of researchers, particularly those associated with the IMP group in Uppsala (Håkansson, Johansson and Wootz, 1977; Hallén, 1979; Håkansson and Wootz, 1979). Their ideas have been further developed in an international project, involving also researchers from the UK, France, Germany and Italy—Håkansson,

1982. This work focuses on what we call holding strategies, and stresses the fact that relationships tend to be stable over a period of time. It is mainly descriptive and does not try to relate strategy and strategy changes explicitly and operationally to explanatory mechanisms and success, which is our main objective. Neither is the need to balance competitive action and buyer–seller interaction dealt with in their approach, which limits its usefulness from a strategic management point of view. Other Swedish researchers emphasizing the role of stable relationships for stabilizing demand and exchanging information are Melin, 1977; and Gadde, 1978. A balanced discussion of marketing strategy is Brege, 1979. He concludes that while stable relationships are most important in this industry, changes in relationships for competitive reasons also must be considered.

In the US, relatively little attention has been paid in the marketing literature to collaborative, compared to competitive, relationships. In recent years, however, the importance of relationship management for industrial marketing has been more widely recognized (Jackson, 1985; Spekman and Johnston, 1986). One reason for this may be the growing awareness that Japanese companies are better than American ones at handling long term relationships, Ouchi, 1981. But again, the balance between collaborative and competitive action is usually not focused on, while it is the basis for our approach, not only to industrial but also to consumer marketing.

4   A model for developer/adopter relationships in new industrial product situations, focusing on negotiation involving information and resource flows, is presented in More, 1986.

5   See Håkansson and Östberg, 1975; and Johnston and Bonoma, 1981.

6   A comprehensive treatment of market segmentation is Frank, Massy and Wind, 1972. See also Arndt, 1974.

7   Webster, 1979, p. 73, states that the most important decision an industrial firm makes is the selection of its customers.

8   An an overview of classical oligopoly theory see Fellner, 1949.

9   Chamberlin, 1962.

10   See Marsh, 1974; Rubin and Brown, 1975; and McCall and Warrington, 1984.

11   See Evan, 1966; Terryberry, 1968; and Aldrich, 1972.

12   Webster and Wind, 1972, discuss organizational buyer behavior in relation to marketing strategy. Bonoma, Zaltman and Johnston, 1977, present a framework for analyzing industrial buying behavior and a review of the relevant literature.

NOTES TO CHAPTER 9

1 This chapter is mainly based on Nyström, 1977b and Nyström and Åhgren, 1983.
2 *cf.* Williamsson, 1975; who discusses how internal organization may be substituted for market mediated exchange.
3 Nyström and Åhgren, 1983, 1984; Nyström, Hellström and Åhgren, 1986.
4 Nyström and Åhgren, 1983.
5 Brege, 1979, is a descriptive case study of a Swedish diversified wood processing company, Fiskeby, which utilizes our distinction between holding and competitive strategies, but does not try to directly relate strategy to outcome.

NOTES TO CHAPTER 10

1 This chapter is based on Nyström and Edvardsson, 1982, 1986.
2 Some major references are Pessimier, 1977; Choffray and Lilien, 1980; Urban and Hauser, 1980; Wind, 1982; Cooper, 1986; and Crawford, 1987. Of these, Cooper and Crawford are the most interesting from a strategic management point of view.

NOTES TO CHAPTER 11

1 This chapter is based on Nyström, 1985c.

NOTES TO CHAPTER 12

1 This chapter is mainly based on Ekvall, Arvonen and Nyström, 1987, Chapters 6, 7 and 10.
2 For instance, Weber, 1947; Burns and Stalker, 1961; and Aiken and Hage, 1970.
3 Ansoff, 1984, provides an overview of the strategic management literature and a bibliography.
4 Ekvall, Arvonen and Nyström, 1987.
5 See Deal and Kennedy, 1982; and Schein, 1984.
6 Compare Payne and Pugh, 1976 and James and Jones, 1984.
7 Ekvall, Arvonen and Waldenström-Lindblad, 1983; and Ekvall and Arvonen, 1984.

NOTES TO CHAPTER 13

1 Many of the ideas in this chapter were first presented in Nyström, 1985d, 1987, 1988b.
2 cf. Sveiby and Riesling, 1986; and Sveiby and Lloyd, 1987.
3 See Grönroos, 1985, p. 19 ff, for a discussion of how service is defined in the service management literature.

Bibliography

Abel, D.F. and Hammond, J.S. (1979) *Strategic Market Planning*, Englewood Cliffs, Prentice-Hall.

Achilladelis, B., Jervis, P. and Robertson, A. (1971) *Report on Project Sappho*, Sussex, Science Policy Institute.

Adams, J.L. (1979) *Conceptual Blockbusting*, New York, Norton and Company.

Aiken, M. and Hage, J. (1970) *Social Change in Complex Organizations*, New York, Random House.

Alderson, W. (1969) 'The analytical framework for marketing.' In Enis, B.M. and Cox, K.K. (eds), *Marketing Classics*, pp. 2–15, Boston, Allyn and Bacon.

Aldrich, H.E. (1972) *Organizations and Environments*, Englewood Cliffs, Prentice-Hall.

Andersson, H.H. (ed.) (1959) *Creativity and its Cultivation*, New York, Harper & Row.

Åhgren, U. (1987) *Strategisk marknadsföringsmix—konkurrens och uppbindning i svenska skogsindustriföretag*. Uppsala, Institute for Economics.

Ansoff, H.I. (1984) *Implanting Strategic Management*, Englewood Cliffs, Prentice-Hall.

Arleth, J. (1981) *Planlägning af nye produkter*, Tåstrup, Teknologisk Institut.

Arndt, J. (1974) *Market Segmentation*, Oslo.

Arndt, J. (1979) 'Toward a concept of domesticated markets', *Journal of Marketing*, **43**, 69–75.

Arndt, J. and Friman, A. (eds) (1983) *Intern Marknadsföring*, Malmö, Liber.

Bart, C.K. (1988) 'New venture units: use them wisely to manage innovation', *Sloan Management Review*, No. 4, 35–43.

Benndorf, H. (1987) *Marknadsföringsplanering och samordning mellan företag i industriella system*, Stockholm School of Economics.

Bernstein, D. (1984) *Company Image and Reality*, Eastbourne, Holt, Rinehart and Winston.

Bhalla, S.K. (1987) *The Effective Management of Technology*, Reading, Addison-Wesley.

Blake, S.P. (1978) *Managing for Responsive Research and Development*, San Francisco, Freeman.

Bolton, N. (1972) *The Psychology of Thinking*, London, Methuen.

Bonoma, T.V., Zaltman, G. and Johnston, W.J. (1977) *Industrial Buying Behavior*, Cambridge, Marketing Science Institute.

Borden, N.H. (1969) 'The concept of the marketing mix'. In Enis, B.M. and Cox, K.K. (eds), *Marketing Classics*, pp. 365–367, Boston, Allyn and Bacon.

de Bono, E. (1971) *Lateral Thinking for Management*, Maidenhead, McGraw-Hill.

Boulding, K.E. (1956) *The Image*, Ann Arbor, University of Michigan Press.

Brandes, O. and Brege, S. (1987) *Nytt strategiskt tänkande—en studie av svenska storföretags förnyelse efter 70-tals krisen*, Linköping Economic Institute at the University of Linköping.

Brege, S. (1979) *Marknadsförändring och företagsstrategi—från produktionsorientering till marknadsorientering*, Linköping, Economic Institute at the University of Linköping.

Brodin, B. (1976) *Produktutvecklingsprocesser. En studie ur marknadsföringssynvinkel av produktutveckling i svenska företag*. Stockholm School of Economics.

Brown, F.E. and Oxenfeldt, A.R. (1972) *Misperceptions of Economic Phenomena*, New York, Sperr and Douth.

Bruner, J.S. (1965) 'Some observations on effective cognitive processes'. In Steiner, G.A. (ed.), *The Creative Organization*, pp. 106–117, Chicago, University of Chicago Press.

Brunsson, N. (1985) *The Irrational Organization*, New York, John Wiley & Sons.

Burgelman, R.A. (1985) 'Managing the new venture division: research findings and implications for strategic management', *Strategic Management Journal*, January–March, 39–54.

Burns, T. and Stalker, G.M. (1961) *The Management of Innovation*, London, Tavistock.

Casson, M. (1982) *The Entrepreneur. An Economic Theory*, Oxford, Robertson.

Chamberlin, E.H. (1962) *The Theory of Monopolistic Competition* (8th edn), Cambridge, Harvard University Press.

Chandler, Jr., A.D. (1962) *Strategy and Structure*, Cambridge, Mass., MIT Press.

Choffray, J.M. and Lilien, G.L. (1980) *Market Planning for New Industrial Products*, New York, John Wiley & Sons.

Cohen, A.M. (1989) *Entrepreneur and Entrepreneurship—The Definition Dilemma*, London, Ontario, National Center for Management Research and Development.

Cohen, K.J. and Cyert, R.M. (1965) *Theory of the Firm*, Englewood Cliffs, Prentice-Hall.

Cooper, R.G. (1986) *Winning at New Products*, Toronto, Holt, Rinehart and Winston.

Cox, R., Alderson, W. and Shapiro, S.J. (eds) *Theory in Marketing*, Homewood, Irwin.

Crawford, C.M. (1987) *New Products Management*, 2nd edn, Homewood, Irwin.

Cropley, A.J. (1967) *Creativity*, London, Longmans.

Crosby, A. (1968) *Creativity and Performance in Industrial Organization*, London, Tavistock.

Dahmén, E. (1970) *Entrepreneurial Activity and the Development of Swedish Industry, 1919–1939*, Homewood, Irwin.

Dahmén, E. (1982) *A Neo-Schumpeterian Analysis of the Recent Industrial Development Crisis in Sweden*, London, Macmillan.

Davidsson, P. (1989) *Continued Entrepreneurship and Small Firm Growth*, Stockholm, Stockholm School of Economics.

Day, G. (1977) 'Diagnosing the product portfolio', *Journal of Marketing*, April.

Deal, T.E. and Kennedy, A.A. (1982) *Corporate Cultures*, Reading, Addison-Wesley.

Drucker, P. (1985) *Innovation and Entrepreneurship*, London, Heinemann.

Duncan, W.J., Ginter, P.M., Rucks, A.C., Jacobs, T.D. (1988) 'Intrapreneurship and the reinvention of the corporation', *Business Horizons*, 16–21.

Edvardsson, B. (1981) *Företagsstrategier för produktutveckling*, Uppsala, Institute for Economics.

Edvardsson, B., Edvinsson, L. and Nyström, H. (1988) *Internationalisering i kunskapsintensiva tjänsteföretag*, Karlstad, Centrum för tjänsteforskning.

Edvardsson, B. and Gummesson, E. (eds) (1988) *Management i tjänstesamhället*, Malmö, Liber.

Ekvall, G. (1972) *Creativity at the Place of Work*, Stockholm, PArådet.

Ekvall, G. (1988) *Förnyelse och friktion*. Borås, Natur och Kultur.

Ekvall, G. and Arvonen, J. (1984) *Leadership Styles and Organizational Climate for Creativity. Some Findings in One Company*, Stockholm, FA-rådet.

Ekvall, G., Arvonen, J. and Nyström, H. (1987) *Organisation och innovation*, Lund, Studentlitteratur.

Ekvall, G., Nyström, H. and Waldenström-Lindblad, I. (1983) *Organisationsklimat och innovativ förmåga. En jämförande studie av tre industriföretag*, Stockholm, FA-rådet.

Evan, W.M. (1966) 'The organization set—towards a theory of interorganizational relations'. In Thompson, J.D. (ed.), *Approaches to Organizational Design*, Pittsburgh.

Fellner, W. (1949) *Competition Among the Few*, New York, Francis, P.H. (1977) *Principles of R & D Management*, New York, Amacom.

Frank, R.E., Massy, W.F. and Wind, Y. (1972) *Market Segmentation*, Englewood Cliffs, Prentice-Hall.

Freeman, C. (1974) *The Economics of Industrial Innovation*, Middlesex, Penguin.

Gadde, L.E. (1978) *Efterfrågevariationer i vertikala marknadssystem*, Gothenburg, BAS.

Galbraith, J.R. and Nathanson, D.A. (1978) *Strategy Implementation: The Role of Structure and Process*, St Paul, West.

Gerstenfeld, A. (1977) 'Interdependence and innovation', *Omega* 1, 35–42.

Glueck, W.F. (1972) *Strategy Formation and Management Action*, New York, McGraw-Hill.

Glazer, B.G. and Strauss, A. (1967) *The Discovery of Grounded Theory*, Illinois, Aldine.

Granstrand, O. (1979) *Technology Management and Markets*, Gothenburg, Chalmers.

Graversen, H. and Trolle, H. (1983) *Produktudvikling. En skabende process*, Tåstrup, Teknologisk Institut.

Green, P.E. (1964) 'Uncertainty, information and marketing decisions'. In Cox, R., Alderson, W. and Shapiro, S.J. (eds), *Theory in Marketing*, pp. 333–354, Homewood, Irwin.

Grönroos, C. (1985) *Strategic Management and Marketing in the Service Sector*, Lund, Studentlitteratur.

Grönroos, C. and Gummesson, E. (eds), (1985) *Service Marketing—Nordic School Perspectives*, Stockholm, University of Stockholm, School of Business Administration.

Gummesson, E. (1977) *Marknadsföring och inköp av konsulttjänster*, Stockholm, Akademilitteratur.

Gupca, A.K., Ray, S.P. and Wilemon, D.L. (1985) 'R & D and marketing dialogue in high-tech firms', *Industrial Marketing Management*, **14**, 289–300.

Hägg, I. and Johansson, J. (eds) (1982) *Företag i nätverk*, Stockholm, SNS.

Håkansson, H. (ed.) (1982) *International Marketing and Purchasing of Industrial Goods*, New York, John Wiley & Sons.

Håkansson, H. (ed.) (1987) *Industrial Technological Development. A Network Approach*, London, Croom Helm.

Håkansson, H., Johansson, J. and Wootz, B. (1977) 'Influence tactics in buyer–seller processes', *Industrial Marketing Management*, 5, 319–332.

Håkansson, H. and Laage-Hellman, J. (1984) 'Developing a network R & D strategy', *Journal of Product Innovation Management*, No. 4, 224–238.

Håkansson, H. and Östberg, C. (1975) 'Industrial marketing—an organizational problem', *Industrial Marketing Management*, 4, 113–33.

Håkansson, H. and Wootz, B. (1979) 'A framework of industrial buying and selling', *Industrial Marketing Management*, 8, 28–39.

Hallén, L. (1979) 'Stability and change in buyer relationships'. In Engvall, L. and Johansson, J. (eds), *Some Aspects of Control in International Business*, Uppsala, Almquist och Wiksell.

Hammarkvist, K.-O., Håkansson, H. and Mattsson, L.G. (eds) (1982) *Marknadsföring för konkurrenskraft*, Malmö, Liber.

Hickman, C.R. and Silva, M.A. (1984) *Creating Excellence. Managing Corporate Culture, Strategy and Change in the New Age*, London, Allen and Unwin.

Hill, R.M. and Hlavacek, J.D. (1972) 'The venture team: a new concept in marketing organization', *Journal of Marketing*, 36, 44–50.

Hippel, E. von (1976) 'The dominant role of users in the scientific instrument industry', *Research Policy*, No. 5, 212–239.

Hippel, E. von (1978) 'Successful industrial products from customer ideas', *Journal of Marketing*, January, 39–49.

Hogarth, R. (1980) *Judgement and Choice*, New York, John Wiley & Sons.

Holdren, B.R. (1960) *The Structure of a Retail Market and the Market Behavior of Retail Units*, Englewood Cliffs, Prentice-Hall.

Holt, K. (1977) *Product Innovation. A Workbook for Management in Industry*, London, Newnes-Butterworth.

Hughes, D.G. (1978) *Marketing Management: A Planning Approach*, Reading, Addison-Wesley.

Hunt, S. D. (1976) 'The nature and scope of marketing', *Journal of Marketing*, 40, 17–28.

Hyrenius, H. (1983) *Entreprenörskap*, Stockholm, MTC/Liber.

Isaksen, S.G. (ed.) (1987) *Frontiers of Creativity Research*, New York, Bearly.

Jackson, B. (1985) 'Build customer relations that last.' *Harvard Business Review*, **6**, 120–128.

James, L.R. and Jones, A.P. (1974) 'Organizational climate: a review of theory and research', *Psychological Bulletin*, **12**, 1096–1112.

Jewkes, J., Sawers, G. and Stillerman, R. (1958) *The Sources of Innovation*, London, Macmillan.

Johne, F.A. (1985) *Industrial Product Innovation*, London, Croom Helm.

Johnston, W. J. and Bonoma, T. (1981) 'The buying center: structure and interaction patterns', *Journal of Marketing*, **45**, 143–156.

Kanter, R.M. (1983) *The Change Masters*, New York, Simon and Schuster.

Kay, N.M. (1979) *The Innovating Firm*, London, Macmillan.

Katona, G. (1969) 'Rational behavior and economic behavior.' In Enis, B.M. and Cox, K.K. (eds), *Marketing Classics*, pp. 91–107, Boston, Allyn and Bacon.

Kerin, R.A. and Peterson, R. (1980) *Perspectives on Strategic Marketing Management*, Boston, Allyn and Bacon.

Khandvalla, P.N. (1977) *The Design of Organizations*, New York, Harcourt Brace Jovanovich.

Kirzner, I.M. (1973) *Competition and Entrepreneurship*, Chicago, The University of Chicago Press.

Klein, B.H. (1977) *Dynamic Economics*, Cambridge, Mass., Harvard University Press.

Knight, F.H. (1921) *Risk, Uncertainty and Profit*, Boston, Houghton and Mifflin.

Koestler, A. (1964) *The Act of Creation*, London, Hutchinson.

Kristensen, T. (1985) *Produktudvikling, omverden og Usikkerhed*, Marketing Institute, Copenhagen School of Economics.

Lagerström, A. and Nyström, H. (1987) *Strategier för tjänsteexport*, Uppsala, Economic Institute.

Langrisch, J., Gibbons, M., Evans, W.G., and Jevons, F.R. (1972) *Wealth from Knowledge*, London, Macmillan.

Lawrence, P.R. and Lorsch, J.W. (1967) *Organization and Environment*, Boston, Harvard University Press.

Leavitt, H.J. (1986) *Corporate Pathfinders*, Homewood, Dow Jones-Irwins.

Liljegren, G. (1988) *Interdependens och dynamik i långsiktiga kundrelationer*, Stockholm, Stockholm School of Economics.

Lindell, M. (1988) *Utveckling av nya produkter*, Helsinki, Swedish School of Economics.

Lindström, C. (1972) *Företagets storlek och belägenhet som determinanter för dess uppfinningsaktivitet*, Umeå, Institutionen för företagsekonomi vid Umeå Universitet.

Little, B. (1974) 'New focus on new product ideas'. In Little, B. (ed.), *The Right New Product*, pp. 1–12, London, Ontario, The University of Western Ontario.

Little, A.D. (1981) *Strategic Management of Technology*, Davos, European Management Forum.

McCarthy, E.J. (1960) *Basic Marketing*, Homewood, Irwin.

MacKerin, R.A. and Peterson, R.A. (eds) (1980) *Perspectives of Strategic Marketing Management*, Boston, Allyn and Bacon.

McCall, J.B. and Warrington, M.B. (1984) *Marketing by Agreement*, Chichester, John Wiley & Sons.

Marsh, P.D. (1974) *Contract Negotiation Handbook*, Gower.

May, R. (1959) 'The nature of creativity.' In Andersson, H.H. (ed.), *The Cultivation of Creativity*, pp. 55–86, New York, Harper & Row.

Melin, L. (1977) *Strategisk inköpsverksamhet—organisation och interaktion*, Linköping, Ekonomiska institutionen vid Linköpings Universitet.

Miles, R.E. and Snow, C.C. (1978) *Organizational Strategy*, Structure and Process, New York, McGraw-Hill.

Miller, W.C. (1987) *The Creative Edge*, Reading, Addison-Wesley.

Mintzberg, H. (1976) *Patterns in Strategy Formation*, Montreal, McGill University.

Mitchell, T.R., Rediker, K.J. and Beach, L.R. (1986) 'Image theory and organizational decision making'. In Sims, H.P. and Gioia, D.A. (eds), *The Thinking Organization*, pp. 293–316, San Francisco, Jossey-Bass.

More, R.A. (1986) 'Developer/adopter relationships in new industrial product situations', *Journal of Business Research*, **14**, 501–517.

Myers, S. and Marquis, D. (1969) *Successful Industrial Innovations*, Washington, US Government.

Nelson, P.E. and Preston, L.E. (1966) *Price Merchandising in Food Retailing: A Case Study*, Berkeley, California.

Normann, R. (1977) *Management for Growth*, New York, John Wiley.

Normann, R. (1983) *Service Management*, Stockholm, Liber.

Nyström, H. (1970) *Retail Pricing—An Integrated Economic and Psychological Approach*, Stockholm, Norstedt.

Nyström, H. (1971) 'Bara effektiv eller innovativ', *Ekonomen*, **4**, 17–28.

Nyström, H. (1974a) Uncertainty, information and organizational decision-making, *Swedish Journal of Economics*, **76**, 131–139.

Nyström, H. (1974b) *Företagskreativitet och innovationer*, Stockholm, Norstedt.

Nyström, H. (1977a) *Company Strategies for Research and Development*, Uppsala, Institute for Economics.

Nyström, H. (1977b) 'Market strategy and market structure—learning and adaptation in marketing relations', *Marknadsvetande*, **8**, 41–45.

Nyström, H. (1977c) 'Strategisk marketing mix', *Ekonomen*, No. 10, 26–37.

Nyström, H. (1979a) *Creativity and Innovation*, Chichester, John Wiley & Sons.

Nyström, H. (1979b) 'Strategier för forskning och utveckling'. In Otterbeck, L. (ed.), *Marknadsföring och strukturekonomi*, pp. 171–183, Lund, Studentlitteratur.

Nyström, H. (1979c) 'Company strategies for research and development'. In Baker, M. (ed.), *Industrial Innovation*, pp. 417–440, London, Macmillan Press.

Nyström, H. (1980) 'Success factors for successful research and development'. In Vedin, A. (ed.), *Current Innovation. Policy, Management and Research Options*, pp. 149–165, Stockholm, Almquist & Wiksell.

Nyström, H. (1983) 'Positional and innovative elements in product development'. In *Creativity and Innovation Network*, January, pp. 21–23.

Nyström, H. (1985a) 'Strategies for developing and marketing new products in the electrotechnical industry'. In Langdon, R. and Rothwell, R. (eds), *Design and Innovation*, pp. 18–26, London, Francis Pinter.

Nyström, H. (1985b) 'Product development strategy: an integration of technology and marketing', *Journal of Product Innovation Management*, No. 2, 25–33.

Nyström, H. (1985c) *Product Development Strategies in Swedish Paper Companies*, Uppsala, Institute for Economics.

Nyström, H. (1985d) 'Marketing strategies for service companies'. In Grönroos, C. and Gummesson, E. (eds), *Service Marketing— Nordic School Perspectives*, Stockholm, University of Stockholm, School of Business Administration.

Nyström, H. (1986) *Balancing Competition and Cooperation—The Key to Successful Marketing Strategy*, Paper presented at the 3rd International IMP Research Seminar on International Marketing, Lyon, Graduate School of Business Administration.

Nyström, H. (1987) *Creativity, Entrepreneurship and Technological Change*, Paper presented at the Rice Symposium on Research and Development, Industrial Change and Industrial Policy, Karlstad.

Nyström, H. (1988a) 'Company creativity and innovation'. In Colemont, P., Gröholt, P., Richards, T. and Smeekes, H. (eds), *Creativity and Innovation: Towards a European Network*, pp. 25–31, Dordrecht, Kluwer Academic.

Nyström, H. (1988b) 'Byggklossar eller kinesisk ask'. In Edvardsson,

B. and Gummesson, E. (eds), *Management i tjänstesamhället*, pp. 139–144, Malmö, Liber.

Nyström, H. and Åhgren, U. (1983) *Marknadsföringsstrategier i Svenska skogsföretag—tidningspappersindustrin*, Uppsala Institute for Economics.

Nyström, H. and Åhgren, U. (1984) *Marknadsföringsstrategier i Svenska skogsföretag—kraftliner industrin*, Uppsala, Institute for Economics.

Nyström, H. and Edvardsson, B. (1978) *Forsknings och utvecklingsstrategier för företag som tillverkar lantbruksmaskiner i Sverige*, Uppsala, Institute for Economics.

Nyström, H. and Edvardsson, B. (1980a) *Research and Development Strategies for Four Swedish Farm Machine Companies*, Uppsala, Institute for Economics.

Nyström, H. and Edvardsson, B. (1980b) 'Research and development strategies for Swedish companies in the farm machinery industry'. In Sahal, D. (ed.), *Research Development and Technological Innovation*, pp. 39–53, Lexington Books, Lexington.

Nyström, H. and Edvardsson, B. (1982) 'Product innovation in food processing—a Swedish survey', *R & D Management*, No. 2, 67–72.

Nyström, H. and Edvardsson, B. (1986) 'Developing and marketing new food products'. In Kaynak, E. (ed.), *World Food Marketing Systems*, pp. 190–196, London, Butterworth.

Nyström, H., Hellström, F. and Åhgren, U. (1986) *Marknadsföringsstrategier i Svenska skogsföretag—sågverksindustrin*, Uppsala, Institute for Economics.

Nyström, H., Tamsons, H. and Thams, R. (1975) 'An experiment in price generalization and discrimination', *Journal of Marketing Research*, May, 177–181.

Nyström, H. and Willén, E. (1987) *Kunskapsintensiv tjänsteexport*, Uppsala, Institute for Economics.

Onkvisit, S. and Shaw, J.J. (1989) 'Service marketing: image, branding and competition', *Business Horizons*, January 13–18.

Ouchi, W. (1981) *Theory Z, How American Business Can Meet the Japanese Challenge*, Reading, Addison-Wesley.

Oxenfeldt, A.R. (1975) *Pricing Strategies*, New York, Amacom.

Parker, R.C. (1982) *The Management of Innovation*, Chichester, Wiley.

Parnes, S.J. (1981) *The Magic of Your Mind*, New York, Creative Education Foundation.

Payne, R.L. and Pugh, D.D. (1976) 'Organizational structure and climate'. In Dunnette, M.D. (ed.), *Handbook of Industrial and Organizational Psychology*, pp. 1125–1172, Chicago, Rand McNally.

Pessimier, E.E. (1966) *New Product Decisions*, New York, McGraw-Hill.

Pessimier, E.E. (1977) *Product Management*, Santa Barbara, John Wiley & Sons.

Peters, P.J. and Waterman, R.H. (1982) *In Search of Excellence*, New York, Harper & Row.

Pfeffer, J. (1978) *Organizational Design*, Arlington Heights, Harlan Davidson.

Pinchot, G. (1985) *Intrapreneuring*, New York, Harper & Row.

Poincaré, H. (1913) *The Foundations of Science*, New York, Science Press.

Porter, M.E. (1980) *Competitive Strategy*, London, Free Press.

Porter, M.E. (1985) *Competitive Advantage*, London, Free Press.

Quinn, J.B. (1984) *Strategies for Change*, Homewood, Irwin.

Ray, M. and Myers, R. (1989) *Creativity in Business*, New York, Doubleday.

Rhenman, E. (1973) *Organization Theory for Long-Range Planning*, New York, John Wiley & Sons.

Ries, R. and Trout, J. (1981) *Positioning: The Battle For Your Mind*, New York, McGraw-Hill.

Riggs, H.E. (1983) *Managing High Technology Companies*, Belmont, Lifetime Learning Publications.

Rogers, C.R. (1959) 'Towards a theory of creativity'. In Andersson, H.H. (ed.), *Creativity and its Cultivation*, pp. 69–82, New York, Harper & Row.

Rokeach, M. (1960) *The Open and Closed Mind*, New York, Basic Books.

Rubin, J.Z. and Brown, B.R. (1975) *The Social Psychology of Bargaining and Negotiation*, New York, Academic Press.

Rumelt, R.P. (1974) *Strategy Structure and Economic Performance*, Cambridge, Mass., Harvard University Press.

Salancik, G.R. and Porac, J.F. (1986) 'Distilled ideologies. Values derived from causal reasoning in complex environments'. In Sims, H.P. and Gioia, D.A. (eds), *The Thinking Organization*, pp. 75–101, San Francisco, Jossey-Bass.

Sandkull, B. (1970) *Innovative behaviour of Organizations: The Case of New Products*, Lund, Studentlitteratur.

Schein, E.H. (1984) 'Coming to a new awareness of organizational culture', *Sloan Management Review*, Winter, 3–16.

Schon, D.A. (1967) *Technology and Change*, London, Pergamon Press.

Schumpeter, J. (1934) *The Theory of Economic Development*, Cambridge, Mass., Harvard University Press.

Shackle, G.L.S. (1957) *Time in Economics*, Amsterdam, North-Holland.

Shanklin, W.L. and Ryans, J.K., Jr. (1984) *Marketing High Technology*, Lexington, Lexington Books.

Sjölander, S. (1983) *Innovation och företagsförnyelse*, Malmö, Liber.

Skinner, W. (1982) 'Technology and the manager'. In Tushman, M.L. and Moore, W.L. (eds), *Readings in the Management of Innovation*, 464–475, Boston, Pitman.

Smith, W.R. (1956) 'Product differentiation and market segmentation as alternative marketing strategies', *Journal of Marketing*, **21**, 3–8.

Spekman, R.E. and Johnston, W.J. (1986) 'Relationship management: managing the selling and buying interface', *Journal of Business Research*, **14**, 519–531.

Steiner, G.A. (ed.) (1965) *The Creative Organization*, Chicago, University of Chicago Press.

Sveiby, K.E. and Lloyd (1987) *Managing Knowhow*, London, Bloomsbury.

Sveiby, K.E. and Risling, A. (1986) *Kunskapsföretaget*, Malmö, Liber.

Taylor, C.W. and Barron, F. (eds) (1963) *Scientific Creativity*, New York, John Wiley & Sons.

Terrebery, S. (1968) 'The evolution of organizational environments', *Administrative Science Quarterly*, **12**, 590–630.

Thompson, V.A. (1969) *Bureaucracy and Innovation*, University of Alabama Press.

Thompson, A.A., Strickland, A.J. and Fulmer, W.E. (1987) *Readings in Strategic Management*, Plano, Business Publications.

Tushman, M.L. and Moore, W.L. (eds) (1982) *Readings in the Management of Innovation*, Boston, Pitman.

Twiss, B. (1974) *Managing Technological Innovation*, London, Longman.

Uhlmann, L. (1977) 'The innovation process in industrialized countries'. In Stroetmann, K. A. (ed.), *Innovation, Economic Change and Technology Policies*, pp. 21–37, Basel, Birkhäuser.

Urban, G. and Hauser, J.R. (1980) *Design and Marketing of New Products*, Englewood Cliffs, Prentice-Hall.

Utterback, J.M. (1977) 'Dynamics of process and product change'. In Stroetmann, K. A. (ed.) *Innovation, Economic Change and Technology Policies*, pp. 7–20, Basel, Birkhäuser.

Utterback, J.M. and Abernathy, W.J. (1975) 'A dynamic model of product and process innovation', *Omega*, No. 6, 639–636.

Utterback, J.M., Allen, T.J., Hollomon, J.M. and Sirbu, M. A. (1976) 'The process of innovation in five industries in Europe and Japan', *IEEE Transactions in Engineering Management*, **28**, 3–9.

Valdelin, J. (1974) *Produktutveckling och marknadsföring*, Stockholm School of Economics.

Vedin, B.-A. (1980) *Corporate Culture for Innovation*, Lund, Studentlitteratur.

Vernon, P.E. (ed.) (1970) *Creativity*, Middlesex, Penguin.

Weber, M. (1947) *Theory of Social and Economic Organization*, New York, The Free Press.

Webster, F.E., Jr. and Wind, Y. (1972) *Organizational Buying Behavior*, Englewood Cliffs, Prentice-Hall.

Weick, K.E. (1969) *The Social Psychology of Organizing*, Reading, Addison-Wesley.

Wallas, G. (1926) *The Art of Thought*, New York, Harcourt Brace.

Webster, F.E., Jr. (1979) *Industrial Marketing Strategy*, New York, John Wiley & Sons.

Wertheimer, M. (1959) *Productive Thinking*, New York, Harper & Row.

Williamson, O.E. (1975) *Markets and Hierarchies: Analysis and Antitrust Implications*, London, Free Press.

Wind, Y. (1982) *Product Policy: Concepts, Methods and Strategy*, Reading, Addison-Wesley.

Zaltman, G., Duncan, R. and Holbek, J. (1973) *Innovations and Organizations*, New York, John Wiley & Sons.

Appendix 1

COMPANY AND PRODUCT BREAKDOWN OF STUDIES A–E

	Industry	Number of companies studied	Number of new products studied	Time period
Study A	Pharmaceuticals	3	24	1941–1975
	Industrial electronics	4	31	1952–1975
	Industrial chemicals	2	13	1948–1975
	Total	11	91	
Study B	Farm machinery	140	166	1968–1977
Study C	Food processing	20	121	1969–1978
Study D	Pulp and paper processing	4	17	1972–1982

Study A is summarized in Chapter 4, Study B in Chapter 5, Study C in Chapter 10 and Study D in Chapter 11.

Appendix 2

METHODOLOGICAL NOTE ON DEFINITION AND MEASUREMENT

Marketing Strategy

[1] Most closed	[3] Intermediate value	[5] Most open
Defensive and product modification (variation of existing product to existing customers)	Defensive and product diversification or Offensive and product modification	Offensive and product diversification (new products, new customers)

More open marketing strategies are thus aimed at generating new business by product and market development. More closed strategies are aimed at maintaining existing product types and markets.

The distinction between product modification and product diversification is based on product usage, as reflected in how companies themselves view the products in their technical descriptions and sales promotion.

Technological Strategy

[1] Most closed	[3] Intermediate value	[5] Most open
Internal R & D orientation and isolated technology use	Internal R & D orientation and synergistic technology use or External R & D orientation and isolated technology use	External R & D orientation and synergistic technology use

More open technological strategies are thus aimed at generating new technological knowledge and competence by cooperation with the outside environment and the combining of technologies. More closed strategies are aimed at efficiently using the companies' own technological knowledge and specialized competence.

The technologies companies are working in and the extent to which they are utilized to solve critical problems in developing specific products are given by company representatives. This is also the case with regard to information on R & D cooperation for specific products.

Technological Innovation

[1]	[5]
Conventional technological solution, based on existing knowledge	Unique technological solution, based on new knowledge

As in the case of market innovation, technological innovation is measured on a scale from 1 to 5, based on company information. With regard to each specific product, companies provided detailed information on the extent to which solving the critical technical problems required solutions novel not only to the company, but to society. Essentially this is a measure of technical creativity, similar to that required by patent law. A direct measure of technological innovation was used to avoid the incompleteness of more indirect measures such as patent data. Companies, for competitive reasons, often do not apply for patent protection, even if it is likely that it might be granted.

Market Innovation

[1]	[5]
Product essentially similar to competing products	Completely unique product

Market innovation is measured on a scale from 1 to 5 based on information from the companies. This refers to how unique a product is judged to have been at its market introduction, compared to existing competing products. In this way competitive response and the effect of marketing promotion and price is eliminated from our measure of market success.

This measure then becomes a pure measure of how successful a company has been in developing a product which at the time of market introduction fulfills previously unsatisfied buyer needs. The extent to which this market potential is actually realized by the companies and transformed into profit is determined by competitive parameters, such as price and promotion.

Commercial Success

[1]	[2]	[3]	[4]	[5]
Large loss	Small loss	Break-even	Small profit	Large profit

The commercial success for the products studied were assessed by company representatives on a scale from 1 to 5. This outcome refers to estimates over the total product life cycle and requires that the product has been on the market for some time.

Index

299